In the

Memories, Moments, Milestones

Childhood to Cambridge

Martin Hearne

Winterbourne 56

Book and cover design by The Author

Published by Winterbourne 56

Printed by Book Printing UK www.bookprintinguk.com
Remus House, Coltsfoot Drive, Peterborough, PE2 9BF

Printed in Great Britain

ISBN 978-1-7398028-0-6

Cover painting: *Une Noce Chez Le Photographe* (1879), Pascal Dagnan-Bouveret

Definition: *In the Picture*

: involved or playing a part in something (Merriam-Webster)

Contents

Prologue

July 2nd 1960 fell on a Saturday. My childhood ended that day. By the time we had finished breakfast, two Robinsons removal vans, black with large gold writing on the side, were parked outside 60 Newport Road, Balsall Heath, Birmingham 12. Most of our furniture and possessions were loaded into the first van, to be stored. I was ten. Maybe that was how my childhood and happiness were carried away from me. Nearly all of my favourite toys certainly were: my Tri-ang scooter, my electric train sets and so on, though one or two very special things were removed to under the bed in my uncle's and aunt's house in Great Barr, like the toy yacht, which sailed so well on Bourneville pool. Clothing, beds and other essentials went into the second vehicle. At least, I think that's what happened. There had to be some means of carrying those things across the city to 202 Burbury Street, Lozells. My sister, brother and I were taken by our parents in Dad's black Morris 1000, XOJ 516, the firm's car of W.G.Sice. The red geranium, given to me three years earlier by my father's mother, Grandma Lily, to mark my First Holy Communion in May 1957, and dutifully cherished, watered and repotted when necessary, went with us. Upon arrival at Great Aunty Annie's, where dad's 57-year-old maiden aunt, a short and stomping Hockley factory worker of limited intellect (she assembled ladies' powder compacts for a pittance paid in notes and duodecimal coins), had lived alone since her step-mother's death six or seven years earlier, the plant was taken up the second staircase, so rickety that we were really not supposed to use it, to the attic. There, forgotten and unwatered, it shrivelled and died. What was expected to be a six weeks' stay until we were rehoused turned into an eighteen months' exile of haunting misery. We descended to the last step above homelessness. But I anticipate.

Under a decade later, on Sunday 5th October 1969, my father drove me from home in South Staffordshire to university in the Fens. My shiny, metal-plated trunk in the boot was so heavy that, when the lights changed and he had to stop fairly abruptly for the first time in the journey, we slid on two or three yards after the white line at the traffic lights. There was nothing wrong with the brakes of the almost new dark green Ford Cortina 1500, the one automatic car he had out of a lifetime's total of nine or ten, and his clear favourite. I suppose the weight of all my essentials, with dozens of books, including an almost full set of cheap inherited hardback Dickens, impaired the handling. That was not the end of my trunk for my father that day. Though as a rare exception we were allowed to take a car into college grounds for just a few minutes, to unload, my first-floor room was a long way up many steps and across the court from the car park. I pitied his tottering struggles, two hands trembling with the leather handle on his side. It was too much for him. When the car drove away, I did not look after it.

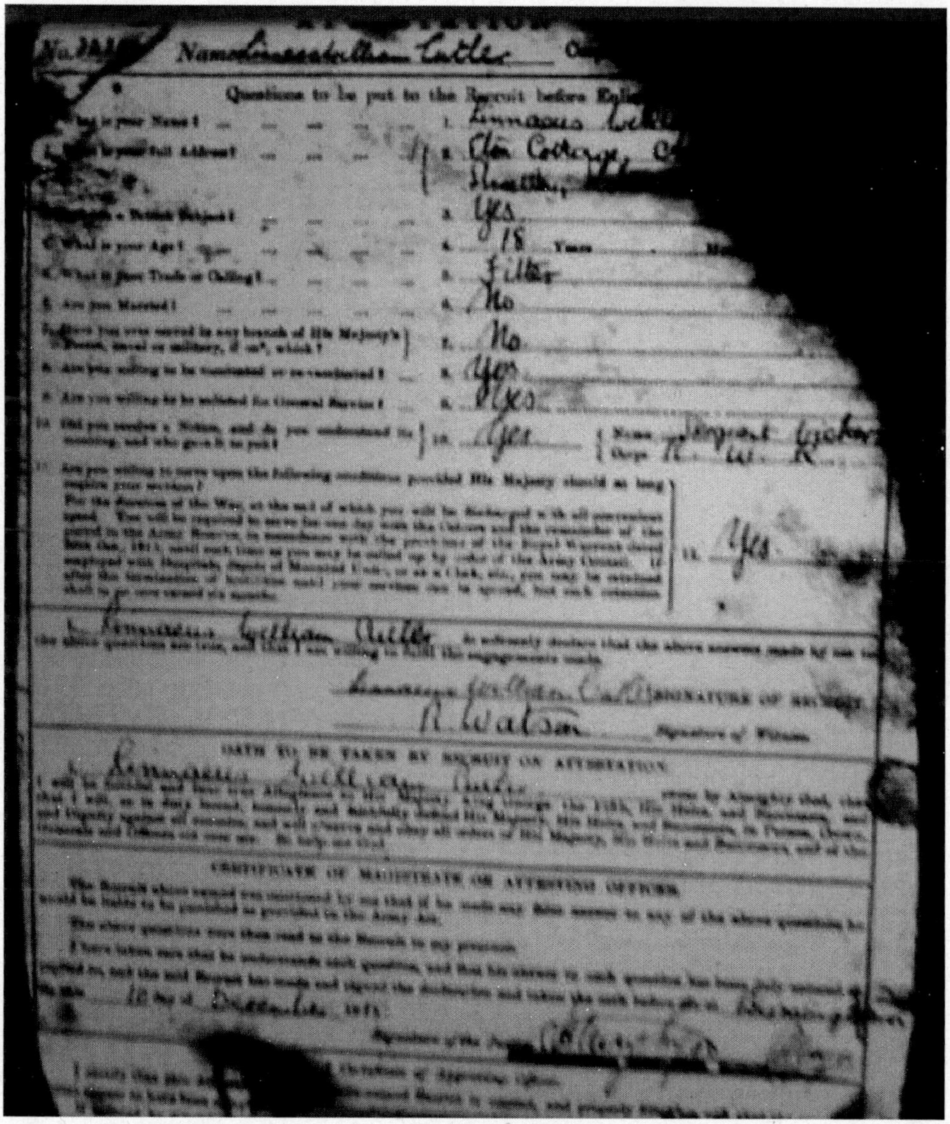
Name Linnaeus William Cutler

Questions to be put to the Recruit before Enlistment

1. What is your Name? — 1. Linnaeus
2. What is your full Address? — 2. Elm Cottage
3. Are you a British Subject? — 3. Yes
4. What is your Age? — 4. 18 Years
5. What is your Trade or Calling? — 5. Fitter
6. Are you Married? — 6. No
7. Have you ever served in any branch of His Majesty's Forces, naval or military, if so, which? — 7. No
8. Are you willing to be vaccinated or re-vaccinated? — 8. Yes
9. Are you willing to be enlisted for General Service? — 9. Yes
10. Did you receive a Notice, and do you understand its meaning, and who gave it to you? — 10. Yes
11. — 11. Yes

R. Watson — Signature of Witness

OATH TO BE TAKEN BY RECRUIT ON ATTESTATION

CERTIFICATE OF MAGISTRATE OR ATTESTING OFFICER

10 day of December 1915

The Attestation of Linnaeus William Cutler, 10th December 1915

The Road Taken ...

'Everything
Would have been different. For it would have been
Another world.'
- Edward Thomas, *As the Team's Head Brass*

In the beginning God created the heaven and the earth ...

In the beginning, which you could say was the 1st of September 1939, a charismatic madman sent his soldiers into Poland ...

'Mom, how did you and Dad have me?'

'Ah well, I was working for your grandfather. Your father used to talk to me on the office telephone ...'

Linnaeus William Cutler, my maternal grandfather, gives his age as eighteen when he volunteers to fight in World War 1. The photograph I have of his damaged enlisting document, dated 10th December 1915, describes him as an unmarried fitter. That is his handwriting completing the same minimalist form that sent so many hundreds of thousands of teenage boys and young men to premature oblivion. His signature on the 'Oath of Attestation' is witnessed by R.Watson.

I cannot remember Grandad, for reasons which will follow, though there are photographs, and even some silent film clips, of us together. His gravestone, in the churchyard of St Peter's Church, Little Aston, records that he died on 2nd February 1956 aged 57 years, when I was 6. But there something does not add up. Even if he had signed the Oath the very day of his eighteenth birthday, he must have passed his fifty-*eighth* birthday in December 1955 before he died later that winter. Did he, like too many others, falsify his age to join the industrialised slaughter as early as he could? Or did whoever commissioned the monumental mason in 1956 keep his mittens on during some elementary arithmetic? It does not really matter; we can be clear that he was very young when he put on uniform.

Grandad liked motorbikes. To begin with, he wanted to be an army dispatch rider. That dream apparently was never realised; he became instead a tank driver, entering action at the Somme at some time in 1916. It is said that on something like fifteen occasions his vehicle lost a track, meaning the crew had to bale out and scamper back to their lines for cover. The first tanks advanced at walking speed, but at least were not stationery targets for artillery when they were inching over the battlefield: When it was dark, some men had to crawl over no man's land, replace the track and rescue their vehicle.

One of Grandad's stories that is passed around the family concerns a battle incident when chivalry was indeed its own reward. The tank commander spotted a wounded enemy soldier on the ground in the direct path of their 14 tons. He gave the urgent order to swerve in order to avoid crushing him. After being narrowly missed, the German raised his rifle and fatally shot the very man who had preserved him. He died in Grandad's arms. Either before or after that, they put the tank into reverse and crushed the man. That was when he had lost his faith in God, Grandad said. He was twice mentioned in dispatches for noteworthy acts. Having risen to sergeant, he was reduced to private when he let a prisoner he was escorting escape: he trusted him when he said he needed to relieve himself, but the man somehow climbed out of the latrine or over the lavatory wall and disappeared. I do not know where this occurred, though Grandad did get himself made back to his old rank, presumably by worthy conduct.

Once a civilian again, he met and married my grandmother, Elsie May Hall. Their first child, my mother Valerie May Cutler, said that she was conceived in Streetly Wood somewhat in advance of her parents' nuptials, arriving on 14th March 1921, to be followed fairly closely by three brothers: Raymond, Brian and Roland. Elsie probably thought her child-bearing times were over, and was well into her forties when my Aunty Kate, Kathleen Cutler, arrived in September 1941. By this time Grandma, an increasingly frail asthmatic who was to develop a failing heart fairly early in life, had been sufficiently weakened physically through hard work to pass much of the infant and child care over to big sister, my mother.

To support his soon growing family, Grandad started up a business. With the mechanical skills he had acquired it must have been simple enough for him to open a crate of bicycle components and assemble new models, all from parts. What a comment on the times too, that the demand for bikes was so great and urgent the manufacturers could afford to forego the extra profit they would have secured had they assembled and sold the complete items, to retailers or individual purchasers. The early 1920s market must have been rapacious.

Grandad became more ambitious. He acquired a partner surnamed Packer, and started a business in the rapidly growing world of motor cars. His garage, which supplied, serviced and repaired cars as well as petrol, oil and all the other consumables, was the first one on the Chester Road in Streetly for miles, though others were to follow. No doubt he was able, inventive and hard-working, for shortly the family was moving through a succession of increasingly large and impressive houses. By the time World War Two broke out, they were living in Aldridge Court, a grand and luxurious ex-millionaire's house just outside the village of that name, with a sweeping drive, spacious rooms (one of which was converted into a cinema), extensive grounds, fields, an attached farm and a stable of horses, pure-blooded Arabs. For a challenge from Grandad, my Uncle Brian rode the stallion Riffael all the way from Staffordshire to the White City, sleeping overnight in stables with him, to compete in the Horse of the Year show. I think this was in the mid-thirties, but whenever it was, the beautiful creature won first prize in his category. A wealthy South African lady fell so deeply in love at first sight with Riffael that Grandad could not turn down the price she offered. Brian had to take Riffael to Southampton, see him installed on board and bid a heart-tearing farewell to his best friend. He had become as much a pet as a mount, highly intelligent, trained to do tricks like unbolting the lower part of the stable door, lying down 'dead', rolling over to a hand signal and so on.

Clearly a remarkable man of considerable energy, Grandad even made his own cars, including a single-seater racing car of the bullet-on-wheels type, which he used to test at up to 100 mph on the otherwise fairly quiet Chester Road. ('He'll kill himself, that young fool, our Billy!' his own father shouted from the pavement, waving his stick.) Various of his vehicles were entered in rallies, races and hill climbs at venues like Donnington Park. With a co-driver, he won the 1934 RAC John O'Groats to Lands End rally in a tuned up production Triumph. (He had become a main agent for the Triumph Motor Company.) I even know of one of his cars that survives, a four-seater roadster using a Triumph engine and other components. I learned about 'the Cutler Special' from a chance meeting with the then secretary of the Pre-1940 Triumph Owners' Club, at which time the car was in the possession of a Sussex farmer called Michael Power. I should love to see, even more to own it.

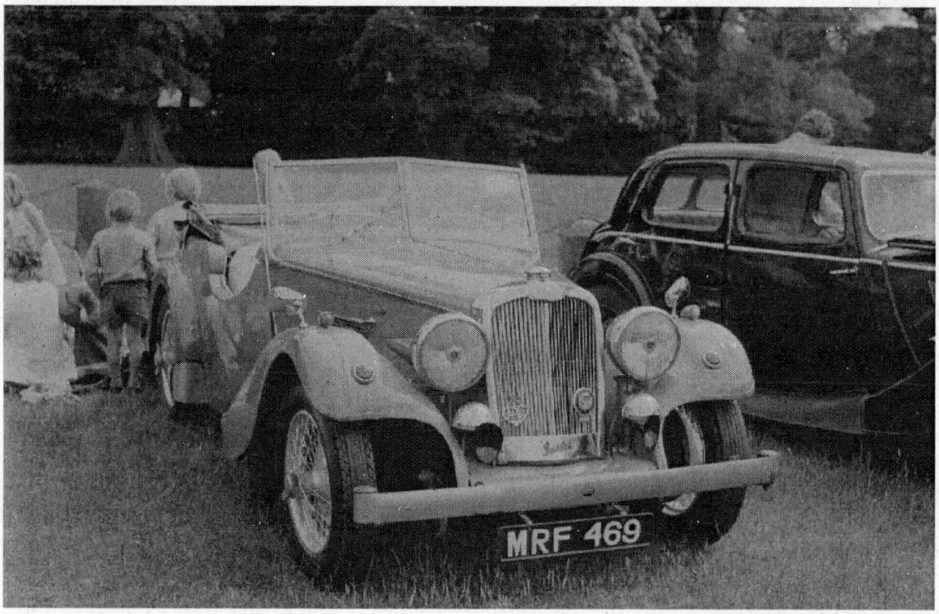

The Cutler Special

Difficult to keep up with, as well as, according to report, impossibly changeable in his moods, Grandad walked with a permanent limp following a motor bike accident at a roundabout, which must have been after the War. His knee being very badly smashed, the surgeon gave him the option of amputation or a new technique whereby the surgical fitting of a silver wire would save the limb but lock the joint eternally. The latter was agreed upon, with the stipulation that the leg would in future be slightly bent. Your ears identified Mr Cutler coming down the stairs, one step at a time, the damaged one always carried trailing. No impediment to most normal activities, adding horse riding to driving any vehicle, this minor handicap did not prevent him from roaming in his relationships either. I think I must have been a very young baby when he started a relationship with an eighteen year old girl who worked with his horses. She moved in, and my Grandma Elsie, along with her youngest, Kate, was exiled to a relatively modern terraced house bought for her at 97 Wilmore Road, Perry Barr, Birmingham, now B20. That led to consequences, as shall appear.

Part of Grandad's plan before that was that my mother, leaving school at 14, would receive secretarial training as a shorthand typist, and then work for him at the garage. That came about a couple of years before WW2, by which time she had passed her driving test first time and been supplied with a racy little Singer Roadster. That was how she came to be answering the telephone for Cutler's of Streetly when my father rang.

*****

Douglas Clifford Hearne, my father, was the first born of Clifford Harry Hearne and his wife Lilian May, née Smith. The Hearnes may not all have personalised car registration plates, but several of them do have rather neat birth timings. Clifford Harry managed to appear at the start of the century in 1900, and my dad at that of a year, on 1st January 1922. Grandma Lil predated the only love of her life, being delivered by Anne-Maria ('the Old Pot') Smith on 11th January 1898. They lived first in Nursery Road, Hockley, where Dad was born. Lil was a milliner by trade and Clifford a toolsetter, rising to foreman toolsetter, which gave him responsibility for 100 machinists and an extra £1 a week, that is, a comfortable 40% more than the average male machinist's £2 10s. They managed to move around the corner from what was Clifford's parents' home to a house in Brougham Street, where second son Gordon John emerged on 29th December 1925. I am not sure whether they were still there when Kenneth Paul was born on 6th September 1933. They may have just moved to a brand-new house at 10 Windermere Road, Handsworth, the tree-lined, tidy, respectably quiet and well-kept residential road, with hedged or walled small front gardens, a gate and entrance path shared with only one next-door neighbour, three rooms downstairs, as many above, with a kitchen and large walk-in brick built pantry downstairs. The lavatory adjoining the kitchen was reached by exiting the back door and walking a little way down the rectangular back garden of slightly more than cricket pitch length. Clifford and Lilian bought the freehold for an extra £30, making the all-in purchase price £250, met by a mortgage.

A Catholic convert, strait-laced Grandma Lil contrasted dramatically with Land Army veteran Elsie, who had started work in service at 13. Eyes habitually twinkling, the latter stayed spirited even when fighting her spasmic lungs for breath. Of a neighbour, shrewdly perceived to be a hypocrite: 'She wouldn't say *cock* for a farthing, but she'd tek it for less!' In her younger days, she had been at music halls, used advisedly to carry a hat pin in her lapel to ward off unwanted amorous advances, had stories of the girls laughing so much at the men's Saturday night antics that their urine trickled across the floor ... I quickly add that she always appeared impeccably smart, and was equally proper and ladylike in her behaviour, certainly in front of us children, whom she would sharply correct:

'Come on, our Martin. Your mother says you mustn't do that!'

Invariably merry, she battled on, frail yet feisty, tackling heavy housework that should have been beyond her, relishing gossip and tales, shouting excitedly at Saturday afternoons' televised wrestlers, enjoying the fun of being ever so slightly naughty, which she would call 'wicked'. So, a small whisky once a week, maybe just one cigarette if a visitor came, three or four chocolates in the evening ('I know I shouldn't'!). She somehow kept her house and garden perfectly.

Whereas, dad's mother …

Abstemious to a fault, Grandma Lil liked everything to be done 'correctly', which meant the way she wanted. Lacking Elsie's more daring and colourful background, she sometimes betrayed an hilarious naïveté, as when she innocently used her ex-soldier brother's, Alf's, trench expressions:

'There we all were, a-rollicking and a-bollocking …'

Remarks like that certainly caused a few splutterings into visitors' tea cups. This placid ingenuousness endured with her right till her final hospitalisation, at the age of 73, when she once asked my father, visiting her, to look after a rather expensive looking ladies' watch, hastily slipped into her bedside cupboard drawer ('to keep it safe for a moment') by a ward cleaner, who was never seen again.

Driven by the wish to be seen doing the right things, she would broadcast that she had not sanctioned the consummation of their marriage until twelve months had elapsed after the ceremony. 'I didn't let my dear Cliff touch me; I wouldn't want the neighbours to think I *had* to get married.' Though later to prove an excellent and entirely devoted mother – my own mother could never understand how such a flat chested woman could have won a reputation as a superb breast feeder – she boasted that when pregnant with her first child she had *no idea* how the baby would exit her body. But then, if you also trumpet that you still believed in Father Christmas when you were fourteen years old …

Church and her version of religion were everything to Grandma Lil. She scrupulously and unthinkingly followed the daily and hourly practices she had been lessoned in. Her voice lowered into quiet reverence when she spoke of Our Lord, Our Lady or any one of the saints. She would pause and bow her head, hesitating before she said in a hushed voice a 'holy' word [*pause, bow*]: 'Mary'. She brought back little things she had noticed. The bus driver *must* be a Catholic: 'He could not take both hands off the wheel to make the Sign of the Cross when he drove past St Chad's, where [*pause*] Our Lord's body is stored in the tabernacle, and so he put his thumb up. Wasn't that grand?' She would not have it that he was being courteous to another driver. Though I quite liked staying overnight with her, bedtime was a heavy ordeal. By the time we had put our hands together, bowed our heads, said several prayers together, remembered mommy and daddy, our uncles and aunts, all the other little girls and boys, and the poor children who don't go to Catholic schools, and the Jewish people who don't accept [*pause, bow head*] Jesus, and the soldiers away from home, and ... and … and … I think I should much more willingly have sat through a mime of the whole of Wagner's *Ring* cycle than go through this dreary, drawn out, monotonous, nightly adagio trail of dutiful reverence! She undoubtedly believed that if you carefully and punctiliously followed all the instructions and procedures about going to mass and all the rest, you would go to heaven, which was a beautiful place: midsummer Christmas all day and every day! The totality of trust and acceptance was just the same as the terrorist's, who *knows* that instantly disintegrating himself and as many 'infidels' as possible will get his prescribed allocation of virgins queuing up and loosening their clothing before you can say 'ammonium nitrate'. In many matters you just could not reason with her.

Priests and nuns lived an immeasurably superior life, the best on earth. In her later years she went every industrial fortnight with a friend on a coach to Blackpool, for an annual holiday with The Sisters, who were perfect in every way. Her favourite film was *The Sound of Music*, which she went into Birmingham to see every week for months on end, later watching it repeatedly on a video machine supplied by one of my uncles.

One of Grandma's most cheerful claims was that she had never read a book! She *could* read and write, very clearly and quite beautifully. Technically, she was very literate. She seems to have been a successful school pupil, there being as evidence – unopened, of course – several books awarded as prizes. According to Dad and brother Gordon, these were mostly late Victorian moral stories, about sweet, golden-haired little girls who somehow found themselves in hard-boozing, rough-living Australian mining towns and cleaned them up in a few weeks by the example of their innocence and piety, occasionally assisted by a few well-chosen words of stinging rebuke. How much more productive the workers must have become now they went underground stone-cold sober early every morning, how much happier everyone instantly was – apart, maybe, from the bar owners! When some of these virgin volumes were sacrificially bestowed upon my younger sister (who went on to gain two degrees in English Literature), she left them unviolated, but arranged their titles in thoughtful order on her shelf: *No Ordinary Girl*, *The Lady of Delights, The Horses Loved it Too* … the other three or four elude me. I think I was in my own last year of English Literature at university when Lil deviated from a lifetime's pattern by buying me a *fictional* book instead of a devotional publication to use at mass or a mind-improving treatise by some Monsignor or other, e.g. *The True Meaning of Christmas*, and other rib ticklers. The story book, incidentally, was a jumble sale paperback police story, originally 2s 6d, which followed naturally on from Chaucer's *Boece* and the translations of Greek tragedy that I was at that time immersed in. I imagine that since policemen are *ipso facto* and by definition *good*, the cover sketch of a smiling fat bobby got this one past the censor! By curious coincidence, an aunt by marriage, also RC, in her young days expressed her disapproval and dislike of a popular television weekly because 'policemen don't swear'. Welcome to Planet Zog!

She was a worthy womman al hir lyf. Unlike Chaucer's *wholy Venerien* cloth maker, Lil actually was highly admirable in many, many ways. When my father went down with polio one hot 1930s summer, aged ten or eleven, and had to spend about a year in Birmingham Children's Hospital, his parents kept the family going, visited their Douglas every day, never flagged. Whether hospital food was as foul as dad maintained, he struggled or plain refused to eat it, and so Lil took him a cold meal that he would eat every single day. Brougham Street to the hospital in Steelhouse Lane is just over a two mile journey. It would have meant some walking and possibly a bus or tram ride in about 1932. I do not know what routes there were then. Even if the infrastructure were as good in those times as when I knew the area, it would still have required appreciable efforts to look after five or six year old Gordon, run the house, cook, clean and launder for the three remaining at home – and attend Sunday mass, of course. Remarkably, she did all these things, all the time carrying the massive load of worry over her eldest born, whose prolonged hospital spell added a bout of sleeping sickness to the crippling virus. Dad missed a whole year of schooling, having to drop down a class. For the rest of his life his left arm and shoulder were to remain small and withered, with severe muscle wastage. His soft hand always communicated a gentle tremble when you held it. It had little strength or grip; he could not raise it above about chest height – apart from his party trick of lifting it behind his neck with his good, right hand, which probably grew a little larger to compensate.

Even more devastatingly, only a short time after moving to Handsworth and the mortgage, with third son Kenneth only three years old, Clifford died, the day before my dad's fourteenth birthday, from a sudden kidney infection. With no savings or mortgage insurance or life assurance, other women might have despaired. Lil's heart was indeed broken for ever; since they met, Clifford had been everything to her. Dad remembered his unfailing knack of getting her out of the most fearful downs and sulks, often by an inspired piece of impertinence, even scurrilous rudeness which she could not resist melting at. Once she smiled or better, the vaporous clouds dispelled. The three sons were not so skilful or lucky. 'Oh God – she's in one of her moods!' or just the sudden wide-eyed glances to each other were the *sotto voce* or unspoken alerts.

The family, principally in the guise of Grandpa Smith, offered lifelines. Lilian set up a bench in the third, small bedroom. It remained unchanged for years after she no longer needed it. I trespassed into 'the spare room' many times before it was converted into a bathroom (with indoor lavatory) in the early 60s. Until the mortgage was paid, and as long as she needed the income, Lilian looked after the house and her boys during the day, then did jewellery outwork in the evenings and at weekends. As one of Birmingham's many small manufacturers of middle-to-high range jewellery, Grandpa Smith could easily use her services, as he sometimes did of other home workers. For my sixteenth birthday, Grandma gave me a pair of gold-plated silver cufflinks she herself had made, inscribed for the occasion with my first initial. They are well looked after, but have nevertheless been worn many times. I should think that her role in their production was silver soldering the tiny retaining brackets to the backs of the panels, and then the delicate yet durable chains between them. Her fingers were very nimble and skilled, as her sewing, knitting, embroidery, finely detailed cake decoration and other productions illustrated.

Because of his lengthy hospitalisation, Dad did not take his School Certificate in the fourth form until he was 17 in the summer of 1939. Since he passed all subjects (excepting mine, English Literature!), with special strengths in Latin and French, and had been top of his grammar school form fairly consistently, he could easily have progressed to the sixth form. He loved learning and would have jumped at the chance. But their circumstances required him to earn money, and so Lil found him a job, first at BSA, manufacturer of small arms, bicycles and many other items. War was about to break out. Whether it was during his work in the offices there or at a steel stockholder's he moved to, possibly Charles Wade Steel Limited, as a booking clerk he took written and telephone orders during the war.

Most businesses with even a modest workshop were encouraged or required to provide what they could for the war effort. Grandad Cutler would have been keen to contribute, I am sure. Some of his men in Streetly started to turn out small metal items, like bullet cases. For these, steel had to be ordered. Valerie Cutler's call was answered by Douglas Hearne.

*****

I was told or picked up fragments about the War from my earliest days. Being rated medically unfit to fight (he couldn't even hold a rifle up or even less keep it steady), Dad had played his part at work in the day by assisting with the provision of steel to various manufacturers of arms and military necessaries, and sometimes overnight by fire watching, being sent to various locations. One happened to be his old school on the Hagley Road, where he spent the hours of darkness on the roof, constantly peering up and around. Incendiary devices dropped on parachutes were a considerable hazard. Even round the corner from their house in Windermere Road one had once became entangled in some telephone wires, mercifully failing to ignite. To help provide some diversion and entertainment, Dad also joined in with the volunteer talks at the Midland Institute in Birmingham city centre. How he managed to get away with his talk on Wagner, illustrated from 78 rpm records, has always puzzled me! The Anderson shelter in Windermere Road, like many others, had been brought to ground level by the time I was around, being used as a garden shed.

Though some miles north of a major city, the Cutlers still were near enough to the Black Country and potential targets like railway lines to be at risk, and so Mom too spent nights in the Cutler shelter, which was of the larger, more expensive kind, improved by her father. I have no idea when the phone conversations between them started. Perhaps it was towards the end of the war. At some point Douglas asked Valerie if she would go out with him. She met him off the bus in Sutton Coldfield for a walk in Sutton Park.

Even by wartime standards, Dad immediately struck her as underfed. At around 5'6" tall, he just about weighed 8 stones. However, they got on well. The meeting was followed by many more over months. At some point, Mom took her boyfriend to her house, to meet the family. By then they were using the word 'courting'.

Mr Cutler was disappointed and unimpressed. The slight, lop-sided, timid and self-effacing man in his mid-twenties, unsurprisingly overawed by the scale and splendour of Aldridge Court, must have shrunk before him, inwardly and externally. They were so opposite: the softly-spoken grammar school boy who could read Julius Caesar in Latin and play classical pieces on the violin, and the battle-hardened soldier who had fire in his belly, a rich store of practical accomplishments, the ability to electrify individuals and teams into doing things, forever budding ambitions and schemes. It may still have been wartime, because on at least one occasion that was mentioned Dad missed the last bus home, and had to walk all seven miles *in the blackout*, a double hardship. If that was the case, Valerie's father would have been almost more impressive or intimidating, since he was running the Home Guard in the area. He loved drill, and was very strict, with both his men and any of the public who were slow to comply with regulations, though capable of some humour. Once, when a drunk middle-aged woman outside *The Elms* pub refused to be quiet and go home, after several previous occasions of rowdiness, he crept behind her and discharged a blank, supplied for training. She simply had to go straight home after that; she had wet her knickers! I cannot suppose that Dad's Catholicism would have gone down particularly well either. Billy Cutler was used to men who *did* things, not made a point of eating fish on Fridays. He thought Douglas Clifford Hearne rather a dud.

He refused to bestow his blessing upon the intended marriage. That hurt and troubled Valerie no end. But Douglas was kind and gentle. He seemed to like and love her as she was, plumpness or not. At least he had not shown her violent changes of mood and favour. Whatever Elsie's feelings, she would have been powerless to alter Billy's. She attended the wedding at St Augustine's in Handsworth, Dad's family's parish church, on Easter Saturday, March 27th 1948, as did young Kate as bridesmaid. Both looked stunningly, even expensively fine. Valerie, who had slimmed down to a Personal Best Since Girlhood of barely eight stones was accommodated by friends called Dutton, who helped with the dresses and other necessaries, and from whose house she went as a bride. Little June Dutton was her other bridesmaid. Wilf Dutton gave her away. Dad's Best Man was Ray Curly from school, who had come safely through the war as a naval wireless operator. Among the wedding telegrams was one from Linnaeus, addressed not to the married couple but Valerie alone:

GONE STOP BUT NOT FORGOTTEN STOP

The ambiguous nature of *how* Valerie had not been forgotten – in love or anger – was never, to my knowledge, ruminated on. It could, of course, have been both simultaneously, either equally or in some unspecified ratio. I am sure the deep hurt of her father's treatment never left my mother. Until Douglas, she had loved him more than any other being.

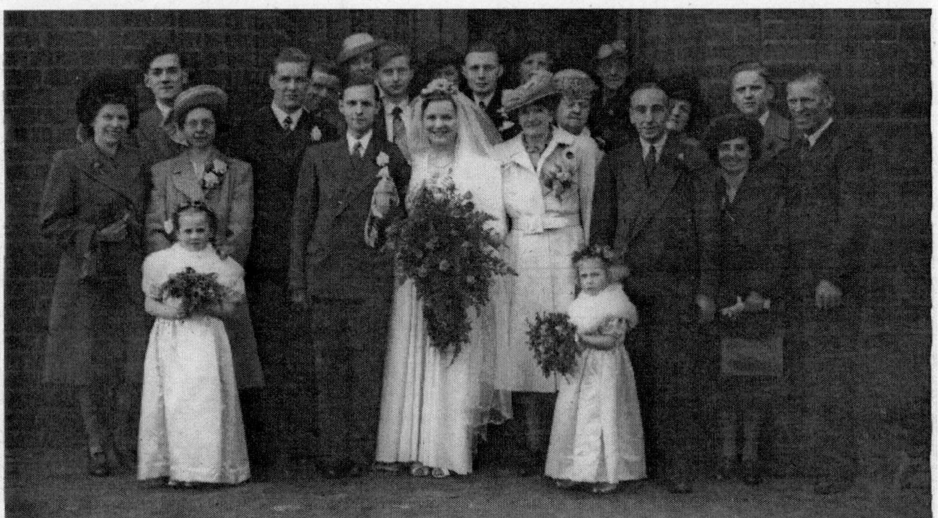

St Augustine's Church, Handsworth, 27th March 1948. My grandmothers are the nearest ladies to the bridesmaids, Lillian May on the left with my Aunt Kathleen. Elsie May Cutler had a fine wardrobe.

After the reception, Mr and Mrs Hearne took a British Rail train, perhaps for the first time together, from Snow Hill Station. The 1947 Transport Act would see all Great Four railway companies lose the identities they had proudly sustained since 1923, being merged and nationalised in 1948. Tired but happy, the newlyweds leaned and swayed for some miles against the carriage wall in the corridor. Because of the holiday period, the train was heavily crowded. After some time, Douglas said he would not be long, and entered one of the compartments. Minutes later, two men emerged with him, insisting that their offers of seats be taken.

When in their Aberystwyth hotel room, Mom asked Doug what on earth he had done to get them seats. She had been so glad to sit down. It was just a pity that everyone had been staring at her legs, though. She had felt so embarrassed. And her stockings were not at all laddered.

'I told them you had an artificial leg and were too shy and nervous to mention it yourself. I didn't expect to get two seats. They were probably trying to work out which was your real leg.'

Were married women not expected to work in those days? It seems incredible to me that Mom, given her abilities and with almost a decade's experience of at least basic office work, did not find a job. With only Dad's income to live on, they had no choice but to rent lodgings, with Mr and Mrs Trueman, at 151 Linwood Road, Handsworth. Far less attractive than Dad's Windermere Road home just under a mile away, this redbrick terraced Midlands house did not even boast a bijou front lawn or flower border, the street door being only two steps from the kerb. Even if the Truemans had no children or other family members living with them, just two couples living under the same roof must have been horribly on top of and always aware of each other. What did Valerie do all day, apart perhaps from go shopping for food, prepare meals, attend to the weekly wash and so on? She must have felt stunned by her constriction: no lively office, no whistle or song of mechanics nearby, or revving engines, clanking tools being dropped, ringing phones, arrivals and departures of cars and people … however tense her father had made home at times, with three brothers and a baby sister, not to mention her father's workmen and farm girls, it had always been animated … she *loved* Doug, but her heart still ached for Linnaeus William …

When Dad came home from work one evening, there was no Valerie, nor any note or word to explain where she might be. Maybe there had been some friction between them before he went to work that morning; he certainly feared she had gone for ever. He did a completely uncharacteristic thing: went to a public house, probably on his own.

Until I was in my mid to late teens my father was almost teetotal. Alcohol was rarely in the house. At Christmas one bottle each of Co-operative Society sherry and port would be bought, offered mostly to family and other visitors. They might not be finished for months. Perhaps once or twice a year, on a summer evening, Dad would walk to the off licence in our road, run by ancient, tottering Mr and Mrs Downes, shrivelled like quivering mice, to buy a small bottle of Ansells beer and one of Mason's or White's lemonade, to make up two glasses of shandy. So it would not have taken much more than a pint or two of draught beer that miserable evening to work a considerable effect, especially if he had not eaten. When my mother returned before bedtime, she found him in a woeful state: unco-ordinated, ill, emotional. I expect she had to find a bucket.

My birth at Dudley Hospital, in the Sandwell area of Birmingham, on Saturday 1st October 1949 was registered the following Monday week by Douglas Clifford Hearne, a steel stockholder's office manager. Did I make a distinguished entrance? HMP Winson Green was half a mile away, while just over 5000 miles further off the Chinese Revolution starting its very first day, when the communists entered Beijing, known to us then as Peking. I am not so sure I should earlier have claimed that Hearnes manage notable birthdays!

One day in my teens, whilst rummaging in a long-neglected cupboard, I came across a pencilled letter from my mother to my father. Written from her hospital bed, it showed her bathed in joy over and love for her beautiful baby, who resembled his dear, darling father etc. The tides of a woman's hormones reach their widest extremes in the season of parturition! Mom and Dad were happy.

Whatever the confines of early childcare were at 151 Linwood Road, I am sure my mother did an excellent job in those early days, actually nursing me for a whole year. The few photographs suggest I was bonny and reasonably bright eyed, albeit usually pensive. The main concerns in those times arose from the landlord's dog, which not only regularly barked me awake, but also was not prevented from fouling the hallway and landing outside our rooms. When Grandma Lil, on a visit, came to see for herself the filthiness of the Truemans' ménage, she uttered one of her inviolable fiats:

'We can't have this! You're coming to live with me!' She raised her voice. 'I won't have *my* grandson living in …' There followed an emphatic anagram of "this", the first of only two such indulgences reported in the whole lifetime of Lilian May Hearne. She probably made a flash judgment that it would be worth a few extra weeks in purgatory just to ease her feelings that moment.

That may have been the end of the matter in one sense, but there was a small preceding incident that deserves inclusion. After a series of canine horrors, Dad had spoken to a friend at work who knew all about animals … he subsequently supplied something, perfectly harmless in itself, but to dogs … Dad took it home, poured the stuff on a glove, dropped it outside the door. Some time later, padding paws and doggy pants could be heard from inside the room … then a sharp whine of distress, followed by a sustained flurry of howls and barks as Bonzo Trueman removed himself *prestissimo assai*.

'Whart have you dun to moy darg?' shouted Somerset-born Mrs Trueman from downstairs.

How everyone was accommodated, never mind rubbed along, at 10 Windermere was never explained to me. The figures are not easy to process: one obsessed female Catholic in her early 50s, one married couple, one weeks' old baby, two sons/brothers/brothers-in-law either side of 20, two double bedrooms. Where did we all sleep? I suspect parents and child were allowed the larger bedroom at the front, overlooking the trees; the 'boys' (my uncles) stayed in their own room, the second bedroom; and Grandma nightly converted the downstairs front room sofa, blue and velvet-covered, into a single bed for herself: you unscrewed and removed a little black knob in the outside middle of one side, allowing the whole arm to hinge down and lengthen things out for a shortish person to sleep. I did it several times when I was an older boy. To me it was an adventure; to a work-wearied, poor-sleeping late middle-aged woman who had had a hard time for years, it must have been tough.

With the enforced close proximity and limited facilities (I should think chamber pots were essential overnight), not to mention tension over the disturbance caused by a crying baby, my parents, particularly Mom, must have found it heavy-going too. Lil could be infuriatingly assertive in her quietly insistent way. 'Leave the baby to me, Valerie' was for decades afterwards a source of painful mirth between my parents. When Dad went down with the 'flu one winter, Lil kept vigil on a bedside chair all night. My mother never forgave her. Used to a household where feelings could be let rip and high spirits released, she must have felt permanently suppressed, unable to breathe fully. When I was grown up she confided in me the reason for her ultimatum to Dad that they must get a place of their own: his brother Gordon was behaving increasingly creepily to her, getting too close in the kitchen, saying how fond he was of her … Nuisance or not, he was an economical man, as well as generous. He had saved £200 to lend his brother towards the purchase of his first, mortgaged, property. He would own only one more before his death. In twenty years, most of the mortgage on that would remain unpaid.

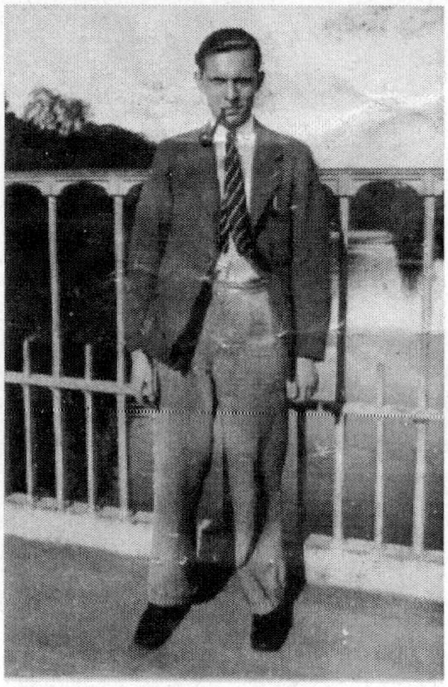

Dad at Tewksebury, circa 1946

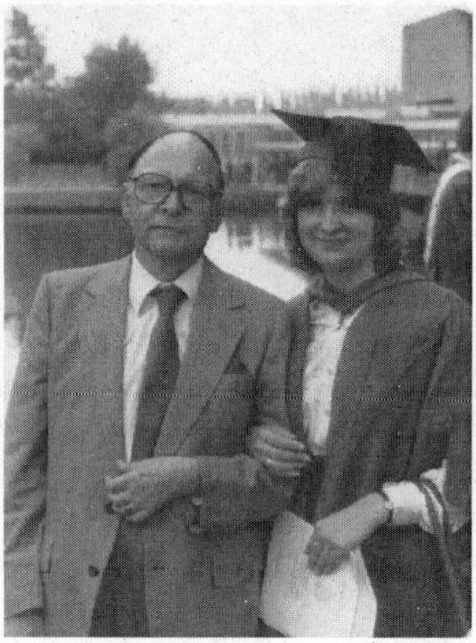

And at Sylvia's M.A. Graduation, York 1980

First Stop

The forest ended. Glad I was
To feel the light, and hear the hum
Of bees, and smell the drying grass
And the sweet mint, because I had come
To an end of forest ...
Edward Thomas – *The Other*

Newport Road was perfectly straight and about 350 yards long. I still occasionally dream of number 60, the first house I identified as home. I regularly dream I'm still there. Viewed on Google Street Map in the 21st century, it appears a reasonably respectable area, where many householders have troubled to replace windows, extending bays where possible. Some reconstruction has occurred towards the Ladypool Road end. In the 1950s a few lock up garages were accessed via an entrance between houses; Dad rented one for a time. In our last few months there, I frequently joined him at the end of the day, when he drove the black Morris Minor 1000 to be locked up for the night. Once the car was inside the single garage, we would sit while he wrote up his record of his day's dealings out on the road for W.G.Sice, Steel Stockholder, Oldbury. These were handwritten into a carbonised Champion book, often taking several pages, with the top copies for the office removed and placed in his handwritten envelope, to be posted at the corner of the road. Whilst Number 60 has been extended across its whole width at the front, to incorporate the front door and bay window, Number 62 shows the original construction. Unlocking our front door with the usual brass Yale key, you stepped directly into what we called our front room. As far I as knew, most of our neighbours maintained their front rooms as the best room in the house, usually carpeted and with more comfortable furniture, though rarely used. In all the years we lived there, our front room was used on only a handful of occasions. One Christmas family gathering around the rarely lit coal fire succeeded so well that I felt mystified we did not repeat it, though for at least two birthday parties, rowdy, physical events when a rough neighbour boy stamped on balloons, and games involved rushing around, screaming and pushing, it came into use. Otherwise, it simply became a storage area for the pram, the push-chair, my pedal car, a sideboard, some boxes containing unused wedding presents, my scooters, my train sets and other toys, articles of furniture and ornaments. On the floor was chill turquoise linoleum. It was a daily ritual to say goodbye to Dad, both in the morning and after his midday dinner, when Mom and I would go to the front door with him. I quickly learned to join in the litany of questions and checks: 'Got e keys? Got e money?' It seemed then that I should never be tall enough to reach the oval Yale l knob; then suddenly the day came when I did.

Like most of our other rooms, the front room was never decorated. Reasons will emerge. One early morning, whilst lying in bed, we heard a crashing noise from downstairs. Bizarrely, the whole of the ceiling paper had come down in one piece, spreading white dust lavishly. Declared a disaster, the mishap was never remedied; the mess was cleared away, and anyone whose gaze wandered upwards would see the yellowed patches, streaked with ageing and stains from an under-adhesive paste.

The interior door that faced the front door led to an enclosed and unlit square area. A black door on the left, made of planks like a garden gate and opened by lifting a latch, revealed the steps down to the coal cellar; the ordinary door opposite opened into the living room. This was the only room where we habitually lit a coal fire, and so where we spent most of our time. We ate at the reddish-brown polished oval table, later replaced by one of the typical square utility kinds, stained dark brown, with an extending leaf at each end, and six accompanying chairs. Two green, imitation leather armchairs faced each other across the fireside, a rug between them affording insulation from the lino. A door in the corner gave access to the stairs; the kitchen was reached by continuing to walk in a straight line from the front door. Whenever electricity was installed, it must have been minimally done. Apart from the single central light to each room or on the upstairs landing, there were only two power sockets, both in the living room. When, in 1958, my Christmas presents included the Tri-ang RFX set, with its R42 controller, I acquired a mains transformer, which meant that my mother's ironing and my table-top railway play could not occur simultaneously. No-one had thought of an extension lead in those days and the other socket was too far away in the corner. Plugs and sockets, incidentally, were two or three-pin round and definitely not fused. Flexes were commonly twisted and fabric-covered. The adaptors my father bought to take power from upstairs light fittings would surely not meet modern safety standards. We had to be kept warm somehow, especially when a baby arrived. Equally, the various paraffin heaters (Sankey, Valor, Tilley) were inherently highly dangerous and unhealthy. Flare ups alarmingly occurred when the Tilley had been insufficiently pumped. Sometimes flames rose threateningly high if wicks needed adjustment. But the greatest risk must surely have been presented by the very design and structure of 'Big Ginger', the Sankey Senator Paraffin heater. Behind and underneath the wick was an open metal tray into which paraffin drip-fed from a valve in the inverted tank. By rights we should have been immolated or poisoned by the stinking fumes and oxygen deprivation. Paraffin fires made the windows run like Alpine streams, though less freshly.

The kitchen, narrower than the other two downstairs rooms and one step down, was almost a working museum in those days. With one cold tap above the white vitreous sink, all water had to be heated on the antiquated black gas stove, or, for washing, in the gas boiler. The walls were of standard house brick, painted a pale green stale with smoke and other kitchen exhaust. The floor was dull red tiles, about a foot square. An old-fashioned and battered heavy door, constructed of planks fastened to one diagonal and two horizontal pieces of timber, opened to the grey-brick-paved yard. On its side against the brick wall dividing us from the yard of Number 58, The Mawbys', lay the full-size zinc bath, brought inside weekly to be placed in front of the open fire and filled, bucket after bucket, from the gas boiler. My earliest memories of being bathed involved a smaller zinc affair, vaguely oval in shape, with a looped handle at either end. To this day I do not forgive my mother for inviting a neighbour in while I was luxuriously immersed and soaping before the open fire. I was eight, and completely unaware that the same neighbour, nondescript enough, not to say tedious, would figure so devastatingly in my later life.

This kitchen, as may be easily visualised, was the traditional half-width of the main part of the house; the third bedroom was above. Integral to this structure but accessed from the yard was the outside lavatory. Thus inconvenienced in at least two senses, we compromised overnight with chamber pots, both china and enamelled metal. The morning's rituals included taking them outside to be emptied, rinsing them (rather unhygienically) from the only tap in the house, and freshening them with a slosh of (usually) pine disinfectant or Dettol. This chore inevitably fell to my mother, along with all the other household tasks, especially (in the colder months) cleaning out the grate, and laying and lighting the fire. Though Dad was skilled at encouraging and maintaining a fire, he normally engaged in affairs of the hearth only at the end of the day. So my mother's mornings were busy, even arduous. For, apart from the above and looking after me, she was also called upon to lay and prepare breakfast. At this period of her life, I never heard her complain. She would have been in her early thirties, and still apparently in love with my father, accepting the consequential duties and labours.

The outside lavatory was, of course, unheated and unlit. To venture there after dusk in the darker months meant taking a lit candle, stuck to an old saucer by melted wax, from the house, even as a seven-year-old. I once accidentally set fire to my fringe, being alerted by a new and pungent smell rather than any other sensation. The only other lavatory experience deserving mention must be my disgracefully wilful dispatch of my teddy and sundry other cuddly toys – all the ones I could locate, including Rabbit – into the lavatory pan. Why did I do such an outrageous thing? I knew it was a major violation. Perhaps I was three or thereabouts. I think Mom rescued the poor creatures and then boiled them in a galvanised tub on top of the gas stove for a sufficient time. Somehow they survived.

Happy times spent in happy places meant our back garden or the beach at the seaside. I had no idea how untended our garden was when I spent whole mornings and afternoons in solitary play. The wooden fence put splinters in your fingers. The one rose bush, which must have been a common, small-flowered floribunda with masses of pink flowers no more than an inch across, mounted thorn attacks. The whimsical ground dragged you summarily down to graze your knees. But I dug, with my seaside spade, rode my blue Vindec tricycle, my cream and red Mobo two-wheeler child's bike, imagined roads amongst the grass clumps for my Dinky cars. I played in the garden soil, my mother as innocent as I was about bacterial infection. I did rapidly learn, though, that earth did not really serve as an after-breakfast top up.

Mrs Williams, from Number 62, planted violets for me, which I ignorantly dug straight up. On one or two of the hottest summer days, the zinc bath was filled with water, as a miniature pool. The Williams son, Derek, was blind in one eye, from an accident. The family moved out in about 1953 or 1954, but somehow I later learned that Derek had qualified as a lawyer and then taken silk. The Wilkinsons replaced them: tall, angular Hilda, with her glasses and twitching nose, and her Lincolnshire husband, the ill-tempered and taciturn chauffeur who sometimes parked shiny black cars, mostly luxury Austins, outside the house. A practical man, he soon erected a shed, the end of which abutted the beginning of our garden. He maintained the privet hedge on his side of the fence between our gardens, and took pride in his flowers, particularly the roses. I remember with some interest watching him hand drill an empty bottle so as to feed the wire through for its conversion to a table lamp. Soon after their arrival, Hilda began to swell with her sole pregnancy, which produced the fair-haired and equally nervous Michael (he commenced every utterance with a hesitant 'erm' and some blinks). Even his infant bow-ties hinted at the family's pretensions; they wanted things to be special. Did I really (with a friend) throw earth at their washing on one occasion? There was certainly a lunchtime, when back home from school for my dinner, I knowingly lay low near the hedge and allowed Hilda to douse me with a half-bucket of water intended for our cat, Sooty. Though quite properly on our side of the hedge and fence, our male marauder was no doubt suspected of and maybe even contemplating feline offences in their well-turned rose beds. This sneaky manoeuvre gained me a twofold victory: too traumatised to be subjected to an afternoon in school, I inwardly rejoiced to hear that Dad had gone round to 'have a word' with Hilda.

The last tram to run in the City was on another Saturday evening. At least, that's what my mother and father told me. I was to make sure I remembered it. 'Look at that!' my mother said. 'Remember it. It's the last tram in Birmingham.' We were travelling back from Lil's in Handsworth, which meant two bus rides and a walk. Research reveals that the last tram ran on 4th July 1953, which was indeed a Saturday shortly after the Coronation, making me three months short of my fourth birthday. This significant siting of the cream and navy vehicle, no doubt festooned and feted, occurred in Digbeth, just down from the Bull Ring, still, like many other streets all over the city, cobbled. Until redevelopment in the 1960s, the area around St Martin's church was a gathering point, with thronging pedestrians, the women headscarved and the men with mackintoshes and flat caps, buying fruit or flowers, or perhaps on Sunday evenings listening to open-air talks or sermons.

Rides on buses and trains were relished events. When we waited outside Snow Hill Station for the second bus, the 70 to Oxhill Road, I would sit on a convenient green wooden box, probably a cupboard housing something electrical, inside the glass shelter. But it was *my* seat, always looked for. Even at two or three I bitterly resented it when some ignorant citizen stood too obstructively close for me to claim it. Birmingham City buses were also cream and navy, with rows of spherical light bulbs and chrome–surrounded 'Press to Stop' buttons. At night, drivers lowered the fan-folded black leather screen behind them, to prevent glare.

When Great Grandmother Anne-Maria Smith ('the Old Pot') was hospitalised in Kidderminster, we travelled to visit her from Snow Hill, probably on an ex-GWR train. I suspect my earliest memories are of going to her cottage at Bromsgrove. I must have gone more than once, since I recall being there with my parents but was also separately taken by her daughter Lil, I believe on a Midland Red bus. That would have been before the illness. To my young eyes she was a formidable figure: largebosomed, wavy-grey-haired and salmon-pink-cardiganed, with clucking chickens and prolific flowers in her garden. I think I was two. Or maybe I go back as far as the holiday at Brean in Somerset, when they bought me a green Jaguar toy car, and I was definitely two. I said the word as 'Jaggy-one'. I do not think it was Dinky 157, the Jaguar XK20; the shade of green is too olive.

Though she did not use the expression 'Rhesus incompatibility', my mother did explain to me, when I was still quite young, why after my arrival she experienced recurring pregnancy troubles. She was always very open and informative about such matters, stressing that it was all very natural and that I should know what happened. She had two serious miscarriages in my very early days. I still see her on the stretcher, having been somehow carried down the extremely narrow stairs with the 90° bend before the final step into our back room, where I was told to stand back. She looked pale and weak, faintly saying something reassuring to me. The first time, she was taken to the hospital at Marston Green, the second to the fairly new Queen Elizabeth, which she much preferred. Her blood group being Rhesus negative and my father's Rhesus positive, her first pregnancy had been as safe and satisfactory as you may consider the writer to be! As then is frequent, though, her body developed antibodies to any subsequent foetus which had a blood group with a positive factor, causing a miscarriage usually quite late into the gestation. My father plainly had the positive factor, since my blood group is O+. These days, after ante-natal blood tests, the mother is routinely given an injection of Rh immune globulins at the appropriate number of weeks, and another at delivery. I am not sure exactly what procedure or treatment my mother was given, but she did say the doctors at the QE had done something that prevented any further problems of that kind. This must have been before her second successful pregnancy, and so somewhere between 1949 and 1955. I hated what must have been her dramatic and loud bouts of morning sickness, when I could hear her vomiting into a two gallon white enamel bucket in the kitchen; an opera singer at full extent could not have made more noise. I used to slam the door, rush to an armchair, put my head on the seat and hold a cushion over my head to try to block it out.

'Don't be sick, Mom!' was a fairly pointless and unhelpful thing to shout through!

*****

It was not necessarily only hatching babies that caused both our throats to convulse, though happily mine unproductively; Mom also suffered migraines that wiped her out in more ways than one, a genetic transfer she need not have troubled herself to make to me! Like her, incidentally, I have noticed a change in the nature and frequency of attacks over the course of my life. One factor is probably hormones, or hormonal changes. One mid-morning in the second form at grammar school, just as the room was emptying for break, I could not see properly: dazzling patches of light were fixed on my eyes; they moved with them, blotting out my vision. I felt dazed and weird. I had to tell first Chris in front of me, then the teacher. I was taken to the medical room. No one explained what was happening or calmed me down. After receiving the phone call Mom prevailed upon a neighbour to do the taxi work. I should normally have been exhilarated to ride in a newish Jaguar! Those first occasions, when thirteen or fourteen, were probably the worst. Though I did not vomit, I was laid in a darkened room without being able to eat till the next day. When life continued, a throbbing slice across my forehead and eyes if I forgot myself and bent down to tie my shoes, went from four to nine on a scale of ten. Some months later there was a recurrence, though whether Mr Southall in his luxury car again did the pickup I cannot tell.

From my mid-teens onwards, the spasmic blood vessels in my head behaved themselves, until the last day of my first year at college, when the summer's light, flashing off the trunk's lid, pulled the firing pin. It just had to be cheap night in the bar, when kegs were sold off laughably cheaply to dispose of the contents; instead of Double Diamond pints for pennies I was reduced to cautiously sipping a small lemonade on a soft chair!

Two first year friends crashed into the JCR, dressed in faultless evening wear, faultless except that their suits, shirt, bow ties and everything else were utterly sodden and squelching. Les Irvine, the Scottish distance runner and University Athletics Captain from his very first term, walked right through a Parker Knoll without noticing it, flapping briefly on the floor like a landed salmon before flopping back into the seat and declaring delightedly:

'We've been swimming in the Cam!'

The explanation was simple. As Captain, Les had hosted the end-of-year stand up drinks party by white-clothed tables with white-jacketed waiters on a college's lawn, the sort of session that usually lasted just an hour, frequently before the college serves the evening meal. His roommate and buddy, Peter Hamilton from Northern Ireland, had gone along as guest. At the end of the hour, it seemed an obvious thing to borrow one of the free punts from Queens' College, and go up or down the river. A boat even awaited them in its mooring. Les undid the rope and stepped, perhaps rocking a little more than usual, on board. He knelt on the flat platform and called up to the bank:

'Get in, Peter! I'm holding it for you.' He was clinging to the wall.

That would have to be the very moment the wall moved. Les toppled forward flailing into the water. Peter's laughing fit was possibly only a nervous reaction, not mockery. Les slid and tumbled back on board.

'Give us your hand!'

As he pulled Peter forwards, he shoved the bank with one foot. The gap widened, too large even for the long leg of a drunk super-athlete. River Cam 2: Athletics Society Revellers 0.

Split raw temples or not, someone had to look after them. Incapable as babes, they benignly allowed me to take each by the arm, exit the building, travel the covered walkway, enter Garden Court and, after many alarming stops, when Les attempted to disengage himself to lean over the chasmic stairwell (they were on S corridor, the fourth floor) and spread his news two floors below:

'Oy, Rich! We've been swimming in the Cam!'

He was a good six feet tall and heavy, with the shoulders and rib cage of a Michelangelo statue. I clung shakily on to him … Did he ever realise how lucky he had been?

When I called in on them next morning, they had not budged from their beds. They were able to laugh, but not too heartily.

For most of my adult life I have gone for up to a decade without an attack. Then out of nowhere I notice the dazzles. On several occasions they have been switched on just when I should have been able to relax … One summer, after the term and school year finished at midday, I drove two miles into town. On the way back I had to stop the car in a bus stop pull in, and wait for my sight to return. That was it for another ten years. No axe-splitting headache afterwards either. Another time, I had just driven 260 miles to a Cornish holiday venue: temporary wipe out. Bright lights, stress, high humidity are all risk factors.

I said my mother's experiences changed. In her middle to late years she used to go numb around the mouth and could not speak. She had pins and needles in her hands. Whilst I never enjoy the business, I have become fascinated by its effects. It must, in my case at least, hit some language centre in the brain. Especially in the first few minutes of an attack I cannot work out how to spell even the simplest of no-trick words.

One Friday morning, soon after arriving at work, I noticed the ripples of the loathsome thing surfacing as I sat in my office, just a few minutes before our weekly meeting in the Headmaster's study. The full works did not actually immediately set themselves into incapacitating motion. I thought it might be all right to try putting in an appearance at SMT. I went along five minutes before the time, to explain to the HM that I might not say much, or even just get up and walk out, if that would be all right with him. I was having a migraine. It could go either way. The kind old cricketer said stay.

When, during the meeting, I started to comment on some agenda item, my six colleagues around the oval table all suddenly look shocked. Three or four even quickly stood up.

'Are you all right? Shall we call Sister over?'

The more I tried to reassure them, the greater their alarm. The Second Deputy took my arm and gently walked me over to the Health Centre. They made me lie down for a few hours and suggested I see my GP as soon as I could. I think the Nurse made the phone call for me. As the Head of Upper School put it the next Monday:

'You were doing an Eric Morecombe. They were the right syllables, but not necessarily in the right order!' The Second Deputy thought he had said something to upset me and that I was having a stroke!

*****

By searching the internet and contacting Birmingham Public Records Office, I have discovered the dates of my brother Nicholas's birth and death. He was born at 60 Newport Road on 7th July 1952, and died aged twelve days old, on 19th July in Selly Oak Hospital. I do not know whether Mom went to Selly Oak with Nicholas after his birth, but she was, I think, said to have come away from the hospital without him. Dad then visited the hospital every day after work. His occupation is described as 'steel stockholder's order clerk', which makes me suspect that he was still working for Charles ('Charley') Wade. Since Dad probably worked on a Saturday morning, one can only guess the distress he experienced at having to open the front door of 60 Newport Road and break the worst news to my mother. It would probably have been mid-afternoon, and he would still not have had his midday meal. I cannot imagine how my mother passed the days and hours alone in the house after she was separated from Nicholas. Her physical and mental condition must have been very raw. Even thirty-nine years after Dad's death, his signature on the certificates is very familiar, the florid capital D and the even more ornamented H of his surname suggest a stylish self-consciousness in line with his idea of himself as a cultured and artistically interested, though poor and lowly, gentleman. After what can only have been a wretched weekend, he must have taken time off work on Monday 21st July for the sad business of the dual registrations, though it is possible that date occurred during the annual industrial fortnight holiday. That would be consistent with my uncle's freedom to look after me, as I shall explain.

Nicholas's cause of death is given as: I a Bronchopneumonia, b Oesophageal atresia & Trachio oesophageal fistula. II Embolism of Aorta from Ductus Arteriosus. P.M. [presumably Post Mortem] Certified by J.E.Openshaw, B.M.

The Great Ormond Street website informs us that 'Oesophageal atresia (OA) is a rare condition where a short section at the top of the oesophagus (gullet) is closed off. This means food cannot pass from the throat to the stomach.' From the U.S. National Library of Medicine's site, we further learn that oesophageal atresia, a congenital defect, is a 'disorder of the digestive system in which the oesophagus does not develop properly. In most cases, the upper oesophagus ends and does not connect with the lower oesophagus and stomach. The top end of the lower oesophagus connects to the windpipe. This connection is called a tracheoesophageal fistula (TEF). Some babies with TEF will also have other problems, such as heart or other digestive tract disorders.' Mom several times commented that Nicholas was a poor and sickly baby with a variety of problems, but that he quite possibly could have been saved by surgical intervention had he arrived some years later. Perhaps there is no point in repining at Nature's habitual wastefulness, though some consolation derives from believing that the tiny being who quickened and grew in my mother, umbilically sustained until he entered daylight, and who came to breathe, weep, agitate his puny limbs, only to find himself utterly unable to take vital nourishment, can have had little, if any, understanding of what was happening to him as he starved and choked his way to an early death. His ticket expired before he had travelled even one stop down the line.

I was told by my parents that Nicholas was buried in New Oscott cemetery. For quite a time I could not trace the record of his interment. It was possible that he was included in an existing family grave. New Oscott Cemetery was opened in 1939 for Birmingham Catholics, and so too late for my grandfather, Clifford Harry Hearne, who died 31st December, 1936, aged only 36, and cruelly the day before my father's fourteenth birthday.

I am indebted to my former pupil Pat, whom I taught as Patricia Heal in the 1970s, for putting her research skills into motion. After tracing many branches of her own family tree she had the knowledge and website membership necessary to come back to me with the information that Nicholas was buried in a communal grave, giving me the grid reference. I shall visit one day. I hope to find something like a rose garden.

Around Nicholas's birth, I was taken by Lil and my father's younger brother, Gordon (born 29th December 1925), by train to New Brighton, where we stayed with Great Aunty Elsie, Lil's sister. As far as I understand, Gordon sacrificed his annual summer fortnight to playing on the beach with me, making sand boats, with shells for dashboard dials and a steering spade, for me to sit in. In those days, men commonly wore suits or blazers on the beach. Gordon additionally sported an idiosyncratic navy beret. Men did wear hats in the 1950s. Dad's was a trilby. Was Gordon's quirk a relic from his Army days in Singapore and Burma? Did he ever forgive his mother for gifting his curved Japanese sword to the rag-and-bone man? She said she was glad to get it out of the house. I have only recently begun to wonder why she felt uneasy. I shall mention his breakdown in a later narration. The other members of the family were Great Uncle Eric and his two daughters, Joan and Rita. Their house was on the corner of a steeply sloping road that went down at right angles to the water. One day we took the ferry to Liverpool. Early in the morning, ships' sirens resounded over the water, waking us up. When we drew the curtains we beheld the magnificent new arrivals with their colourful funnels. What would otherwise have been the Bradleys' New Brighton downstairs front room was one of their two shops selling jewellery and timepieces. (The other shop was at Liscard.) Upstairs, with windows on two sides, was a large, long lounge, complete with pianola, which Rita would pedal too fast for Uncle Eric's approval. When our stay was over, they all escorted us to the station, giving me some little toy plastic vehicles to play with on the train. Their kindness extended to sending me two jigsaw puzzles, one of the Queen Mary liner and the other the Golden Arrow train, for my third birthday, 1st October 1952. Opening the brown paper parcel afforded me powerful delight.

My mother was so distraught at having to leave hospital without Nicholas that after his death she entered a depression and was inconsolable for some time. So, on return from New Brighton, I lived with Grandma Lily at 10 Windermere Road, Handsworth, sharing her double bed in the front bedroom, with its two windows overlooking leafy trees, a diaphanous-green screen in the early morning light. Unheated, despite the provision of a grate and chimney, it was ever chill, with cold linoleum underfoot, and smelling of must and moth-balls. It was part of my morning fun to join Gordon in his bed for a few minutes before 'the boys', as Lil invariably called them, had to get ready for work. I assumed from hints given by my mother that I was away for several weeks and that the grief for her lost baby meant that she just did not want me. From the knowledge I now have of when Nicholas's birth and death were registered, it seems that it cannot have been that long. The day came when, with one of her characteristic rushes of strong feeling, my mother suddenly wanted me back. Since neither household had a telephone, I am not sure how communication occurred. Perhaps Dad called the corner shop from the red kiosk at the corner of Newport Road and Church Road, asking for the message to be personally delivered by the shopkeeper. Or maybe he phoned one of my uncles at work. We boarded the bus on Oxhill Road to the city centre, took a second one to Moseley Road and walked the rest. I may have been in my blue push-chair.

I think it was from this time that I stopped eating meat. Maybe Auntie Elsie was an incompetent cook. (Oh yes, she was! Anyone who sniffed the air in her house, as I later did in 1959, would have instantly known that she should not have been allowed in a kitchen without a security guard. Her ham boiling might have emptied provinces.)

Ah, food! Earliest home memories are of three definite meals a day, eaten at the oval table, properly laid with a laundered tablecloth. Rice Krispies had sugar and milk added to them. My child's cutlery set had a green-handled knife and chrome-plated spoon and fork, each with a pig embossed on the fat part of the handle. Write your own caption. Though he left Wade's to work in town, at J.L.Brearley, Steel Stockholder, Dad came home for lunch, as he bizarrely did almost every single day of his working life. How many men do that, I wonder. How many would want to? For at least three or four years, until Mr Brearley told him he must acquire a car and learn to drive if he wanted to keep his job, Dad relied on walking and buses. Five feet six inches tall and skinny (I think he weighed not much more than eight stones then), he was physically fit. Like other 1950s mothers, Mom stopped working when she married. As a stay-at-home housewife, she walked to the shops every day to buy food, which always included fresh meat or fish. Afternoons often saw baking sessions. Our copy, a small paperback book of probably 100-200 pages, of the revered Mrs Beeton must have been a selection of her recipes, only part of her complete *Family Cookery.* I suspect some enterprising post-war publisher identified a market possibility, and provided a popular selection. I enjoyably participated in stirring the mixture of eggs, flour, sugar and butter, adding dried fruit for the small round cakes, six or twelve to a baking tray. Soon, enticing aromas floated from the kitchen into the living room. The first sample – 'Be careful, our Martin, it's hot!' – invariably melted into deliciousness. A treat was to scrape the last traces from the bowl. We had not heard of salmonella in those days. Apple pies, rice puddings and various crumbles were frequently made. Fruit and vegetables were seasonal. My mother did not have the use of a fridge until the 1970s. No second invitation was necessary to shell the peas (and eat as many of them, wonderfully sweet, as I could filch) into the aluminium colander. As the day's vegetables were prepared, pieces of cut-up and washed carrot, swede, turnip and even potato were handed to me in the kitchen as informal *hors d'oeuvres* to be eaten there and then standing up, likewise trimmed runner beans or whatever else was to hand. Though, as you will see, we were not far from the edge of poverty, the quality and freshness of our food reached admirably high standards. We relied little on prepared foods, with the exception of tinned fruit (peaches, tangerines, apricots), eaten with that curiously viscous and tangy evaporated milk. Other tinned items were Heinz baked beans and (occasionally) their Cream of Tomato soup, which has not changed in well over fifty years. I might mention here that Mom's soups, or broths as she called them, with minutely diced vegetables, were exquisitely fine, though I have no idea how she coaxed those extra flavours out of the ingredients. Boiled eggs appeared at breakfast; cheese salads were accompanied by finely grated carrot as well as something nutty and also grated I cannot recall (hazel nuts?) on shredded lettuce, with perhaps dried fruit, sultanas or currants, sprinkled around; tea (we called the midday meal 'dinner') might involve something with toast: cheese, baked beans, a poached egg.

Food, of course, means shopping – or perhaps deliveries. Joe the Co-op milkman, in his brown cow gown, placed three bottles of milk, two of pasteurised, one of sterilised, on our doorstep every morning, rattling the reclaimed rinsed empties. If he did not visit some houses, then Wacaden's man did. He drove a whining, three-wheeled electric vehicle; Joe had a large, snorting horse. We saved our cut grass for him.

The coalmen, who might also have been from the Co-op, also delivered from a horse-drawn wagon in the early days. My job was to count the number of one hundredweight, heavy-duty rope and jute sacks that were carried on their backs and emptied rattling down the opening in front of our house, clumping lumpily down into the cellar. In just a few years delivery horses were phased out, though the rag and bone man's lingered on for years. We did not have bread delivered by the Hovis van that regularly drove past. Our laundry, meaning sheets and larger items, was collected in tied up bundles, returned a few days later in another parcel, brown-paper wrapped and cross tied with string. Every Friday, the greengrocer, Bratton's, from around the corner delivered our order of fruit and vegetables in a cardboard box. My mother had given them her handwritten list the previous day.

At least once every day we walked to the shops in Ladypool Road, between Church Road and Brighton Road. In perhaps 150 yards you could find most things that you might normally want. Wrensons was a provisions and food store, with marble counters along both sides, like the old-fashioned Sainsbury's. The Co-operative store, larger and further down the road on the other side, offered more. Watching the payment and change zing along wires never failed to fascinate me. I have mentioned the greengrocer's. Add a fish monger that spilled its stalls onto the broad pavement, an ironmongery, shoe shop, draper's, butcher's, bakery (which always smelt wonderful), newsagent, confectionery and provision shop, motor bike showroom, pharmacist/post office and others I am probably overlooking, and you will see that most things necessary were within ready access, certainly walking distance. The chemist's, owned and run by Mr Kerkhoff, who lived above it, sported rows of huge stylish glass containers containing vividly coloured transparent liquids, for display only then but once working vessels. Medicines were still mixed from a multitude of stock bottles on site, usually on the very shelf behind Mr Kerkhoff, white coated at the counter. He measured and poured small amounts of colourless, radioactive-looking yellow stuff into a glass bottle, added some powder from a rolled sachet, inserted a cork with a twist and shook it up, inverted. The self-adhesive label was written on the counter, peeled off its backing sheet and pressed around the flat, shouldered bottle, which you returned, washed, after use.

In the window was a small selection of Kodak and Ilford roll film cameras: a Brownie box, the same manufacturer's 127 (at 25s 3d, taking 12 photos 1½ in square on 127 film), the 44a and Cresta 3. The Ilford models were more expensive, as much as £12 or even £15 with the leather case, and used 35 mm film, like the Sportsman. As at many other chemists', films were accepted for developing and printing, being sometimes processed on site.

The typical red telephone kiosk on the corner outside the shop really was a lifeline, since hardly any house had its own phone. At any hour of the day or night, local residents would run panting to it to summon help after a serious accident, medical emergency or to alert the midwife when labour started. My father must have done the last mentioned at least five times! When a rare necessity arose, Mr Kerkhoff allowed his out of hours privacy and even sleep to be broken in order to relay vital messages in the neighbourhood. Dad did have to knock him up once. I do not recall the crisis.

Not long after Christmas 1954 my mother must have confirmed with a visit to Dr Fraser Brown on Moseley Road that she was pregnant. One afternoon we walked to book the midwife, just over half a mile away in Esme Road, a hill to climb. In an ordinary house lived a number of unmarried midwives. Though not attached to any religious order, in other respects they were just like the ones in the mawkishly nostalgic television programme, with similar uniforms, belted raincoats and so on. When they visited our house in the later months, to check my mother and ensure that all the preparations for a home delivery were being made, they propped their basket-fitted bicycles against the front wall. Of course everything was ready: Mom had been through all of this before with Nicholas and possibly some of it before her two miscarriages. The appointed date approached: 1st August.

It was a hot summer. My mother had been very big for some weeks, smiling and rosy faced. She walked more slowly and with a waddle. She gave little puffs and noises when she stood up or sat down. July went by … the swelling grew. So did the craving for chocolate! Almost every afternoon I was dispatched to the bottom of the road opposite to buy a block of Aero chocolate from Skiffington's newsagent's. Children as young as five were trusted to go to the shops on their own then.

Saturday 30th July saw the start of the Bank Holiday weekend. No movement. Same the next day, Sunday. The predicted day, the holiday Monday, dawned.

Mom was feeling energetic and expansive in more ways than one. She ordered my father to take us out for the day. She had always wanted to go to Tewkesbury, for a ride on the river. My father hesitated. Should he really risk a round trip of eighty or so miles? He called upon good sense. He tried persuasion.

Half an hour after breakfast, we were doing 50 mph in his grey Austin 8 Tourer, with the hood down. At some point we passed Dr Brown as he drove the other way past us. The weather remained superb all day. I sat between my parents on the top of the river cruiser, looking at the frothing white waters of the Severn – or was it the Avon? The town stands at their confluence.

I had been sleeping for some weeks in the little third bedroom, moved away as far as possible from the front one.

In the morning of Tuesday 2nd August, my father came into my bedroom.

'You've got a little sister,' he said.

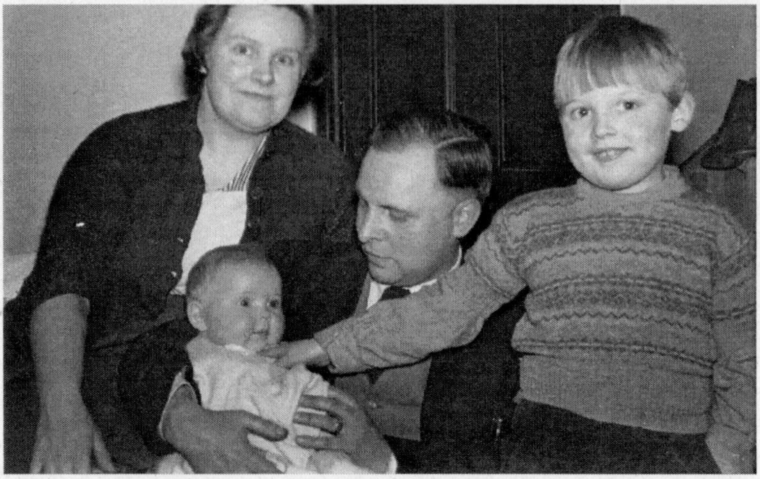

Sylvia's Bathtime, 1955

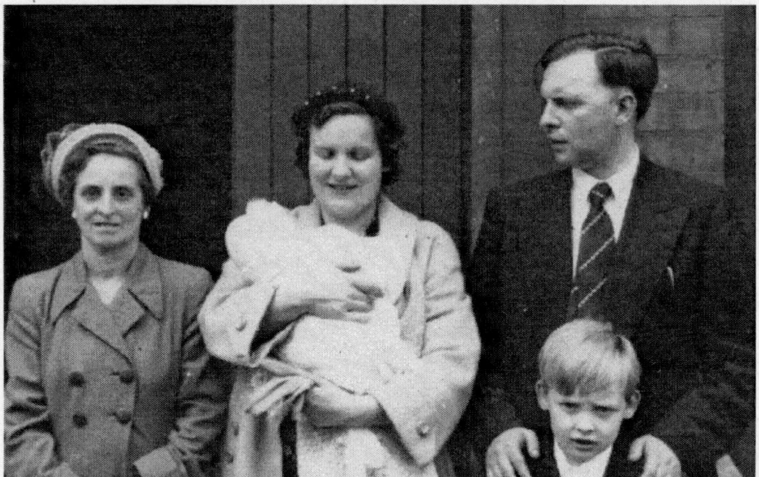

Her Christening, with Godmother Great Aunt Annie

Occupation

They fuck you up, your Mom and Dad,
They may not mean to, but they do.
- Philip Larkin - *This Be The Verse*

Intentionally or not, Larkin achieved a productive ambiguity with his first four famously shocking words: your parents really do bring you from nowhere and nothing into a being before everyone's eyes, like conjurers raising spirits, only with a different spell. And with total reliability they make a pretty rotten job of it! Even more uncomfortably, you may well be the sort of accident that could have been avoided by a driver's last moment swerve, but this time on a vehicle's back seat! (My parents were not to have a car for a few more years.)

One school of child psychologists legislates that, to ensure a perfectly balanced, happy, charming, well-adjusted near facsimile of yourself – a *homunculus idoneus* perhaps – all you have to do is trowel on the approval and smiles tirelessly. What a good boy! How clever you are/he is! My word – did you do that *all on your own*? That's wonderful! Make sure he wins at Ludo and Draughts most if not all of the time. My father did.

We need water to survive, but too much of it ruins our biochemical balance. I was a horrible brother. Sylvia Margaret, whose second name I suggested since I was soft on the gap-toothed classmate across the room, was a perfect, bonny baby, blue eyed and fair. She gave her mother no undue trouble at all; she slept, fed, bubbled and gooed; then smiled, sat up, became even more winning. Valerie May was delighted with her new creature, Nature and the doctors, probably even with herself. Dad almost injured himself with grinning. At the evening's bath time he removed his jacket, rolled up his shirt sleeves, put a towel on his lap and did the full honours of washing and playing. He could use ordinary baby soap to blow from the extended joined first fingers and thumbs of both hands the most enormous bubbles, bigger than balloons, for the splashing infant to pop, blinking. When his daughter was beginning to speak, she first pronounced her name as *Tull* and then *Ulvia* (like Mark Antony's wife missing the first letter). In drying her, Dad laid her across the towel on his lap and 'played the Ulviana', singing his own invented lyrics and tickling her theatrically, as if playing the piano, to the tune of the Hokey Cokey:

O, the Ulviana (repeated) etc

I had been the first child of my parents, the first grandchild of two grandmothers and one grandfather (after a reconciliation, which proved only transient), the first nephew to five uncles and an aunt only eight years older, not to mention neighbours and family friends who had been Greek chorusing my virtues and charms relentlessly for over five years. I was spoiled. I could not have put it into words. I felt a difference. I was jealous, as revoltingly difficult and complaining as I could manage.

My two youngest grandchildren, only eighteen months apart, are as harmoniously happy and secure as any pair of that age can be. Petty irritations apart, they look after each other automatically and rather touchingly. I had had everything and everyone to myself for just too long.

My first nasty trick was completely accidental. A few weeks after the birth, we went for a week's holiday to Bryn Glas Farm in Bangor. Nellie, the black and white working sheepdog, and I were equally white-eyed and wary of each other, the farmer's wife the only adult I have ever seen outside a care home for the so-sadly-demented to flaunt nostrils perpetually blocked with viscous grey-green snot.

Wales in the last week in September never disappoints. The winds, mists and rains make sure of that. We dared the beach once or twice. Wellingtons, a thick jumper, woolly hat and even a school mackintosh did not proof me enough to excavate the toffee thick sodden sand to fashion pies and forts. I lavishly contributed my moodiness to the misery.

As you might have foreseen, my father had written to request special permission for me to miss a week of school, since the autumn term had started on about 6th September. We had been back a good two weeks. It was not only the weather and my disgruntlement to have become a brother that were consuming me within. I made sure the Saturday drive home was doubly unbearable for my father, whose gastric volcanoes had dramatically erupted before we left and remained bubbling all day, so that he did not dare eat a mouthful. It was my sixth birthday, and I had not yet had my present! I whined more all the way back more than the pre-war 900cc Austin engine and transmission. We did just reach Burton's, the toyshop in Ladypool Road, before closing time. My parents' present to me was a large, silver-finished space gun that fired caps and generated sparks from flint behind a ruby red transparent plastic panel.

Children are unhealthy things. My first gift to Sylvia was the whooping cough I had been incubating in North Wales. To warm up my weary mother, I first took her through the full experience of tending a feverish and querulous child for some days. Then, under ten weeks old, my innocent sister had the full works visited upon her, including one enormous explosion of cough-induced projectile vomiting I can still visualise. My mother sat motionless in the armchair, dripping. Thereafter, the poor mite was left with a squint, one eye wandering inwards. The corrective operation could not be performed in the children's hospital until she was two years old. It upset my father horribly to leave her screaming after him, trying all she could to get past the legs of nurses blocking her. The muscular repair worked, though glasses were needed afterwards. They tested little children by getting them to manipulate pictures on a screen, putting Bunny in the Box and so on. The first specs, NHS supply, were the standard 'owl-eyes' round ones, with a petrol blue frame weakly attempting to make a brave show of things. Optician Uncle Ken dispensed a far more stylish and feminine pair, with red wavy tops. It was part of the family conspiracy: make them *very* smart and she will want to wear them!

How many nappies does a newborn baby get through (sometimes too literally) in twenty-four hours? It must be ten or twelve. We had three dozen or so terry ones, the last dozen starting off brand new this time. Even with what my wife and I used to call the 'two bucket system' in the 1980s, that meant doing a nappy wash every other day. My mother did not have a washing machine or spin dryer till her first twin tub in the 1960s. Even without a baby, Mondays and Tuesdays were major labours, using the gas boiler, a zinc tub brought in from the yard, a dolly (or posser or posher), the hot-water-tapered boiler stick scalded to the pith, wood and metal tongs, a wringer, scrubbing board and brush … The back door was left open in all seasons. Windows steamed. The kitchen floor swilled and frothed. It had to be mopped and wiped afterwards. When rain would not allow things to be hung outside, they were draped on furniture or on a clothes airer in front of the fire, where they steamed and occasionally dripped.

Just for nappies, we had a lidded zinc cooker-top boiler, almost always percolating. You filled it from the mains gas boiler with a bucket. How there were not more accidents, with tired mothers, screaming children, a soapy-slithery floor and a huge, high placed vessel with gallons of water boiling stuns understanding. It was perilous work, and highly arduous. The regular dilemma whether to risk hanging out nappies to dry *on a Sunday*, when the neighbours might be offended, seemed incapable of resolution. The words of the Scaffold's droning number *2 Day's Monday* get it wrong very near the beginning: Tuesday was never soup but *always* ironing. My mother and both grandmothers obeyed this law. Less disruptive and uncomfortable, it still caused upheaval, with piles of clean laundry waiting, items airing, others waiting to be taken off airers and put away. As a curious aside, Grandma Lil used to iron on the dining table, which was natural, unpolished wood. She would remove the cloth and place an old heavy grey blanket on it. Clothing was all hand washed or boiled. Till well into the 1960s, Dad wore detachable collars, attached by two studs. To restore their whiteness and stiffness they had to be scrubbed and starched. Amid or around all this, shopping had to be fetched, meals prepared, children occupied, crying babies fed …

It was Nurse Pedrick who delivered Sylvia Margaret. David Ian followed on 18th March 1958. Though a normal baby, his arrival was not without some anxiety: the umbilical cord was wrapped around his neck, impeding the delivery and his vital supplies. Nurse Brown (on this occasion) had to work very swiftly and expertly to set my little brother going. Whether his birth trauma caused lasting distress or insecurity, in his early days he proved, though physically perfect, indeed very beautiful, an unsettled and anxious baby. Mom had nursed Sylvia and me with plentiful ease, but Nature did not suit David or was not working so well. Quite early on, the clinic or doctor suggested switching him to SMA, which proved successful, though at nine shillings a pink tin from Mr Kerkhoff, costly. Dad's weekly gross pay would not reach even £20 until nearly two years later. For the cost of one tin of SMA you could easily have bought ten of either sliced white loaves or tins of Smedley's baked beans, or even (overlooking the diabetic risk) a festive binge of eighteen Mars bars!

Solving the issue of nutrition was not all. For an unusually large portion of the next three years or so her youngest production could not bear to be put down. When rarely not asleep, he had to be held. Mom found no other way of doing things than clasping him permanently to her left side while she was working in the kitchen or around the house. Certain tasks were massively difficult or just impossible.

Jealousy apart, watching my younger sister and brother develop from birth onwards and the experience of helping with some of their care were fascinating then and have proved useful in looking after our own children – and now grandchildren. Though the tiredness and tedium of an inconsolable teether or endless repetition of a mind paralysing playroom ritual mercifully evaporate into the past – you know that they happened, but like toothache cannot feel it now – some good things remain. Our daughter-in-law dubbed me 'the baby whisperer' for settling young ones to sleep; I have used the same methods of rocking and crooning, the same lullabies and songs, as I heard my parents and grandparents use, even to me. If I begin to sing *Bye Baby Bunting* to three-year-old Elise, she plays the game of swiftly stopping my mouth with her hand: 'No, Papa!' It did work on her, though, at the right period. Family life continued, too predictably for further detail.

There were special events. Since I came across the Romans' impersonal *accidit* ('it happens' or 'it happened') I have mused at how language affects and alters thought and thereby feeling. Our derivative *accident* is so charged with urgency and distress.

I was seven. It was a holiday afternoon at Easter time. I had gone to play in the garden of Pat and Susan Smith, who lived five doors away. We were kicking a plastic football back and forth. I have no idea why I was wearing my school blazer.

Behind me was Wilf Smith's garden shed, I should think six feet by four feet, sideways on. A pane of glass in shed windows these days is 2mm thick, about 5/64 inches imperially: very thin. An large irregularly shaped piece of one pane, about a quarter of the whole area, had somehow been knocked out, then precariously replaced. Wilf had deftly reseated it, suspended on its wavy edges, balanced by gravity on its own scant thickness.

When a little more than twice my age then I could have worked out, with a glass sample, balance and basic physics formulae, how much sideways noise vibration would have been needed to exert a sufficient force to dislodge the piece. I have always liked pointless little games! The slightest amount of ordinary common sense should have immediately blasted with a ship's siren lack of ambiguity: not just with his or anyone else's little children around but just anyway, that this was a Very Silly Idea. Maybe tiredness from his night shift as a Cadbury's electrician at Bournville made it bypass his judgment.

At different times I fancied myself as a goalkeeper, perhaps because you don't have to run around too much. In practice, any goal I guarded was as little protected as the ground by gravity! The shed side was my goal.

For a girl of my age, Pat Smith kicked pretty well, at least as well as I could. Her first shot slammed into the wood behind me.

The dislodged pointed shard hit first the double material thickness of my blazer's collar. Deflected, it somehow continued its plunge to bite the outside of my right calf, a couple of inches above the ankle bone.

I had had many cuts. Blood, even my own, did not trouble me. Grazed knees, hands and forearms ripped on thorns or sharp wood, a finger's lost skirmish with a penknife (at my age!) – these and other unsought slices and piercings, though initially sore, were actually quite interesting. I *liked* the attention of having plasters applied.

The glass blade had known its business. Unknown colours and textures of subcutaneous material gleamed whitely up at me. Screaming girls fetched Mrs Smith. My mother was summoned.

I do not know who looked after toddler Sylvia. I suspect Canadian Edna Smith. At the nearer end of our road, on the other side, was Jones' garage and taxi service. Such small, family businesses must have died out years ago. In a road of terraced houses, the corner pair - or perhaps three - had been converted into a workshop and living accommodation. The kerb along the garage's length had been dropped down, to allow vehicles to draw up to the fuel pumps and tyre compressor. Two black Austin Princesses, four litre gas guzzlers that at their best could manage only 23 seconds for 0-60 mph, were kept dazzlingly immaculate by the younger Jones son, Bunny, clean cut in a black two-piece suit with a shiny-peaked chauffeur's cap. He regularly parked them on the pavement while he tied on the white wedding ribbons on Saturday mornings. Their less glamorous taxis were 2 litre early post-war Austin 16 HPs. It was in one of these that the older son, Don, drove me with Mom to Birmingham's Accident Hospital. Though very ordinary looking, unlike his dashing young brother, it was later Don who surprised many, especially the Newport Road ladies, by abruptly moving in further down the road with a film-star-stunning young bride.

I soon saw I was not the sole holidaying pupil to have suffered mishaps. As we moved past the partly-screened bays of assessment and treatment bays, we glanced at some highly distressing sights of children needing repairs. The very worst was a poor little soul of about my age who had received the poleaxing momentum of an older child on a wooden swing seat full in the face. It must have been the back swing, because you could see the outline of the wood across the blood covered and already bruising face. Her lips and teeth looked like minced meat. I hope she was helped to a total recovery.

Several injections. Five stitches. A dressing not to be moistened or removed for a number of days.

Slowed down for a day or two, I soon more or less forgot about my sporting trophy, except when it started to itch under the bandages, or worse I accidentally banged the site. After the stitches' removal, everything carried on. The scab diminished; the scar faded. Over time it went from a vivid purple, through pink to an almost undetectable pale depression about two inches long. You can still join the ten dots of the pale pink stitching punctures.

Sylvia's hospital experience was scheduled and altogether more helpful, David's very much something else.

There being no hot water tap in the kitchen, indeed only its solitary cold tap anywhere at all in the house, water for cooking had to be heated or boiled on the gas stove. We had a new, shiny kettle …

One Saturday morning when I was nine or ten, I was in my bedroom, engaged in gluing together a balsa wood model aircraft kit. I became aware of extraordinary downstairs noise. After a while, there was a shout for me to come straight away. Mom and Dad were taking David, eighteen months, to hospital. Too young to be left, Sylvia and I would have to come as well.

Mom had been in the middle of preparing lunch when someone knocked on the door. She went to answer it, placing the new and almost boiling kettle on the floor. In only seconds, David had toddled in, gone straight for the shiny toy, and tried to lift it. He emptied scalding water on to his ankle and foot, hence the screaming and commotion.

The only fortunate aspect of this appalling occurrence was that the Accident Hospital had special expertise in treating burns and scalds. Dad said they were leaders in the whole country, maybe more widely. So while David received the best possible care, he had to endure a long and very painful time over many weeks before everything was healed. He will carry the quite extensive area of scarring for the rest of his days. What prolonged his pains and the family's was that, every time he went to have the dressing changed, the healing layers of skin were ripped off by the nurses, leaving it as raw as before. Eventually Dad took over, treating his baby son at home much more gently and actually speeding up his recovery.

Before the other two were born, Dad learned to drive. He had to, for work; it was get a car or new job. L-plates were tied on to the dull, black 1930s Morris 10's bumpers. Mom gave all the lessons, with me aged four on the back seat. I could hear and see how Dad struggled, for example, with the weight and stiffness of the incredibly long gear stick for his weak left hand and arm. He was once sweating to make a hill start in traffic at the top of steep Lawley Street with the cantankerous non-synchromesh gearbox that was standard then. A whole queue was behind him. He stalled. He stalled again. He crunched the gears and lurched a couple of feet. I put a crumpled sweet paper down his neck. (There no child seats or seat belts then.) In his remaining thirty-seven years he never forgave me. He failed the first test. He succeeded at the second attempt. Driving from then on was a regrettable necessity; he rarely enjoyed it. That old Morris was a sluggish lump. Even so, Mom once got 70 mph out of it on a dual carriageway. Cutlers were drivers. Her oldest brother, Uncle Ray, had followed Grandad Cutler into motor racing.

Being a driver did make a difference. Gone was the morning sprint to the bus stop on Alcester Road; gradually arriving was extra weight. Dad was never as fit again as before he took to wheels. The nature of his work changed too. Previously based in offices, from now on he was on the road for years, driving around stockholders and manufacturers, buying and selling steel. He had years before taken an order marked 'Top Secret', having previously signed something to pledge his compliance. That was, he later discovered, to supply metal for Sir Frank Whittle's first jet plane. Years on, a more humdrum deal got his firm to supply the metal for all the 'Ban the Bomb' rear light cluster pressings for the Mark 1 Cortina. In time he built up as much knowledge of the trade as anyone in and around the Midlands – and further afield – highly developing his skill at handling potential customers. P.G.Woodhouse's Jeeves called it ‘the psychology of the individual’; Dad knew whom to tease, which old boy liked a risqué joke, who the passionate gardener or golfer was – and with surprising skill adjusted his approach suitably.

He always believed he would be very successful in the trade, even though he never found it congenial scrambling over oily bundles of steel sheets in starkly lit warehouses, micrometer in hand - very successful indeed, and make his fortune, if only he had the capital to start with. He called that ‘the wherewithal’. Looking after the family was always financially stretching. We lived from week to week. In about five years’ travelling, though, Dad had become well known, liked and respected in the trade. He was educated and looked smart. When he landed a job with W.G.Sice in Oldbury, he would have a firm’s car and £1,000 a year. We were happy. Family and friends were pleased. On the Wednesday before Christmas 1959, he left his own car, the grey Austin he had run since spring 1955, at work, and drove home in a brand new black two-door Morris Minor 1000. This was the era when all three Hearne brothers had Morris Minors: Uncle Gordon’s older pea green saloon, NOV 134, had the split windscreen, while younger Uncle Ken more sportily bought himself a shiny, light grey convertible, OON 62. It disappointed me that he had to sell it after a short time to pay for his wedding. The next day, Thursday, was Christmas Eve. Dad left the Morris outside our house after lunch, while I walked with him to catch buses to Oldbury, to collect his own Austin, soon to be sold. After the number 50 from Alcester Road, we took a Midland Red double decker to Dudley, getting off at Langley, where JOP 800 was parked outside the firm’s single-storey brick-built offices.

When we arrived home, we had to park a little way up the road. An Austin A35 had been abandoned at an erratic angle some way from the kerb. The first thing I noticed in our living room was someone sprawled in the facing armchair. Our white bucket was by the side. Every so often the drooping man groaned, opened his eyes, leaned over the arm of the chair and added some mouthfuls of watery vomit to the bucket.

My mother came out of the kitchen, carrying David. ‘Mr Knight’s not well,’ she explained. ‘He can’t go home yet.’

The son of Tom Knight the shoemender, whose workshop was eleven doors down at number 38, Frederick John Knight lived at that address with his mother. Though his father worked there on weekdays, where Mrs Knight cooked his midday meal and supplied him with cups of tea while he hammered and tapped at his last, even fetching him his lunchtime draught beer in an open jug from the off licence exactly opposite, Tom shared the bed of his other woman, who had borne him a half-brother to Fred. Could you properly call such an arrangement *un ménage à trois* if two households were involved? We knew Fred because he and Dad had started talking in the road on one occasion. Eventually he must have come to our house for a cup of tea.

Pale, sharp-nosed, and wearing National Health glasses, he did not cut an impressive figure. He talked to Mom and Dad for hours, exhausting my patience. I had not forgiven Mom for allowing him to come into our room one evening when I was naked in the bath, aged eight. A weedy specimen younger than Dad, he had nevertheless been conscripted into the Army, trained at Bugrooke and Plymouth, then dispatched to India on a troop ship as Signalman Knight. Nervous and of limited physique, he could never have been a boy among boys, kicking a football all day or getting into playground tussles. Among manlier, coarser adult men in uniform, he can only have been a complete misfit.

Soon into his spell abroad, he became so ill he was sent to the medical people. Tuberculosis was diagnosed. His Army days were instantly over. So, most people would have judged then, would be his entire existence. As the troop ship was carrying him home, he opened the cabin window and threw his rifle bolt into the Indian Ocean: *Goodbye to All That* with a difference! It looked like goodbye to everything.

In the military hospital, the doctors told Fred Knight one day that they had a new drug they wished to trial on him. It might not work but was highly unlikely to make things worse. This must have been before penicillin was habitually used, in combination with other drugs, to tackle the killer. Until then, there was no cure; it was just a question of time in this sorry world:

> 'Where youth grows thin, and spectre pale, and dies.'

We can begin to estimate the impact of tuberculois from famous victims, and therefore everyone's dread. The death in 1818 of Keats's much loved younger brother, Tom, broke the poet's heart; he was fated by the same infection, called 'consumption' then, to follow him after an achingly short time feasting his senses on this world's beauties, in 1821. His experience of the implacable life-shortener charged his late, best works with the fullest realisation of the transience of seasonal and earthly beauty in *To Autumn* (1819) and *To a Nightingale* (1819). The youths and maidens on the Grecian urn are frozen in a moment of time but unliving; the ceramic artist's work lives on for him. Keats had to cling to something.

The new drug worked. Gunner Knight survived. Hardly robust before the war, he was nevertheless sustained by his lungs well into his seventies, as I shall one day reveal. He also sobered up enough that afternoon for my father to walk him home and explain to his mother where he had been and why. The last morning of work before the holiday, someone at his place had produced a bottle of whisky. This jolly soul, a hardened drinker, pressured everyone to have a Christmas drop with him – from white teacups, which he generously kept topping up. When Fred stood up to leave for home, he was barely able to walk. His normal limit was half a pint of Mitchells and Butler's mild, and that infrequently. Somehow he made it to his car. Even more remarkably, he drove the seven miles from Small Heath to our house. As fuddled as he was, he knew he could not go home, and so knocked on our door. Mom said he had to slide along the wall to the chair in our living room, where he had been for a couple of hours. Mrs Knight always held my father responsible.

During their interminable talks, Dad somehow mentioned a steel trade acquaintance who wished to set up on his own but was looking for a partner with money. Fred knew diddly squat at that stage about metals, but had been steadily saving for years, with no appreciable expenses. The introduction was made. Eric Parker accepted him as partner in W.E.Parker Steels. Accepting Dad's promise of help and advice, Fred thereafter visited us often, notepad in hand, to jot down details about likely outlets for his available stock, and useful approaches. It does not seem to have occurred to our kind father that he was giving away hours of his and our time and, of more material value, years of expert knowledge. Naturally hospitable, Mom ran around supplying cups and plates of refreshments, cakes she had made for the family. At the same time she regularly complained about the imposition upon our time and lives. Saturday afternoons were worst. Just when we expected to have the use of the living room and our parents' attention, a two-hour session would be heralded by the knock on the door. In those days, we took it to be a strange friendship with wearisome claims.

Dad's liberality worked against him in another way. Out of kindness he would stop at the corner shop on his way home to buy us comics and sweets. The latter continued well into my teens. If you added up all the shillings and pence that must have amassed, you would definitely have an appreciable sum. Cut off by her very wealthy father at marriage, practically if not legally disinherited, my mother had no independent means; Dad gave her cash every morning for the day's food and other necessaries. Otherwise, in time, she had the Children's Allowance, collected from the post office. Relatively well off in her previous life, she did not have the habit of economy which other women, like her mother-in-law, must have been given at birth. It seems treacherous of me to write it now, but a useful portion of what was given by both my parents to indulging me and my siblings could – and most would say should – have been better used.

Never mind the garden, the house was *always* neglected. It needed decorating throughout, a more modern and labour-saving kitchen, maintenance and repairs. Genial to a fault, Dad did almost nothing. There was a remarkable moment when, before Sylvia's birth, he painted the smallest bedroom for her, using the novel patent spray gun attachment that came in the box of tools with our cylinder vacuum cleaner to cover the existing bland wallpaper with peppermint green emulsion. He thought it would be a brilliant way of making the job easier. He actually succeeded after a fashion, in that the walls changed colour acceptably. If only he had *completely* cleared the room and covered the floor and what remained! His pile of 78 rpm records as well as the floor, a wooden chair and footstool, not forgetting the now discordantly turquoise linoleum received a considerable amount of overspray. When we later acquired an HMV wind up record player and I started listening to his records, I never got to hear the ending of Wagner's *Rienzi* overture, which had been on top of the stack, having to wait until that piece was broadcast on the radio many years later!

Apart from the Great Front Room Ceiling Paper Collapse, the leaking roof was never effectively attended to. A local builder was called once, but not judged particularly competent and anyway expensive. There's was always objection or refusal to pay the standard rate for things. Everyone tried to *diddle* you. Now and then, there might be a discovery. Some chance acquaintance just 'happened to know a chap who would do it on the cheap'. They always did do something; it rarely worked! In heavy rain, a light brown patch started to spread in the ceiling just beyond the foot of their double bed. Dad fetched a chair, bucket – and the corkscrew! A couple of well-placed holes made by screwing the thing in and then pulling it out with one tug did the trick. The rogue inflow dripped neatly into the bucket. You just had to remember to empty it now and then.

Another early morning I was shocked awake by a loud thud and shouts from the next room. Some part of the second-hand bedframe had given way, knocking Mom and Dad conscious. The fix on this occasion was somehow to shorten things all round so that the structure sat more or less level again, leaving the mattress not much higher than floor level. The malfunctioning scooter that karated my front tooth provided another example of a good idea that misfired. Saving a few shillings on an ingenious prototype product at a give-away price secured me a dangerous disaster. Though I learned never to squat on it again and could ride it along the pavement for ages at a time, I never knew when it would suddenly jack-knife, wrenching my arms and making me jump off, usually at speed.

Without a toolbox, Dad owned a pin hammer, an electrical screwdriver, a pair of combination side-cutting pliers and a rusty blunt handsaw. The only tool he regularly used was a small penknife, which he sharpened on a stone, for scraping out the carbon cake from his pipes. On the rare occasions he really had to do something physically practical, like break up a wooden box, he retained his jacket and tie. Sighing and panting, he would wield the hammer or stagger to lift and move a heavy object, as when bringing in the coal bucket:

'Ey up! Mind out the way!'

Was the big drama mostly for sympathy? 'Poor Douglas!' according to Mom, was the regular refrain in his mother's house. Frustrating as this was, it could be accounted for. In his early teens he had lost the example of his eminently practical and skilled father, whose ingenuity he illustrated by mentioning things like the potato gun made for him. When he told Clifford that other boys were playing with this novelty toy, his father went to work. In his lunch hour he borrowed a lathe and some tools. On returning home he handed Dad, probably nine or ten, a shiny, heavy toy pistol.

'Don't point it at anyone's face or eyes.'

The next day, with his supply of vegetable ammunition, Dad went out into the garden to see what he could do. The pretend weapon was 'bosting good'. It shot far and true. The garden overlooked Brougham Street, being literally higher than it. By climbing a tree near the wall, Dad had the perfect, lofty sniper's vantage point and leafy cover. A man came along. After he had passed, Dad took steady aim at the middle of the retreating back. He squeezed the trigger and pulled it. Crack!

The result shocked both parties. A sharp yell from the stranger accompanied by a reflex grab at his back made Dad jump too. The victim turned round and peered upwards, face twisted with pain.

'You little swine! You'd better stay up there! If I catch hold of you …'

'What a fuss!' Dad thought. 'It was just a piece of potato!'

He reloaded and stood on one leg to turn his boot's leather sole upwards. Again, he squeezed and pulled. Again, there was a whip-snapping crack.

He said he could not feel his foot for a good half hour afterwards! Clifford Harry Hearne made things sturdily and well. No doubt if he had lived longer he would have passed on some invaluable knowledge and expertise. As it was, Dad was already damaged by his polio and lengthy spell in hospital when he lost his father. It was a double blow from which he never recovered.

In those days, and perhaps understandably in this case, rehabilitation and physiotherapy after physical injuries and illnesses were not so skilled and developed. At least, that is the picture I have painted for myself after what I have seen and heard. Sometimes, tough love may be necessary for those learning to overcome or live with being somehow incapacitated. Dad *could* have painted the house if he had been determined. His standard, even self-pitying explanation was that he could not hold the paint tin. He should never have dreamt of climbing high on a ladder, for example, to clear the gutters, which would have been an inconceivable action in any case. But he could have devised means of standing or suspending a can of paint within usable reach. I have in my garage a heavy-duty piece of wire I bent decades ago into an S shaped paint tin hook for when I need my other hand for holding on. For many years a man in our village ran the DIY store perfectly well *with one arm*. Dad was not utterly incapable. He *could* use a spade in the garden, although his left arm would not lift heavy spadefuls. The garden could have been initially arranged to make maintenance possible for him. If we had ever had a proper lawn, he could have paid a local boy to cut it now and then. He gave up. With few exceptions, that extended everywhere. On holidays in a caravan he did – rarely – cook breakfast, equally infrequently wearing a brown collared jumper instead of a jacket. Beautifully relaxed and smiling, he seemed to relish frying bacon, eggs, tomatoes and mushrooms on the tiny camping gas stove. Otherwise, he was a stranger to almost every household task, choosing to sit and read the newspaper instead of picking up a tea towel after a meal. He never dusted, swept, tidied, made the beds, hung out washing or brought it in. He did clean the car, but out of a resented duty, not pride and pleasure, looking always strained and harassed as he struggled outside with the bucket slopping over its brim.

Did he also think 'Poor Douglas!'?

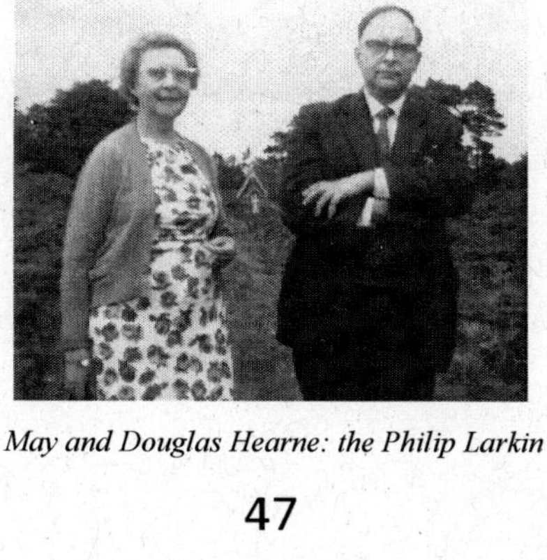

Lilian May and Douglas Hearne: the Philip Larkin pose!

St John's RC Primary

"Give me," said Joe, "a good book, or a good newspaper, and sit me down afore a good fire, and I ask no better. Lord!" he continued, after rubbing his knees a little, "when you do come to a J and a O, and says you, 'Here, at last, is a J-O, Joe,' how interesting reading is!"

Charles Dickens, *Great Expectations*

'Sit there,' Miss Shepherd said. 'Put the apple in the desk.'

It was a dark brown double table, with a shelf underneath. I must have taken my apple out from the new satchel my grandmother had given me the day before, and pushed the fruit out of view, into the woody smelling hollow.

The boy next to me, I eventually learned, was Dennis Hanner, if that was how he spelled his name. He had large, black warts on the backs of his hands, Brylcream-glossy parted black hair, and a home-knitted horizontal-striped pullover. I suppose his mother had smartened him up. I had seen only one or two other children of my age before, certainly not around fifty, mixed boys and girls, at one go. Dennis's purple-stained mouth scab puzzled and repelled me. He sat on my right, while no one was to my left. I was the latest arrival.

The room echoed, its mostly bare brick walls painted a shiny light blue all fifteen or so feet to the ceiling. To enter via the part-glazed shuddering door you lifted and turned the semi-circular brass handle on its pivot. Instantly, a huge hot dog leapt up and smothered you with the tang of massed five year olds: plasticine, wax crayons, unwashed bodies, urine, dried sweat, hot farts – whatever went into cocktailing that prevalent 1950s classroom reek.

The tables were arranged in lines around the rear and two side walls, the beginner's departure station – my place – at the very front on the teacher's far left. In time I would travel clockwise to the front group at the other terminus, though to begin with I faced the left wall, and so couldn't see them. If I could, I should instantly have ached to play in the sand tray just behind them, expecting it to afford some of the absorbed joys of the seaside, though that hope was never realised.

'Don't eat that now. It's not playtime!' She swooped and grabbed the tart green snack before rolling it to the back of the shelf. How very strange she was, if not mad – mad and maybe dangerous! My mother had given me my apple. You eat your apple, biting first round all the middle, then working your way round the top and bottom. You give her the core back. That's what she *told* you to do. Only here you didn't! Peculiar!

'Hands on heads! Stop talking! Stand up! Put your chairs under the desks – SILENTLY! Put your hands together. Now – In the Name of the Father, and of the Son, and of the Holy Ghost. Amen …'

‘Kevin O’Connor! You don’t make the Sign of the Cross with your left hand! Show him, Mary Davis … yes, that’s right. You see? You got that, Kevin O’Connor?’

Morning playtime. A squarish tarmaced yard, mostly enclosed by walls: the school buildings, the block of lavatories, the red-bricked east wall of the church. To reach their doorless cubicles, the girls walked behind a row of boys, one shorts leg lifted, spraying the concrete urinal wall in concert.

Back outside, dozens of children hurtled randomly around, screaming. Girls skipped or tucked their skirts into their navy blue knickers to do handstands against a wall. A freckled boy darted at me. ‘Tag. You’re It!’ The choir shrilled as everyone radiated away at speed from me.

A handbell clanged. Arrest. Silence. ‘Stand still! Quiet! Line up in your classes. And no talking! Miss Shepherd … ’ Our teacher led us back.

At midday my mother collected me for the walk home, and then back for the afternoon. I went home every day for dinner until I started grammar school.

During afternoon playtime a boy I later knew as Edward Hussey punched me in the eye.

‘You’re new,’ he explained. I cried.

*****

I am sitting in the middle of the back row of tables, directly facing Miss Shepherd. She’s wearing a black, buttoned cardigan, a white blouse with some embroidered flowers, and a longish dark grey skirt above flat shining black slip on shoes. Her auburn hair, short and fairly curly, surmounts a fresh and youthful face, the cheeks habitually flushed a strong pink which volcanically spurts to raw beef crimson with temper.

Slighter than my rounded mother, though certainly not boyish, Miss is wearing her pink cheeks this morning. Reading time. We’re all sitting, with our copies of *Janet and John* on the tables, yellow ones to my right and reds from me leftwards. Having to start on yellow Book 0 (*Off We Go*) had slightly offended me. Zero? Was I actually worth nothing? But now I was on red Book 1.

All around, the class are looking down at their pages or up at the walls. Many baby fingers are sliding jerkily across the page or edging handwritten pale blue named reading cards under the words. Young lips are mouthing individual words deliberately.

I have stalled. I’ve done the same page over and over. It’s not much of a story.

> Here-I-come-Mo-ther.
> Thank-you-for-the-ride.
> My-horse-went-up-and-down.
> My-horse-went-ve-ry-fast.

'Martin Hearne! Come up with your book.' She says my name in a funny way, not pronouncing the 't' and making my last name sound like *hairn*. My mother and father say *with* too, not *wid*.

'Stand here. Use your finger. Right then. Read to me.'

After I've gone through the page, she writes 37 in blue biro on the card cum bookmark I keep in my book. She puts a tick next to it.

'Now go back and do the next page.'

Reading is one of the safer and quieter times in the day, but every morning after registration we have prayers. Many days the partitions, folding glazed doors which go all the way from floor to ceiling, are unbolted and taken back, uniting three classrooms, which become the Headmistress's church and pulpit. We bawl hymns, put our hands together, close our eyes, chant the Hail Mary, Our Father and other prayers. We are told what's what, or rather what shouldn't be and what *must* be from now on. Or else, Mr McCarthy.

All morning lessons invariably start with Religion. God made the world in six days and rested on the seventh, which means that we all have to go to Mass on Sundays, and your mother doesn't hang the washing out. Now, put a hand up if your parents took you to Mass yesterday … Come on! I want to see all of your hands!

There was a wonderful garden, with everything you could possibly want in it. Your food grew on the trees and bushes. The animals didn't bite you or wasps use their stings. In fact I don't think they even had stings yet. First God made a man. Then God put him to sleep, took one of his bones and made a woman for the man. They lived together and were *very* good friends. They could do anything they wanted, except for one … and Cain killed his brother Abel, and … people were so wicked, which means really very, very naughty, Joseph, that God made it rain and rain and rain … nowhere for them to sleep, so they found a stable … run away, because the wicked Jewish king was killing all the babies …

*****

Singing. The farmer's in his den … eeee-iii-addio … wants a wife … a child … a dog … Elsie wants a wee … she's trying to squeeze it in … eeee-iii-addio … she's puddled on the floor …

Down by the river bank the green grass grows,
And there Paula Burns washes her clothes.
She sings, she sings, she sings so sweet;
She calls for her playmate across the street:
Playmate, playmate, won't you come to tea?
Come next Sunday at half-past three.

Mrs Davis comes in sometimes to play the piano. Gentle Mrs Davis. We go over hymns, learning them line by line till we know some verses.

A sore neck. Feeling hot and sleepy. Miss Shepherd talks to my mother at home time. The next morning, I don't go to school. Dr Fraser Brown calls at 60 Newport Road. Mumps. Stay at home. Lie in bed watching the clouds slide across the window, passing blurred through the unclear panes Mother said were wartime replacements from remade glass. 'They swept up all the broken bits from the bombing and melted them down to make new windows.' Dark afternoons approaching Christmas. The shops lit up in the afternoon. Snow and wellingtons. *Away in a Manger, Silent Night.* The holidays.

In the New Year, some of us were siphoned off into another room, with kind Mrs Davis: poised and smiling, with short dark hair, glasses and a powder blue fine knit cardigan. A cloakroom or medical room briefly served as the small classroom for, as I now suspect, those of us who were faster learners. But if time has depth as well as length it also varies its pace; all too soon our untroubled, peaceful interlude was over. At some suitable juncture, perhaps half term, we were moved up into Miss King's class. In the Sacristy.

A narrow metalled enclosed path led along the north side of St John's church to the sacristy door, just around a tucked in corner. Presumably on account of pupil numbers, as the birth rate had risen in the immediate post war years, the parish priest, in my time Father Clement Burrett, allowed one overspill class to be housed in his holy tiring house and props store. Overseen by book shelves, wardrobes, and dark wood wall cupboards storing altar vessels, cloths, church paraphernalia and boxes of unconsecrated wafers, and just a door's width outside the north side aisle of the church, we chanted our tables, daubed our poster colours on sugar paper and, like geese being stuffed to fatten their livers, were daily crammed with the knowledge, terminology and superstition that would bloat our minds – and more importantly our souls – for Father Burrett, or his younger assistant Father Williams, to regale themselves with at Our First Confessions.

Before that, many daily sessions of instruction, direly serious, about our risibly slim chances of avoiding eternal pain and tears in the Awful Everlasting.

'Your soul is like the end of a barrel that's been painted white. And every time that you sin – which you can't help, you do it all the time – you hammer an ugly black nail into that white painted circle. So, sin after sin, nail after nail, till it all gets blacker and blacker and you can't see any white any more. When that happens,' declared with gleeful triumph, ' your soul is completely black, which is mortal. And – you – go - to – Hell!'

Our infant hopes being already winded and floored groaning by this point, Miss King bounced joyfully on her elevated captain's chair as she drove the death blow home.

But, wonderfully, we had Confession, or to be more technical, the Sacrament of Penance.

What are the Seven Sacraments, Maureen? Come on! Yes: Baptism, Penance, Communion, Confirmation, Holy Orders, Matrimony and Extreme Unction, which is just before you die. And the very best of all, boys, is Holy Orders, which is when you become a priest.

Now, confessing your sins was clearly another miracle, just like Jesus's special effects displays with water and dead people. Only this time you did the trick yourself, simultaneously extracting away hundreds of repellent and dangerous black headed nails in a jiffy, which must feel a whole lot better. Still, by mid-week your barrel end would all be coal black once more, of course, which meant you would have to toddle to confession again on Saturday morning before Communion on Sunday. Just you make sure you don't do, say or even THINK anything wicked before you take the Lord's body (conveniently packaged as a flavourless pappy disk) at Mass. Of course, I'll be checking every Monday to see who has – or (I hope) hasn't [pause] – been to confession and communion at the weekend!

It occurs to me now, at my threescore and ten, that gaunt and greying Miss King, who, had she ever been a plum of a young woman had long before we encountered her turned prune, never included herself in the sinning business. It was always 'you', never 'we'. What, though, might she have confessed? What could have been on her conscience? She must know all about examining that invisible mystery since she went on so much at us every day about it. Her options being limited by the narrowness of her life, did her towering respect for Father Burrett ever topple crash to the carpet in sensual fantasy? Was she perhaps a petty shoplifter, whisking flimsy underwear into her shopping bag at Marks? A spreader of malicious untruths? A secret poisoner even? I shouldn't think so. Her established and incontrovertible acts of commission, regularly witnessed by fifty of us at a time, sprang from a common source: bigotry. We were to have nothing to do with the pupils at Tindall Street School, our Church of England neighbours, because, 'They're all pagans. Pagans!' I had no idea what that was, but evidently it must be something abhorrent and so to be avoided, an irritating pity, since I had quite liked playing in the pagan garden of next-door Carol. As for Jewish people, they had been so intolerably uncaring and cruel to Our Dear Jesus [bow heads], as the hymn reminded us:

> Have we no tears to shed for Him,
> While soldiers scoff and Jews deride?
> Ah! Look how patiently he hangs;
> Jesus, our love, is crucified.

Perhaps my memory fails me, but I've always recalled 'mock' rather than 'scoff', though it all comes to the same thing. I am confident that the tune we sang those words to was not the Eric Ashley one.

I realise now that, unsatisfactory and wrong-headed as it was, this travesty of religious teaching did enrich my young vocabulary: deride, scourge, immaculate, wondrous, afflicted, grief, petitions, ravishing etc. No doubt many more could easily be added to the list, not to mention learning hymns and prayers by heart in Latin nearly a decade before I knew enough of the language to translate them. Much of it has stuck:

> Adeste fideles

Laeti triumphantes
Venite, venite in Bethlehem.
Natum videte,
Regem angelorum.
Venite adoremus (x3) dominum.

Our next-door-but-one neighbours were Jewish, the Chiswicks. I looked up to and enjoyed playing with their children, a year or two older than I, Geoffrey and Vivian. Their terraced house was twice the width of ours, with a garage, and correspondingly larger back garden, including an apple orchard and swing.

'I've learned to read to myself,' confided Vivian one morning, gently swaying back and forth without holding on. 'Would you like me to show you?'

'Yes, please,'

I waited. The swing was gliding slowly.

'Go on then! Read to yourself!'

'Well, I am doing it! You can't hear me say anything, silly!'

Geoffrey had skills. He could yoyo, roller skate, tell you about the planets. One evening, as we talked on the pavement, I was squatting on my folding red scooter, a new unbranded model obtained directly from a small, back street manufacturer by my steel-trade father. Smack! The handlebars collapsed down under my weight, clouting my face numbingly.

'Your tooth's broken!' Geoffrey discovered, peering down. My top right incisor, one of my 'big' teeth: chopped for ever; six decades-plus, one gold and plastic filling and three crowns further on, the root remains live.

Geoffrey (and perhaps his sister, certainly his baby brother Peter in his turn) went to the Jewish school, founded in 1843 as the Birmingham Hebrew School, on the Alcester Road, and later King David School. At the time of which I write its Jewish numbers were declining, and so it opened its doors to those of other faiths. Ten years ago, over half of the pupils came to be Muslims, the school being praised for its promotion of racial and religious harmony among the young. After my father drove us past it and told me the playground was on the roof, I could think of little else for days. What must it be like to run around up there, far above the streets? Could you fall off? Were there railings, or a wall? What a good school it must be too, for my mother told me, with characteristic tact, how much more the children there had learned than we had! Look what Geoffrey knew, about all the rivers and history. *And* he was learning to read and write Hebrew! I didn't ever mention admirable Geoffrey or his pretty, clever sister to Miss King. She would have forbidden me to mix with them.

I have no idea how it came about, but Miss King discovered that I knew by heart *Tubby the Odd Job Engine* stories, as read to me by my mother from *The Robin*, a children's weekly. On one or two occasions I was asked to stand on my chair and tell the class the latest adventure in Tubby's locomotive life. Eileen Gibb's stories, illustrated by Jill Franksen, may still be available nowadays, at least secondhand, though they don't feature in my grandchildren's library, which includes all the stories by the Reverend W.W.Awdry. I recall absolutely loving them, and yearned to be back home listening to more such readings, or doing jigsaw puzzles quietly to myself. For years as I grew up I believed the fiction fed to me by my mother as she pushed me towards the railway bridge on Brighton Road. It was probably a Black 5 she pointed at when she foretold, 'One day you'll be driving one of those.' I have always loved railways and especially steam locomotives.

The first public performance Miss King rehearsed us for was our First Holy Communion in May 1957, a couple of days after we Examined our Consciences, Made a Really True Confession (religion apparently caring tautologically more for the soul's than sense's preservation), and Entered a State of Grace – all highly appropriate language for seven year olds, who (we were firmly told) were old enough to have moral awareness, though that was just about the only piece of ethical terminology not to be slice served over the spiritual net and whizz past our ears.

St John's Church, now the Church of Saints John and Martin, always seemed to me gloomy, but once you closed the featureless door behind you, the encasing confessional box, resin scented, windowless, speed ferried you to Hades: shadows, stealth, breath and silent dread. You knelt down.

'Bless me, Father, for I have sinned. This is my first confession, and these are my sins' … Two of my juvenile revelations were total fabrications; I had to think of something plausible to say. The third troubled me. My heart raced.

'And is that it?' the green curtain mumbled.

'And … and … I stole a pair of plastic scissors from a friend's house.'

They were not even working ones that someone had bought for use, but tiny replicas, about three-quarters of an inch long and utterly worthless, that a 1d bubble gum vending machine had dribbled down with the one inch diameter shocking pink sphere. I yearned as soon as I saw them.

'Aha! And did you replace them?'

Checkmate. Of course I hadn't!

'Yes.'

'Well, good – that's something. Just make sure you don't take anything else that isn't yours, and put your hands together while I say a prayer. For your penance, say the *Hail Mary* three times. And pray for me. In the name of the Father … '

I knelt facing the altar, trying to look as good and serious as the two headscarfed girls nearest to me, hands together pointing upwards, eyes closed, lips moving soundlessly. They were safe. It had worked for them.

Two days later, Grandma Lil, a fervent convert, came from Handsworth by early bus to secure a ringside seat. At the exact end of a front side aisle, she nodded reverentially at me as we filed past to our places. During the entire mass, I fought to avoid looking her way, terrified she might wave. Every time my glance treacherously flitted at her she was beaming unblinkingly, a transfixed radiance suffusing her apple round face. Outside the church she gave me a potted scarlet geranium, price 2s 9d.

A photographer took group shots of the Lord's latest conscripts with his Sergeant and Corporal, Messrs Burrett and Williams, girls and boys separately. There followed individual photos on the bizarrely carpeted infants' entrance steps. If there was any symbolism in the strawberry pink satin sashes that were pinned across our blazers, it was never explained to us. Maybe we were just gift wrapped for the Almighty. The girls, of course, were all white dresses, cardigans, socks, shoe and gauzy veils, as befitted the Lord's baby brides. According to the dictat of the prevailing Vatican superstition, everyone had been kept faint with hunger, it being essential to fast before accepting what was actually – miraculously! – Jesus's body into our alimentary canals. Ordinary human toast or cornflakes, never mind the indulgent animal luxury of a bacon sandwich, would just have introduced too much mortal corruption for His Holy Body to associate with, though I suspect His entrance into our purified portals was in time followed by a less than glorious departure. If any theologian or logician had followed the unshakeable beliefs and practices of those days, conclusions most preposterous must surely have been arrived at. Only the priests were allowed to touch the consecrated wafers, and then with only their thumbs and the first two fingers of each hand. On one occasion a couple of years later, the bread came to slip between the priest's fingers and the child's mouth in mass – it would have to be mine! – on to the altar floor. A whole pantomime of recovery and cleansing followed the outrageous indignity, though to be fair no one afterwards persecuted me particularly for it. By the same reasoning, though, every Catholic lavatory in the world should have been given more sanctified cleansings than ever Harpic or bleach could deliver.

Another annual public ordeal was the School Concert, given on two nights and attended by parents and other family members. The partitions remained open between three classrooms for two weeks, and Mr McCarthy with some of the oldest boys pushed enough tables together to create a level platform filling almost all of one room space, on top of which sections of stage flooring, no doubt stored the rest of the year, were placed. Stage curtains and even wings were somehow provided. You got backstage by entering that particular classroom from the corridor, then stepped up on to the platform in the wings.

My first appearance, in Mrs Davis's class, was as an unfledged duck, circling an imaginary puddle with several others from what I now understand to be called our paddling or raft, whilst the rest of the class chorally entertained the audience with a suitably pondish number. It proved a disappointment to the wardrobe designer that the flaming orange crepe paper webbed extensions to our pumps fell as flat as the three or four of us kept threatening to do, since they immediately folded under our soles as soon as we essayed our first waddles.

Miss King must have been so struck with the inspired choice of her first concert contribution that she troubled her invention no more thereafter, her class invariably forming the percussion band. When our turn came, we all stood and bashed, jangled or rattled our tools while the record player gave out a military march. After rehearsal skirmishes with a triangle, I was promoted to our only junior marching snare drum. Miss K, vigorously wagging her hands in what she took to be the authentic action of a well informed and practised conductor, awarded me an unusually fierce glare when I descended from my precarious chair-on-table elevation to retrieve a dropped stick. After your class's spot, you doubled back down the corridor to watch the remaining acts from the back of the auditorium. Brendon Garvey, classmate Kathleen's big brother, regularly stole the show with his solo accordion performances, which though still only seven or eight I could tell were genuinely accomplished. He seemed much older to me than he possibly can have been, but then the poise and control of genuinely competent young performers often bestow maturity upon them. Having shot my bolt as a drummer boy, I was to make three more annual appearances.

I have been unable to find any trace of *The Melancholy Princess*, a one-act drama with music that followed our percussive efforts; I retain only patchy memories of it. I know that I had a part with some lines to myself, and that the plot centred on a junior royal's chronic depression. The part of the blue-blooded misery with the droops was given to Susan Cormican, whose vocal part included:

> O woe is me!
> My heart is sad;
> There's nought in life
> To make me glad.
> O cruel fate
> For princess fair,
> This heavy load to bear.

I have always remembered the tune in D minor, but that may be false.

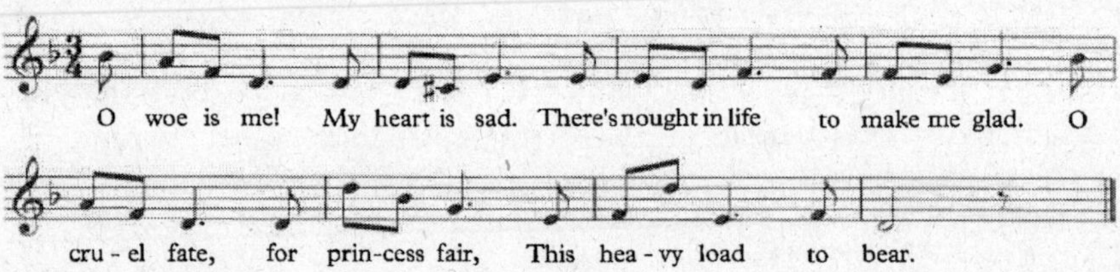

Heavy enough indeed for the poor young thing, though soon afterwards worse befell Susan. One afternoon, happening to go past me in the playground, she fell unconscious to the ground. As she was being carried away limp in the arms of a male teacher, I was summarily accosted as joint prime witness and suspect. Did you trip her? How did you push her?

I have always remembered the difficulty I had in explaining the incident. It taught me then, aged seven maybe, that when we want or need to communicate a fresh, original experience, there are no ready words; either the rest is silence or we resort to inventive comparison.

‘What do you mean, “she fell”? How did she fall?’

‘It was like’ – I fished around –‘ erm – it was like – a fork falling out of the kitchen drawer.’ It was a lame effort, though the best I could come up just then. I saw the old brown drawer at home as I said the unhelpful words.

Following this collapse, Susan was off school for ages. I think the next time any one of us saw her she was again being carried, this time by her father, who brought her, wrapped in a blanket, to another evening event, possibly a Christmas celebration. I don’t think she ever resumed her schooling with us. Relatively tall, with short dark hair and brown eyes, Susan was one of the few girls who wore the bottle green uniform gymslip, the rest being dressed either in the alternative bottle green skirt and checked blouse, with green cardigan, or perhaps more smartly in non-uniform clothes. Most boys wore the regulation dark green blazer, with its yellow-gold SJS letters on the pocket badge, and the matching cap.

They say we remember when we build up neural connections in our brains, that things associate with each other, that the more we supply to our store of life experiences, the more we are able to add, that by using established techniques we can develop and improve our accurate recollection of something we came across, went through or were told. You largely drive your car by a bank of memories: where (without looking) to find the controls, which of them to use and when and how, even how this new vehicle you have been driving for only half an hour is to be treated slightly differently from others you have known. Memories often, maybe almost always, have individual, personal meaning to us: the names Malcolm or Wendy probably say something to you because of real or fictional owners of them familiar to you at some time. Such an item of food or drink reminds you of a long dead relative or friend, or perhaps is to be savoured or shunned, according to whether it signifies to you pleasure or something else. Some humans achieve prodigious memory feats, like the Brazilian I was told of when leading a school trip to Lloyds of London in the 1970s. According to our guide, who himself dabbled in games of mental chess (when neither player has a physical board or writes anything down, but remembers all the moves and plays using agreed notation), the current world record for the greatest number of *simultaneous* games of mental chess was sixty-four, though how adjudication was carried out is unknown to me. Reputedly, the champion kept track of the separate games by imagining a square-fronted eight-storey building with eight windows on each floor.

Actors, sometimes very speedily, secure vast numbers of words, movements, cues and so on. Shakespeare’s contemporary actor, friend and dramatic poet Ben Jonson claimed in age (or at least Drummond of Hawthornden claimed for him) that he could still recall perfectly parts he had learned decades before, though he did admit that he was a trifle hazier over more recent ones. One of my college friends fended off boredom whilst at public school by memorising pretty well the whole of the national timetable for British Railways, challenging others on CCF marches … it’s 3.30 pm on a Sunday. You’re in Peterborough. What’s the quickest way to get to Aberdeen with the minimum number of changes? Baby stuff, to him, perhaps, though whether being a highly accomplished performing and academic musician he had, by nature or acquisition, a marked advantage cannot be determined. Certainly, professional musicians often offer extensive and staggering repertoires of highly demanding and complicated works – all played from memory.

It was my mother who taught me how to memorise words deliberately. I must have been quite young when we were sent home with the task of fixing several lines of a poem or song into our retrieval systems … say the first few words to yourself several times over … go on to the next few words … go back to the first part and repeat that … when you're ready, put part one and part two together, and so on. You could leave school at fourteen and have that ability under your belt. Maybe it indirectly helped me to the equal leading role of the King of Hearts in our concert performance of *The Knave of Hearts* when we were eight: a weighty speaking part, though crushingly serious, all the quips and audience ticklers being accorded to my best friend, John Falkner, who netted the title part.

The actual star of the production was a total surprise: Paula Burns! That dark-haired, dark-skinned, black-eyed deep-voiced female classmate stepped not just into my shoes but into my entire costume, mostly home clothes like my white shirt, when I went down after the first performance with chicken pox! She both was word perfect and discharged the part with verve and gusto – probably much better than I had been doing - and this was *without* any conscious effort by her to learn the words, cues, actions and so on. We remember sometimes just by being there. I wonder, though, whether Paula suffered chicken pox as seriously as I did. I think she also quickly went down with it after the play, wearing my clothes not being the most sensible idea. I had already followed mumps with (in order) measles and whooping cough, which made three serious childhood ailments in under twelve months. *The chickens*, as my father termed varicella, made me very ill, with a prolonged high fever, at the terrifying height of which one evening delirium tortured me so frantically, as the frightening little man raced at insane speed round and round and round my bed, and I was compelled somehow to process overwhelmingly impossible numbers that kept presenting themselves in unthinkable profusion. Hell (if it existed) or insanity could well feel not much different. I have been left with dozens of small scars over much of my body; after I have been in the sun, they stand out, white and hollow against the browner normal skin.

I suppose my mother's memory trick was also responsible for my final role on the St John's stage, as the eponymous Ali Baba. I retain nothing of the business save that again I had pages to learn, was required to wear silly green baggy satin trousers, and my son (John again) gave the audience its only proper laugh on the first night when he stuffed a handful of white sliced bread in his mouth an instant before he had to speak, leading to an impressive fountain of pasty gobbets aimed centrally at the front row and scoring a direct hit on the Headmistress, who not only suffered a massive indignity but also had to squeeze out a smile from some remote anatomical crevice, two things she just never did. Falkner Junior was under unspecified pains enjoined to empty his mouth before speaking in the remaining performances. To our disappointment, he complied. But I have leapt ahead of myself, to when I was ten. I shall rewind.

Miss Fuller to Mrs Smart

With perhaps only two exceptions, all our teachers were curiously distinctive, if not downright odd. When we moved back from the sacristy to the main building, we experienced Miss Fuller. In her late fifties or early sixties, ponderous, strong-voiced, emphatic, and utterly unsmiling, she must have been tiring from birth onwards. Had her father ever rolled her over on the carpet and tickled her? Or her mother once risked a pretty, flimsy dress on her? Or were her nursery clothes also sensible dark shades of brown and grey, with the occasional festive indulgence of dark olive? Stout lace-up shoes, dull suede except in the depths of winter, when they were replaced by black, zipped ankle boots, facilitated the long-striding lumpish gait. Inclining forward, she doddled her head slightly, to one side then the other, with each clumping step, the airborne ends of her silver-grey upstanding hair, shaved close at the back, quivering when the shock waves reached them. Stockings: thick machine knit. Spectacles: silver framed. Nail varnish, make-up, perfume, bracelet, earrings, costume jewellery: none. Wristwatch: men's silver Timex, with black strap. Miscellaneous accessory: one small gold crucifix on a fine chain, worn outside the jumper. Handbag: uncertain – possibly of equine origin, viz. former nose bag.

No incidents, accidents or noteworthy events occur to me from around this time. We carried on with our tables, arithmetic, reading, spellings and all the other routine business. Once a week we had painting: the evidence was pinned up around us. Of course, the beginning, middle and end of everything was religion: prayers to start and close each instruction session, and at assemblies; Benediction on Friday morning; weekly Mass on Tuesday, following Monday's grilling about our weekend's dips in God's pool; and the inevitable calendar events. In May it was all white shirts for us and bridesmaid style dresses for the girls. The cult of the Blessed Virgin and pagan spring celebrations were collapsed together. One girl was chosen each year to be Mary/the May Queen. She enjoyed a place of honour at mass and was led out down the central aisle in a formal procession. I was horribly censured when concentration caused me to poke my cheek out with my tongue. The train bearer's dignity (even more than English, Mr Keats) must be kept up! We even danced around a maypole, another questionable activity for good Christians, more correctly Catholics, since no one is yet sure what that fourteenth century Welsh invention was all about. Phallic symbols? Fertility rites? A marking of the intersection of heaven and earth and the meeting of North, East, South and West?

> O Mary, we crown thee with blossoms today,
> Queen of the angels and Queen of the May.
> (x 2, to a squirmingly mawkish tune.)

When it plays over in my mind, I always hear voices thick with beer and sobbing emotion. Ah! The Lord loves us all!

On 17th March, we had sprays of shamrock pinned to our clothes. Perhaps influenced by my mother, I felt the impertinence. *We* were not Irish! Ash Wednesday had our foreheads all daubed with something sooty, marking the beginning of a particularly miserable time when we had to give up doing something we naturally liked, put money aside and later hand it over for unspecified causes. Church statues were completely covered with purple cloth, prompting my little brother David one Sunday to point and call out, to everyone's amusement, a long wavering 'Ghooosts!'

The best bits of school were story time, when you could be safely absorbed for a while, and, until we moved up to the big playground, playtime.

After a year or two, the boys were separated from the girls and younger boys, to the front playground. Adjacent to the pavement on Mary Street, from where passers-by and those living opposite could see through the railings to our activities, the older boys' play area was all hard tarmac, like the road, with a toilet block to one side and the tall red brick end walls of the enclosing houses on either side. Balls and other play equipment were vehemently prohibited. We ran around, chasing each other, held races between the walls, mingled and moved around, followed crazes, squabbled and occasionally exchanged pushes and blows.

Shortly after we went outside for each session, we were joined by a supervising teacher, almost invariably Mr McCarthy. Short, slightly tubby, light-grey plaid-suited and with parted, slicked-down hair, he may have been still just in his thirties, otherwise a few years older. He terrified me.

Smacking children was freely practised in those times, by many if not most parents. There were occasions when my mother and father slapped my leg, usually when I went way over a clear limit and had been warned several times. I got over it quickly; our love for each other didn't falter. School was different, was horribly worse. From the very beginning, what you did and said was conditioned by fear and threats. Accidental clumsiness might be instantly acknowledged with a stinging swipe, whereas petty disobedience, like forgetting not to talk to your neighbour, would trigger the angry summons to the front of the room, where you held out your hand while a much larger one was raised high above the head to clat down repeatedly. You winced and quivered to witness the execution, keeping perfectly silent, like everybody else. No one spoke to Susan or Harry, Maureen or Johnny, returning to sit in disgraced solitude, tears quietly dropping unwiped.

One or two of the women staff had petrol tempers, probably hormone ignited: the eyes and cheeks flashed, the voice shrilled, the hand crashed. But Mr McCarthy …

Sergeant L.O.McCarthy had served in Wellingtons and Lancasters, as navigator and bomb aimer. He taught Class 4, the top but one. Sometimes he told them of his war experiences. On one raid, he said, a huge bomb, a blockbuster, had fallen from an RAF bomber above his aircraft and gone clean through the fuselage. They survived the perishing cold only because of their wonderful thermal wear, flying home as low as they dared.

By assumption or informal appointment, McCarthy was understood to be ultimately responsible for punishment, if not justice. We understood this from others even before we made contact, rapidly learning that, when he blew his whistle in the playground, you froze and became silent. On the second blast you lined up in your classes with the utmost celerity, mute. You withstood the prolonged glare. Whistle in mouth, cup and saucer in the left hand, he held the pause. He put the cup down on the edge of the steps side wall, pocketed the whistle. We remained motionless.

'Reynolds!' A boy had moved or muttered. 'Come out here!'

The first time you saw the sequel made you blink. From the right jacket sleeve a bamboo cane, about two and half feet long, would flash into his hand, like a flick knife blade when the catch is pressed.

'Hold your hand out!'

The culprit leaned backwards, extended his arm to its limit, maybe hoping to keep the approaching pain as far away as possible. The hand trembled. Using the tip of his stick to raise the target and level it suitably, McCarthy entered a moment of intense concentration, his unblinking eyes fixed in their focus. The cane rose slowly to above his shoulder.

Whoop! Crack! The boy was moving from foot to foot, alternately sucking his fingers and placing his hand under his arm, for about a quarter of a minute.

'The other one!'

Red-faced, holding his breath to contain the sob, the offender complied.

We walked all the way up the steps, into the building and to our own classrooms, death-quiet.

Having the stick or the whack, as we called it, profoundly affected my weekday life. Or rather, constant terror of that unthinkable violation - the ecstasy of pain and humiliation – directed my every move. I paid attention. I followed instructions promptly and exactly. I was never naughty. Luckily, I really liked the substance of the three Rs, did my best and so, by being in all senses a good pupil, fabricated a shield for myself against the perpetual threats and attacks. I am not entirely clear how long this policy of industrious self-protection took to establish itself, though it must have been by the time I was eight, because I remember Mrs Smart, the next-but-one teacher after Miss Fuller, commenting, 'Well, I don't think much of your writing, Martin Hearne,' that being a distorted acknowledgement that not much else could be cavilled at.

On se voit dans les yeux des autres they say over the Channel: for over six decades, my handwriting has been a daily source of disappointment to me!

My most convincing acting displays in these days were neither on a stage nor at normal performance times, but at home in the early mornings. *If you were ill, you didn't have to go to school; you stayed at home!*

'Mom! I don't feel well.'

'Why, what's the matter?'

'I feel sick!'

‘Oh no! Let me feel your head … hmm – maybe a little hot.’

(*A coughing spasm, followed by a stunned stare which I hope looks seriously poorly.*)

‘Doug! Is he well enough for school?’

‘Oh I don’t know. He does look a bit … (*more coughs*) … Is anyone ill at school?’

‘Peter Farrelly was sick on Monday. He was away yesterday …’

‘Better keep him at home. See how he is. What time is Fraser Brown’s surgery on Wednesdays? I don’t think he’s playing the wag.’

But he was, then and on many occasions, so successfully that, with a string of genuine illness absences added, including a nasty bout of bronchitis, a visit by the School Attendance Officer was triggered one lunchtime, when Dad happened to be home. I actually had gone to class that day, and so missed the encounter, though if Dad’s account was accurate, Birmingham Education Committee’s champion hobbled wounded off the field, having foully impugned the genuinely delicate health of an innocent child and his worried parents, as Dr Fraser Brown would vouchsafe. *That’s* how I told him!

One argument for being at home was that I got on very well! My reading ability and general knowledge grew apace, though I suppose I had to catch up on arithmetic on return. (The subject was not called ‘mathematics’ till secondary school.) I quite enjoyed ‘sums’ anyway, remembering the multiplication tables early on, and usually finished exercises before anyone else in the class, with only slipshod mistakes. Multiplying and dividing duodecimal sums, even when the redundant farthing was included, were just matters of manipulation, and so multiply £19 14s 6¾d by 29 and similar games were not uncongenial. I was lucky to have at home a number of hand-down books of the better Children’s Annual sort, which contained stories and features from over the world, with continuous prose to read, not just comic strips and pictures. Of course, I read weekly comics as well: the Beezer, Dandy, Beano, Wizard and others, often brought home by my father. The *ex cathedra* educational condemnation of such entertaining publications was, like many such miserable strictures, just wrong, at least in my case! As Beatie Bryant in Wesker’s *Roots* proclaims, quoting her never-seen boyfriend Ronnie Kahn: ‘There’s nothing wrong with comics; only there’s something wrong with nothing but comics.’ Stuart Miall’s dark green four volume set *The World of the Children*, published by Caxton, was in itself the foundation of an education, with his three volume *Junior Science* proving useful well into grammar school days. Both these sets, incidentally, were bought from a door-to-door salesman, indicating that there was a 1950s market in selling improving books to working class families. What I effectively did in those years by histrionically avoiding school was to foster the useful and satisfying practice of what Dr Johnson termed *filling the vacuity of life*, doing things on my own: reading, making things, acquiring knowledge, in a sense learning to learn.

Though I had quite enjoyed *Janet and John* it wasn’t long before school reading books became vapid. Chicken Licken, Hen Pen and their cronies, in storyline, phraseology and illustrations, were just dud, whilst trees that instantly grew two branches for every one the useless character lopped off impossibly silly. I sat there and thought of other things, turning the pages at intervals. When summoned to read, either to the front or occasionally to the Headmistress's office, I opened at the back page, read it off, went through the list of words, and returned with the next nuisance. If this was naughty, my mother must accept at least half of the blame, for reading much better stuff to me, and so expressively. She made you want to listen, as did the radio *Children's Hour* and Uncle Mac's *Children's Favourites* on Saturday mornings, the latter of which first demonstrated to me that time enjoyably spent travels heart-breakingly fast. The converse is also regrettably true: whilst when you dread a thing it races towards you, once it's there – or you are – a few moments last for ever.

Though the acts of greatest cruelty were committed by our ex-aircraftman, he did not so much differ in attitude from most of his colleagues; he merely rode the prevalent way of thinking further down the line towards the terminus. Not much more than a decade on from the Second World War, and with ample surrounding evidence, even as deeply inland as we were, of uniformed personnel from all three branches of the armed forces, giving orders and enforcing them – summarily telling people what to do and quickly – were unquestioned assumptions of anyone with even a small amount of authority. If some of what we underwent might fulfil the yearnings of those now nostalgic for 'discipline', they surely could not connive at the easy and regular infliction of physical pain on children. How did that come about? Had sensibilities been blunted by the War? Is it in human nature to abuse even small amounts of power over other, and weaker, members of our species? Must we do to others what was done to us? Or does our conviction that we are right and others in error allow us to race several steps further on and ensure that we have things our way and that's that?

You cannot dispute or even reason with rigid religious or philosophical beliefs. The bigot or fanatic *knows* all the answers, and yet there can be no questions. The Book/Party/Ideology/Religious or Political Leader says it; it is Right. My primary school days have helped me to understand how atrocities occur. Auschwitz is nearer to Birmingham than the 928 miles a theoretical crow would wing to get there.

One morning, in assembly, our very Catholic principal, Mrs Knight, a holy priest's almost equally holy mother, stopped proceedings in mid-lurch.

'Mr McCarthy!'

He stepped forward, from the side.

'Yes, Mrs Knight?'

'That girl isn't singing! Will you deal with her?'

'Yes, Mrs Knight.'

Mary was in our class, which by now in 1959 was McCarthy's. I shan't give her surname in case this true anecdote somehow comes back to her; should that almost impossible circumstance arise, she will know how, if at all, she wants to react. She was probably nine years old. One of eight children, she looked much smaller than her age, being usually dressed in droopily over-large hand downs, possibly from a big sister. Her face was regularly smeared, with tears or for want of a wash. Shrinkingly murine, she made little impression in class, saying almost nothing. I don't think she was much of a scholar. Before this occasion, maybe after picking up school gate gossip, my mother said at teatime to Dad that Mary's father laid into his children when he came home full of beer: malicious tittle tattle maybe, but it would have made sense.

We were all silent in our places before McCarthy entered our classroom hut. He walked straight across the front of the room, past his desk, to the corner cupboard. From its interior his voice, not particularly raised, could be heard:

'Mary?'

She neither spoke nor moved.

He emerged, one eyebrow raised, left hand palm upwards, index finger beckoning.

'Come out here.'

She scurried to the centre front of the room, turned to face us.

'Hold your hand out.'

We had seen the stick used many times in that room. One afternoon, during a painting lesson, there had even been a duel between Michael Reynolds (again!) and McCarthy. Summoned for talking to his neighbour, Kevin Broadfield, Reynolds had been hit hard once on each hand, visibly registering the impacts. He was a well-muscled, physical boy who by then had often been caned. Immediately on return to his place, he spoke again to Broadfield, with deliberate clarity.

'Pass me the water.'

'Reynolds!' The voice had multiplied in volume and pitch. 'Come back.'

Two more swooping whacks, as hard as any. Reynolds blinked at each, returned, resumed his seat, and without even looking at his increasingly red hands, repeated:

'Can I have the water, please?'

'Reynolds!' More fury, more disapproval, as if arresting a dog's misbehaviour in mid rampage. 'Get back out here!' You could hear the choke in his throat. 'We'll see who gets tired of this first, you or me!' Four swipes, extremely mighty.

I cannot remember how the contest ended, but it was a fight of several rounds. Reynolds never cried, though I suspect he gave in at some point and stopped talking. In our minds it was his victory.

But this morning, Mary. Puny waif Mary.

With his full strength he struck her on each hand. Twice. It was the cruellest act I have directly seen in over seventy years.

Remarkably, there are forces which apparently wish to prevent the spread of reports of such inhumanity. Some years ago, when I submitted a summarising comment on this pitiless act of McCarthy, Friends Reunited wouldn't publish it on their website. I circumvented the censor with cheery irony:

'What a wonderfully charitable and Christian man our teacher Mr McCarthy was, thoughtfully reminding little Mary that she must sing up in the hymn by allowing her two hefty cane strokes on each hand!'

On a later occasion, when as part of the school's Senior Management Team I heard an elderly Governor inform us all, over the lunch table, that the beatings he had received at his Catholic school were a Jolly Good Thing and that such practices ought to be widely reintroduced, I felt prompted to tell Mary's story again. I shouldn't have wasted my time.

'Oh, that never happened!' the retired City gentleman dismissively corrected me. It was comforting to hear that.

McCarthy's Class 4 layout was typical: rows of double desks, with everyone placed according to ability and achievement, cleverest on the right, near the door and coke stove, as he faced them. Since I had been placed first in Class 3, Miss Coleman's, I had pole position: front table, right side facing the board. My best friend, John, had come second, and so sat next to me, with Harry Barrett and Peter Farrelly behind us, third and fourth, and so on backwards and then sideways across the room towards the teacher's desk and more windows. Furthest from the leading grid were those who, actively or passively, never seemed to get going. Desmond McGrath lived at the other end of our road. His bullet head shaved almost bare, he was well dressed (white shirted and in a light grey, two-piece short-trousered suit), clean and well groomed, but unable even to say his own name distinctly, never mind talk normally. Perhaps birth-damaged and certainly very frustrated, he relieved his feelings with his fists, and had to be accorded a wide berth. McCarthy's attempt to assist Desmond's speaking would have been crudely inspired – had it worked. One afternoon, he called the boy to the front, told him to open his mouth, put a little piece of carefully shaped wood in and asked him to say his name, Desmond McGrath: 'Deb-muh Muh-ga.'

Removal of wood piece. Replacement with a different one. Say 'Desmond McGrath:

'Deb-muh Muh-ga.'

Not even McCarthy won every contest.

Whilst inarticulate Desmond appeared to function tolerably well physically and may, therefore and as I hope, have had something of a reasonable and enjoyable life, at the opposite pole to my fear-secured *primus inter pares* location at one corner of the room lolled little Elsie Trainer.

From another numerous family, this limp shape perpetually half-lay across her desk, her face fixed in a vacant open-mouthed grin. Her participation and attainment registered somewhere between nil and negligible. A piteous soul of immature intellect, she really should have been in a more suitable school, where she might have benefited from effective specialist attention and care. I suppose her Good Catholic Parents preferred her to be where she was, with us, being spiritually prepared and processed for both Life and the Hereafter. She did, with some show of happiness, manage to simper her way through her First Communion in her white dress and get up, but whether her mother proofed the day by fitting her with a nappy or not letting her drink for many hours, I can't say. I am confident Elsie didn't wet herself that morning, though her dripping chair and spreading puddle were well known to us. If I remember aright, in later years one or two of the maturer girls habitually took over at such liquid crises, easing Elsie outside and fetching the bucket and mop. No doubt they became lovely mothers, maybe one or two of them even nurses, in later years.

Whatever the methods, McCarthy, like his colleagues, did instruct and sometimes entertain us. He shared personal stories about discussing the uses of pocket money with his son, David, about three years older than we were. Was he more relaxed in the afternoons because the effects of the night before had receded, or did he just perhaps ease off because the end of the day's formal exigencies was approaching? During one such better-humoured moment he sent me outside with his car keys, to fetch his fishing rod, strapped to the roof inside his unpolished black 1930s Standard 8 car, parked in Mary Street near the school gate. He wanted to show us how something worked, probably the reel. Another time, he spoke about Winston Churchill's writings: if we wanted to know what really happened in the war, those were what we should read … I trusted the recommendation at the time, unsuspecting that, however Great the Man had been, just now and then he might have wished to colour his readers' perceptions a shade or two! *Alii alia dicunt*. Though he perhaps prided himself on his jokes, they rarely rose above mediocrity, losing measurably in the telling: (*Leaning back against the stove cage*) 'Why is it no good buying a Vauxhall car?' (*A fifteen seconds pause, during which the relished smirk swept in slow arcs back and forth across us, head tipping a few degrees from side to side.*) 'Because you always vorks hall the way there … (*more arcing and head tipping*) … and then vorks hall the way back again!'

Though he supplied us with some information that has lasted a lifetime, not all of it has ever in my instance found an actual use:

'How do you tell whether a skeleton belonged to a man or a woman … (*serious expression, head inclined forward*) … by the shape of the pelvis - that's this bit.'

When the afternoons of the late afternoon grew darker, and Christmas neared, the room was partly lit by the red glow of the cast iron coke stove. For several afternoons in a row, McCarthy sat centrally in his captain's chair, reading *A Christmas Carol* to us. Brute or not, he was sometimes capable of magic.

Though the stick might swish so regularly that after some weeks it began to splinter, there was always a reserve of two or three stored in the cupboard. The long, thin, whippy one passed away first, to be succeeded by a thicker, healthier looking individual, more golden than yellow and with a zigzag marking along its length. The thicker the rod, the lower the note of its downward warcry.

One time, it wasn't the stick's swoop that alighted on a pupil's anatomy.

Bernese and Margaret sat beside each other, at the very back of the second across line of double tables, perfectly matched in ability but also in physical maturation. Already turning into young women, being taller and more rounded than the other girls, they were naturally best friends. Pretty blue-eyed Margaret's soft fair curls floated freely down on to her shoulders; Bernese's dark brown, short haircut, the straight across fringe and curving curtain sides, presented the proscenium arch theatre look common then. Always at risk of bubbling over, together they simmered merrily away through their exercises. Their whispers and sniggers frequently drew McCarthy's fire.

He had told them several times, with increasing sternness. Since the last emphasis he had sat facing everyone, arms folded, expression unchanging.

The snort from the back of the room switched our eyes to him. For some moments he showed no response.

'Bernese! Come out here!' He remained seated.

Blushing, smiling, and with one hand to her mouth, she stood and advanced sideways between the rows of tables, catching some with her large hips.

'Stand there!' He pointed to a spot just in front of him and slightly to his left. 'Turn to the window.' She was now facing away from him. 'Hold both sides of your skirt with your hands, and pull it tight.'

Understanding, she didn't immediately comply.

'You heard me! You're a naughty girl! Do as you're told!'

Blushing even more, she looked over her shoulder at him, then pulled her clothes tight about her.

With the flat of his hand, he swung meatily against her, the shock making her cry 'Oh!' and impelling her forward a step.

'Come back!' Still without rising, he struck her seat a second time. She hadn't moved this time, but was biting her lower lip, looking down. 'Just go and sit down. That's what happens to naughty girls.' The voice was not raised, but remained measured, level.

I left the school a few weeks after this, and so it was probably fifteen months after the incident that I next, and for the last time ever, saw McCarthy. By then I had moved from my second primary school to the first year of a Catholic grammar school. At our prize day, on an autumn evening in 1961, there outside Birmingham's Town Hall was Mr McCarthy, about to see his son receive some award. As I stood there with my parents, he spoke more tenderly to me than any of us had ever previously known. He stood, hardly taller than my nearly five feet of height, facing me, close. He had his hands behind my mackintosh collar, endlessly neatening and smoothing it. Without knowing why I felt uncomfortable.

Dad's Cars

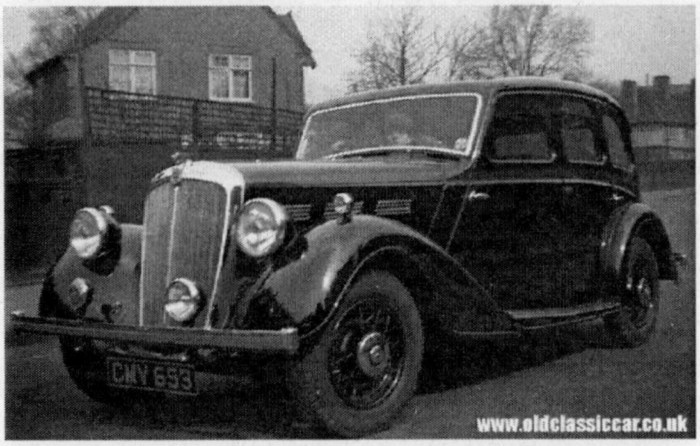

Dad's first car DOX 686 was like this Morris 10

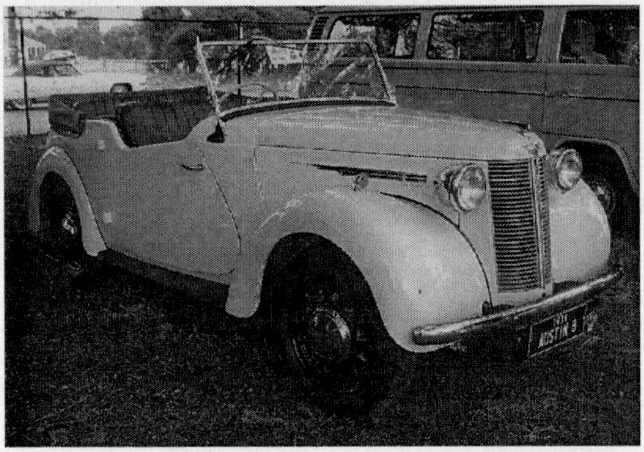

Grey JOP 800 followed – my early favourite!

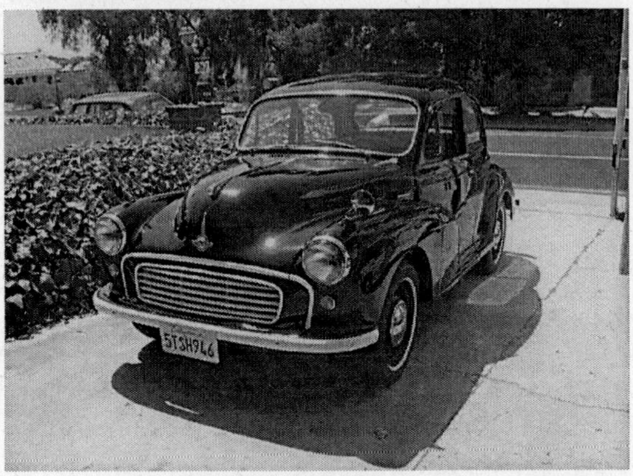

With brand new XOJ 516 in December 1959

Miss King (again!) … and others

Perhaps I should clarify my route, from arrival in September 1954 to departure from St John's on 1st July 1960. Even though it can never be retrodden, I ought not to leave anyone lost in one of Time's blind alleys …

In historical order, our teachers were:

Miss Shepherd
Mrs Davis/Mrs Avery
Miss King
Miss Fuller
Miss King again

The group above taught us for the first three school years, though at this distance I cannot say how or when we were moved or divided up. I am sure about the sequence of rooms and teachers, but not the dividing points in the calendar.

Mrs Smart taught 7-8 year olds, then:

Junior 3 Miss Coleman/Miss Kean: 8-9
Junior 4 Mr McCarthy: 9-10
Junior 5 Mr Wild: 10-11

I left the school just two to three weeks before the end of Junior 4. A decade or two ago, I learned via the Friends Reunited website from Kevin Broadfield, former classmate, that Mr Wild had also left in July 1960, to be succeeded by a much younger and more unpleasant character than even McCarthy.

One might ask oneself what previous life experiences or forces had been necessary to produce such an at least superficially educated person, engaged and salaried to bring about the intellectual and social growth of other people's children (in a professedly highly God-fearing establishment, it might be added). One might well ask, but sadly there have been, and still are to be found, too many instances of other totally unsuitable characters entrusted with young people. Sexual predators and paedophiles will naturally home in on sources of their prey; schools will always therefore be at potential risk, though it is to be hoped that political and professional efforts over the last few decades have raised awareness and imported some safeguards. I am not thinking particularly of such deviants and criminals. It would not surprise me, though, if psychologists identified some sexual elements in attitudes and practices of other unacceptable teachers.

According to what I believe to be trustworthy first-hand report, Mr Wild's replacement used the cane, and possibly other means of physical punishment, freely and mercilessly. He liked using his power over ten to eleven year olds; he enjoyed their suffering. Apart from wielding the stick, he would sometimes give a boy money and dispatch him to the little shop a few hundred yards away, to buy a sponge cake. I think it would have cost perhaps three shillings in those times, maybe half a crown. Upon its receipt, he would cut the family-sized cake up on his desk, and with slow relish eat every slice in front of everyone. Mouths were in reality watering.

The story continued that, just before the end of the school year, on I think a hot summer's afternoon, Kevin himself was picked on for punishment. He had been caned before – I can attest to that from our time together with McCarthy, the previous year. He was told to come to the front of the class and hold his hand out.

Whether this was just one time too many, or the pretext too flimsily unjust to be tolerated, Kevin defiantly refused to be hit. I wish I still had his account in front of me. He told the story better than I shall ever be able to. I think that, once he had refused to take his punishment, his determination rose, almost certainly buoyed by the support the rest of the class would have instantly given him. He was a nice and harmless boy in a class with many other decent young people. I am sure that Harry Barrett and Johnny Ward would have been with him, many others, no doubt, not least the girls, maybe everyone.

I don't know how long the stand-off endured, or whether there was any physical tussle. It may have been near the end of the afternoon. Whatever the detail, the outcome has been clearly passed down: Kevin left the classroom untouched – except, that is, for the embraces and back slappings of everyone else, as he was carried away on people's shoulders, to massed cheering and singing.

This incident I did not witness in a sense links with one I did. This time, it was McCarthy who was not allowed to have his way. It was another school concert, and I was in Class 4. We had done our bit before the interval. I was in ordinary clothes again, back with my family, which somehow included optician Uncle Ken, my father's younger brother, in his mid-twenties. We took our fairy cakes and orange squash outside, on to the playground. Ken had had a sufficient supply of infant posturings and warbles.

'This is a great place for football,' he observed, looking around. 'I bet you have some super games.' Everyone else was resignedly filing up the steps for the second half.

'We're not allowed to.'

'Well, that's just silly, isn't it? It's a top place. Doug, give us your car key. Here, Martin, go and get the ball from the boot.'

The red inflatable Frido plastic ball had cost 6s 6d and was about three-quarters the size of a full adult football, with little raised dots all over and lines representing the panels of the real leather object. As soon as we had the playground to ourselves, led by Uncle Ken, the three of us were hoofing the ball from wall to wall, with shots in and bounces off. Our voices, the shish of plastic skidding over tarmac and the boink of the arcing sphere hitting brick echoed around.

After a few minutes, McCarthy came out and stood at the head of the steps. He looked serious. 'Came to see what the noise was.'

My uncle picked up the ball and grinned. 'Just having a kick about,' he explained. 'It's a super little ball.' He bounced it up and down, reverberantly. *Super* was a word he used frequently. From inside, clapping broke out.

'Righty-ho!' McCarthy returned, with a sickly expression. He turned and re-entered the building.

*****

To have Miss King as our teacher *again* was hardly cheering, though we were familiar with her sharpness and spiritual preoccupations. More of our weekly daubings were selotaped to the glass partition, which vibrated to Miss Fuller's boomings next door. It was curious to me how the best intentioned start to any new painting of mine, with each bright pastel colour briefly keeping its authentic purity, rapidly fused into a more or less brownish-grey silt of sog. Others achieved better patterns, contrasting clear yellow with vibrant purple, orange with green. Their flowers looked like the thing. If any one of my efforts was ever accorded display, it must have been through uncharacteristic charity. We gathered that many of the Lord's affairs went in sevens, like the sacraments: deadly sins, gifts of the Holy Spirit, things seen by God, devils cast out from Mary Magdalene, and so on. We were now in the middle of the three partitioned rooms: only one to go before the Annexe, whatever that was. Before that, Mrs Smart.

Certainly older than both my grandmothers, and weighing more than the two of them taken together, this good Birmingham woman, white-haired and black-framed-spectacled, had, she informed us, been 'brought back' from somewhere or something to the classroom. Maybe that explained her habitual slight grumpiness. However long she had been left untroubled, she had, though, lost none of her assurance. Gruff and hefty, she waddled her way from door to desk, reminding me of my biggest toy electric boat yawing heavily from port to starboard, fighting to cross the pond on a windy afternoon. Once anchored at her tall, dark desk, she generally stayed there, probably moored by her painful hips, sending us all over the room and the building on necessary missions.

'Treanor! Come and get the key. Go and open up the cupboard and bring me those red geography books on the second shelf.'

'Edward! This is a note for Mrs Knight. Now take it to the office.'

'You're tall, John. Stand on that chair and pull the blind down – the sun's in my eyes.'

Neither graceful nor gracious, Mrs Smart was simply effective. Plainly clad in a fine knit apple green button up cardigan, a generous black skirt, thick tights and stout lace-ups, she looked what she was: no nonsense. Straight. In her strong Brummie accent, her instructions clanged round the walls and ceiling. She never shouted, raised her voice or erupted into rage. She knew what you were going to do. She told you. You did it. She didn't imagine you might misbehave – and so you didn't. Whilst this was an unglamorous way to conduct affairs, at least you felt safe. You did your work. She marked it. You made any corrections, following all the rules about using pen or pencil, using a ruler to underline, and leaving the right spaces. You did the next thing.

'You two,' pointing to the boys nearest the door around milk time. 'There's a box in the corridor. Bring it in.'

They were apples from her garden.

'If you want an apple, come up and get one, starting with that row. Only if you take it, there'll be no mess and you must eat it all up.'

No one ever said it, but we all knew she was a good mother and grandmother.

If Mrs Smart wove no enchantment in the end classroom, Miss Strasse provided ample compensation. Eighteen years old, pretty and Austrian, she took us for singing lessons, using the same upright piano that accompanied our morning hymns. Unlike the dutiful teacher who jangled us through our spiritual bawlings, Miss Strasse really could play the piano. Her fingers lit fireworks in the keys. Dazzling runs thrilled the room as she smiled over her shoulder at us, not even having to look at her hands.

The BBC put out a weekly radio programme, I think called *Singing Together*, for classes to tune into and sing along with. Each year or perhaps term or season, booklets of tunes and words were issued to accompany the broadcasts. It was old sets of these that Miss Strasse sometimes used for our pieces, but to her accompaniment, which had extra introductions, embellishments and endings. She was talented, and fun. It went without saying that Mozart ran through her veins; the first time she sang and played Papageno's bird catcher song to us, a wonderful flush travelled throughout me, to my fingertips. What excitement! What joy! Her young woman's voice was itself music, not just what we knew as singing. It travelled brightly on the air. The piano finished with the two little upward panpipe runs, from G to D, answered by two chords, before the bouncing, happy *tutti* ending.

'It's better in German, though, I think.'

I wish I could see again the whole BBC translation that was in front of us. I know it awkwardly began with two notes on the word *I* and the last line ended with the last syllable *-er* unnaturally stressed:

'I-yer am the jolly bird catch*er* …'

And how infelicitously enfeebling the scansion-obliged 'jolly' is!

I would not know any German for another five years, but understand now why the real thing was so much more triumphant:

'Der Vogelfänger bin ich ja …'

In just the first line, the musical stresses, exactly catching the words' tone and sense, along with the alliteration and the fling of *ja*, beautifully communicate his joy at being himself and doing what he does. What more self-affirmation could anyone want? She sang the whole aria without looking at the music or the piano, just at us: Miss Strasse and Wolfgang Mozart, two perfect human beings, both Austrian.

There was another, perhaps even more miraculous moment in one of Miss Strasse's lessons.

In the front left corner of the classroom, stood a plaster statue of Mary about four feet tall and elevated on a table of almost the same height, allowing the Holy Mother to look down in stunned serenity over all our heads. On top of her full length loose cream dress, gold trimmed, a bluebell and white open drape hung from the extended, welcoming arms. At her bare, flesh painted feet a glass vase was weekly supplied with fresh flowers, according to the season's availability. *Above* the Blessed Virgin's head a hinged, brass arm supported the gold crown of the Queen of Heaven, suspended a few inches above the top of the statue.

We had been singing what was described in the book as a Swiss yodelling song:

From Lucerne to Weggis on,
Holdiridia, holdia.
Shoes nor stockings need we don,
Holdiridia, holdia.
Refrain:
Hol-di-ri-dia, holdiridia, holdia.
Hol-di-ri-dia, holdiridia, holdia.

'Wait, wait, wait! Where I come from we don't call that yodelling! Let me show you!'

She took a breath, put one hand on the top of her chest. Next, the most astonishing passage of rich, throaty warbles, flicking from low to high notes was bubbling profusely, profusely from her, making the whole room resonate …

There was a loud creak. Our eyes moved to the corner, to Our Blessed Lady. Slowly, the bracket was swinging to one side, bringing the gold crown right to the wall. Should we breathe? Miss Strasse also heard the noise, despite her singing, or followed our eyes and saw the last stages of the movement. She stopped in mid-phrase. And giggled.

‘Well, that’s never happened before.’

*****

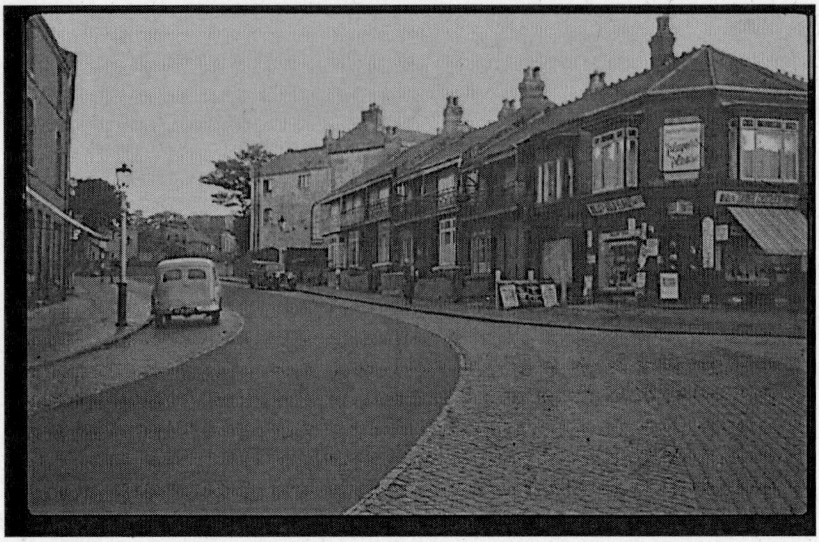

Up the Hill. Like many 1950s Birmingham streets not all the cobbles had been lifted.

If you walked up the hill of Mary Street to the staggered five-way junction with George Street, Edgbaston Road, Park Road and the continuation of Edgbaston Road, taking first left and walking down George Street eventually brought you back round to St John’s Church, behind which was the school. A couple of hundred yards before that, though, you passed the high, chainlink-fenced area of a playground, and then, again on your left, a single storey building with a side entrance. This was the Annexe. Like Noah’s boarding passengers, we formed a two-by-two line as we followed Miss Coleman on the first morning of the autumn term in 1958, to our new classroom, the left-hand one, to this recent addition to pupil accommodation.

Well towards the other end of the Frump-Dolly scale from our previous teacher, Miss Coleman charmed the air when she glided by – or at least fragrance swayed gently in her wake. She did not quite have Orpheus’ power to enrapture all earthly things, but your eyes did naturally follow her around the class, or at intervals flitted upwards from your exercise book to her sitting neatly at her table, ankles crossed. Perhaps in her mid-twenties, trim and light in her movements, she had gracefully accepted Nature’s birth gift of vibrant curly orange hair, and wore it every day. Pale complexioned with bright blue eyes, she intensified the normal red of her lips to a lit up scarlet, matching her nails. Whether blood or blusher warmed her cheeks I cannot tell; the glow was there. Her wrists clicked bracelets. Every morning before the register, the girls craned to see what colourful outfit would be revealed from under the day’s pastel raincoat. In the coldest times, matching angora scarf and hat softened further the femininity.

As far as I can be sure, our learning during these years kept to the straight main roads of progressive exercises, graded reading books, writing called 'composition' and comprehensions, short extracts with ten or twenty questions. Nothing unexpected jumped out and said 'boo!' to you; it was established, thorough instruction, practice. Unless you could not follow or became distracted, you knew and could do more at the end of it. By this time, I was following my own interests, able to ride my red and yellow Triang scooter on Saturday mornings to the Balsall Heath public library on Alcester Road, a rather grand late nineteenth cantury red brick and cream stone building, complete with square tower and four-sided clock. Though on my first visit, taken by a neighbour with her daughters, I had no clue what you did and proudly returned home with a totally unreadable book, I think from the Geography section, before too long I found the junior fiction, and began to work my way through adventure stories. *The Famous Five* rushed rapidly by, followed by *The Secret Seven.* Before long I became aware of Serious People on platforms snootily despising on our behalf Enid Blyton's popular fictions, which they scoffed were hardly better than comics. We should read Robert Louis Stevenson, Charles Dickens, Jane Austen, the Brontës …

We were nine. We did not have the necessary vocabulary and other reading skills, never mind some understanding of older societies or life experience, to crease up at Mr Collins or shiver in the death cell with Fagan. We can all bang the *Daily Mail* drum – if that's all we can read. I doubt whether many of them ever got round to just starting *Anna Karenina, Middlemarch* or even *Oliver Twist.*

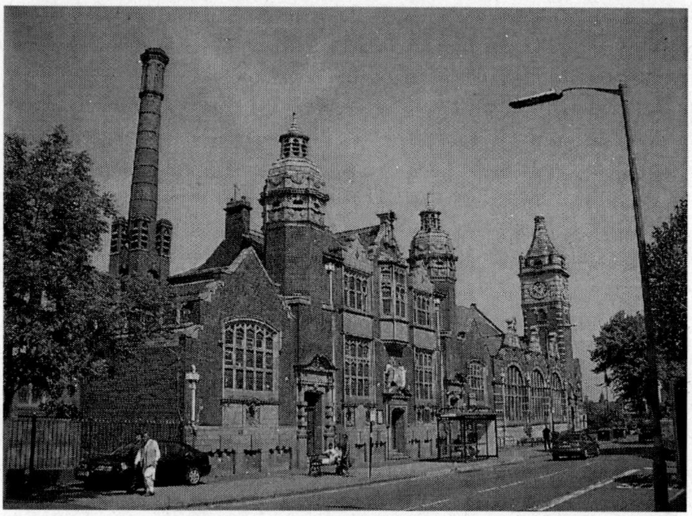

Balsall Heath Swimming Baths (left) and Library

Malcolm Saville's numerous books included the *Lone Pine* series, two of which, along with other stories, (my maximum allowance) I consumed each week, keeping up the habit until I went to grammar school, two years later. I do not recall which authors or works I moved on to, but read and re-read *The Secret of Smugglers' Wood* by R.J.McGregor. My aged copy, intact, is destined for my grandchildren: an exciting mystery story not without some amusement:

> *'Bert was followed by a lady with a violin. She had a fine instrument and played well, but was unfortunately the victim of an accompanist whose ideas were all her own. The piano was so bad that it did not give the violin a chance ...'*

When the music stand collapses, the village hall audience, who have been smouldering, think it's a comedy act, flashing into laughter. If, in four years, you have come from complete ignorance of all letter symbols and sounds, to be able to enter on your own a fictional scene and smile or open your eyes with dread, time has not been entirely wasted.

So, it was possible to supplement our plain but perfectly sustaining standard classroom fare with treats; but to continue the theme, if Mrs Smart's classroom had been a safe and substantial main course followed by pie and cold custard or rice pudding, Miss Coleman's afforded some spicier variety. Her alert and darting eyes missed little. Murmur or begin to turn round during work and, like a worm spotted by a statuesque blackbird, you were darted on.

'Harry! Keep your eyes on your own work!'

'Godfrey! Face the front!'

Sharp and brisk, she shooed us through each day, always poised to strike, but equally liable to flash us smiles. She kept us slightly breathless, though we came to appreciate the pleasure of her company only when she was replaced for some weeks – was it because of family illness? – by Miss Kean!

Angry and angular – even her bosom thrust forward in geometric outline – this red-cheeked, salmon-pink-jumpered lady spat fire. Only a few years the senior of our proper teacher, she enjoyed none of her personal charms. Her black tail of hair swished ferally behind her, with aberrant fringe strands trespassing down over her black, heavy framed glasses. High prominent cheekbones above a lantern jaw, blessed with protruding, over-sized and widely spaced front incisors, might have inspired a Walt Disney cartoon character; they could hardly have favoured her prospects in the matrimonial stakes, though had she practised the occasional smile, whilst carefully reducing the scale of her mouth movements and hence dental and gingival exposure, she might have shortened the odds marginally. I wonder whether, catching sight of herself in the mirror one morning, she had conceived such a grudge against her Maker that she resolved thereafter to take things out on any of his other productions when occasion presented itself. She certainly was very free with her ungainly slabby smacks. One time, when she said we had been talking, she needed to walk up and down all the rows, landing a weighty slap on everyone's hand or arm, before her feelings were eased. This, by the way, was the only time I was ever physically punished at any school, if that's the right word, since I know I had already taken cover at the warning shots and was keeping quiet. *It raineth on the just etc*

Physically awkward, this stand-in also wrinkled my brow with her gauche English. A stress on the *last* syllable of 'geography' *and* making it rhyme with 'cry'? A long 'o' in the first syllable of the *noun* 'project'? I don't think she taught me much, but I do remember her.

Not only were there a mere two classes in the Annexe, but Mr Wild liked his sport and games. So, at playtime, he stood with Miss Coleman while we ran about, having supplied us with balls of different sizes to throw, bounce and kick, shouting encouragement and advice to the boys in the main football game. If the ball came his way, he joined in, passing it on or running it a few steps down the yard. The trick that particularly impressed us was his kick from behind: he was adept at letting a high looping ball drop over his shoulder so he could backheel it over his head and again into play, often with respectable aim.

'Sir? How do you do that?'

'Oh, nothing to it, lad. Just twenty years' practice!'

He was not far off retirement, but still very active, riding a dark green upright Phillips bike to and from work. Our P.E. provision was indeed very poor and patchy; it would make modern inspectors foam and fit with despair. Mr Wild did what he could for us, taking us in groups to the playground for half an hour or so some mornings, where we did forward rolls on mats, threw bean bags at skittles, chased hoops and lined up for whatever it was called.

Stand to Attention! Feet astride, jump!

Running on the spot, begin: one-two, one-two, one-two.

Right: two lines, against the wall. First boy run to the wall opposite, touch it, run back and tag the next boy. Ready? Go!

He looked good: upright, well-made but slim, round-faced and blue-eyed like many Midland men, typically bald except for a fluffy silver valance. At first we mistook his energy, thinking him fierce, but he was brusquely benign. Our year in the Annexe presented relatively few troubles. A spell in the right colony might not have been such a bad thing for a Roman.

*****

Over the years, since from the reception class, we were at times taken off the school sites. Holding hands until old enough not to, we walked to Cannon Hill Park. (I privately objected to Dennis's warty clasp!) I already knew this amenity, which in later years housed the Midlands Arts Centre. My parents had regularly taken me there at weekends and on holidays, to start with in a blue push chair, later walking, until Dad's first car in 1954. Shortly after entering via the entrance at the junction of Edgbaston and Russell Road, you descended past the tropically hot greenhouse on your right. The banana tree or perhaps trees produced impressive pendulous clusters. We usually say 'tree' when thinking of the plant, but someone told me (maybe my father read a label) that it was not really a tree at all, but a very large fruit plant. You can understand that when you look at their parts and structure, though common sense assures you that, on account of its size alone, it *is* a tree!

If you've read *Things Fall Apart* by the great Nigerian writer Chinua Achebe, you will have learned about how Okonkwo beat his second wife, Ekwefi, even during the Week of Peace, because she cut banana leaves to wrap food. The Umuofian warrior has too much energy and pent up tension because he cannot work during the obligatory sacred holiday. His overreaction is characteristic:

> 'Who killed the banana *tree*?' he angrily shouts.

As much as I respect the botanists, I wouldn't have argued with Okonkwo!

On school outings, we turned left just after the greenhouses, walking along the road to the café on the left (Garden Tea Room), where if we had the money we could buy an ice lolly. The main business of the afternoon seemed to be rolling down the grassy hill towards the café building, which looked much more fun than it proved after a few descents, when you had to sit still because you felt so giddy and sick. In autumn we collected big leaves, taking them back to make plaster of Paris casts the next day, using Kraft Dairylea box bottoms or tops for moulding shells. We also brought back items for the Nature table: leaves, cones, berries … Understandably, we didn't explore further, to the two ponds or lakes, it being not only some distance to walk to them, but also to prevent the possibility of someone's ending up soaked and shivering. Nor was everyone else shown, as I had been, the River Rea, shallow-looking, green and some way down in its engineered channel, or the big lump of stone my father said had fallen from the skies, a meteorite.

Annually, there was the optional chance of a day trip to the coast, I think always to Weston Super Mare. My parents would have paid for me to go, but as easily allowed me to have my own away day at home, haranguing teachers and irritating other pupils being conveniently removed by coach or bus from the county. Since I dearly loved the seaside, to forego the opportunity of even a few hours on the stretching sands of an open beach only confirmed the antipathy I felt towards the regime. One amusing, almost alarming story was brought back one year, of the headmistress getting stuck in the sands and having to be heaved out by other teachers. The word 'quicksand' was even mentioned, immediately bringing to mind knife-edge scenes from children's television dramas: the masked hero having to be rope-pulled from certain suffocating fatality thanks to the local expertise of his resourceful redskin chum, stallion Silver and a rope. As a curious footnote, I supply the following Tripadvisor extract, from a comment on the resort's Sand Bay:

> ' … if the quicksand, fast tides, crumbling cliff isn't [sic] enough to put you off, I guess this is a great place to get rid of your family forever!!!'

Maybe I had been better off at home after all, even though Mrs Knight was still at school the morning after that trip!

Mrs Knight! Margaret Knight, M.A.(Oxon)! I only wish I knew the details of her background and education. From the perspective of my own life and career, I seriously ask whether she really was an Oxford graduate. In what subject, could that have been? Modern languages, perhaps? There was no indication whatever. Why oh why, or how oh how, did a supposedly bright young woman, leaving the oldest (and some would claim greatest) university in the realm, professedly qualified, spend the last stages of her career in a very basic, far less than glamorous primary school more or less in Birmingham's red light district? (Though I didn't realise it at the time, I saw my first working woman one lunchtime, unbelievably short skirted and open bloused for the times, on stilt-high heels and leaning on the arm of a smirking uniformed sailor at the top of George Street.) Mrs Knight did not in any way fit the bill of some very dedicated intellectual women I have come across over the years, who chose to teach little children from poor or worse backgrounds for altruistic, vocational reasons; or if she did, she never showed us their sensitivity, insight and interest in young people. Was she just a plodder, then, who had somehow scraped through to a low-class degree by dull application, and defaulted into teaching at an elementary level? Or was it that her servile adherence to and thoroughgoing application of the Catholic Church's doctrines, strictures, prohibitions and pronouncements gained her the favour of (in her chosen limited field) a top appointment? While *Better to rule in Hell than serve in Heaven* might not quite apply, I can more easily credit the likelihood that, if any frumpy, late middle-aged woman in the whole of our Second City knew the Catechism pretty thoroughly, parroting it on reflex, it was Mrs K. If her priest son, Michael, was as young as he looked, perhaps early twenties, that might have made her anything between, at the greatest extremes, late forties to approaching sixty, a woman's normal retirement age. If I had to put £10 on it, I'd venture 55, based on what has so far not faded or been erased from my mental gallery.

My mother was five feet two and a half inches tall in her young days. My impression is that Margaret Knight was even a little shorter, though her bodily proportions might have created some distortion. Plump and rounded all over, she may not even have been flabby, though the tightness of her well-buttoned tailored suit tops, usually Cambridge blue, though sacerdotal black on very special occasions, suggested a meaty solidity of substance. On the 1950s principle that, if you can't shoo your unwelcome fat away, you might as well trap it where it can't move for a few hours, she was probably corseted. Everything else was visibly tight: the polished stout-heeled lace up shoes, the opaquely thick quasi surgical stockings. Even her facial skin struggled to contain the bulging flesh of her shiny face, making her eyes appear even smaller behind the round National Health spectacles. Well permed, her tight, colourless hair curled rigidly against her head, she made me think of a Pekinese dog or Pong Ping from *Rupert Bear* annuals.

She pleased the priests.

We were never given much, or perhaps any, warning of a fairly common, if not regular class outing in better weather. The lunchtime parking of a Birmingham City Transport cream and navy double decker outside the railings meant an afternoon off site at what were called the playing fields. There must have been two classes on the bus, one on each deck, as we ascended Mary Street, went up Park Road to the Alcester Road, turned right and found our way through Moseley Village, turned right into Reddings Road and past the old ground of Reddings Rugby, later Birmingham Moseley Rugby, eventually to a large green expanse. Once released, for some time we just ran around. Sometimes we roamed over towards a small detached house, furthest from the entrance, where I suspect the groundsman lived. A low palings fence defined what must have been his little cottage style flower and vegetable garden, while, on the edge of the fields themselves, a deranged goat on a tether, possibly a tractor rope secured to a stake, disported itself, by turns grazing or gazing thoughtfully towards us. The dare was to creep to within its reach. The girls and feebler sorts, resolutely including me, kept well away. The word 'capricious' justly deserves its existence and origins: at any moment, even when the ring of spectators kept perfectly still and silent, it would suddenly leave feasting and rocket head down in a straight line at one small group of us, producing screams of mingled fear and delight as we scattered. On one occasion, McCarthy, as always the male teacher with us, in the unfamiliar role of protector, actually intervened to effect a rescue by hoisting a stumbling straggler up and away from his would-be first-degree assailant.

I cannot remember what the girls did with Miss Coleman, but with only her male colleague she must have been in charge of two classes' worth of eight and nine year olds, a staff to pupil ratio of between 40 and 50 to 1! (We had travelled three to a seat.) In an emergency, the groundsman could have been summoned, as presumably could our driver, who sat in his cab or under a tree, reading his newspaper.

When the single ball was produced, all of us kicked it about, without instruction or sportswear, even a change of footwear, for the putative game. Our referee, McC, still wore his grey two-piece suit. To borrow from Shakespeare's Mark Antony, our procedure was pretty well 'boys unto a muss'. We swarmed back and forth after the ball, rarely getting to touch it. As tiredness and despair felled us, we dropped out of the charge, some taking to the ground, breathless and sweaty.

*****

Anyone, amateur or professional, who has played an instrument in orchestras or under conductors can be guaranteed to have witnessed, or quite likely been the target of, the humiliating fury and scorn unleashed upon players – most commonly of the orchestra's solo instruments (wind and brass especially) – though just as possibly a whole section:

> *'Second violins, you have no sense of rhythm!' screamed Andrew Davis passionately at a Festival Hall rehearsal of the New Philharmonia in summer 1975.*

I have seen it and borne it since my mid-teens. Understandably, to survive long as a working professional you have not to be just a very proficient and adaptable player, but also bullet and acid proof. That ruled me out on both (unintentional pun) scores! Yet the world – or perhaps evening and weekend activity – of the willing amateur does not necessarily remain more comfortable. You may well have paid your appreciable membership subscription, humped chairs and stands about, functioned as librarian, supplied, prepared and served the teas and coffees taken at breaks, washing up after the whole rehearsal, and still be publicly butchered alive into all known joints to relieve the feelings of a social misfit of risible appearance and physique, who happens to have electronically perfect pitch as well as the whole of Mahler's Second Symphony committed to working memory. Even at humble levels the arts have their costs!

A combined schools' event was being prepared at Birmingham Town Hall. From schools all over the City, selected pupils had learned songs for a massed children's choir. Without asking my permission, of course, I was one morning transported with our fairly small contingent to a rehearsal. Like other school happenings, there was little or no notice – probably not even a letter home with a parental consent slip to sign and return. Who even imagined nonsense like that!

My place to sit and stand was (as you faced the tiered auditorium), to the right of the massive Victorian organ pipes, a row or two back from the level of the console and half a dozen children away from it.

I was not talking or doing anything other than look up and around me at the quite wonderfully grand place. We had not even started to sing. The suited man in the middle facing us suddenly held his arm out at me for a long time, shouting very loudly. I knew I was in trouble. He was warning me very seriously.

We were singing the first song, several hundred of us. Imagine all the choir steps completely packed. After a short time, he stopped us all and fired a bolt of hot fury at me. I needed to open my mouth widely. I really thought I had been, but even if not, he could have asked more gently. I do not suppose one reduced-volume child's voice out of hundreds impaired the total effect that much! A few minutes later on, he did the same sort of thing: 'O why (with a stamp) can't you *look* at me?' I was reading the words. In the whole of the rest of the morning he did not single out anyone else.

Perhaps later, when he was congratulating himself in the bar to his chums or even his admiring date, he explained how his success was largely attributable to the principle Voltaire describes in *Candide*, referring to the execution of Byng, shot on board the Monarche at Portsmouth on 14th March 1757:

> *Mais dans ce pays-ci il est bon de tuer de tems en tems un Amiral* ***pour encourager les autres.***

I missed the actual performance because one of the roaming infections caught me. I was eight.

One of my friends habitually twits me for the 'stream of consciousness' nature of my emails to him. I do not mind; it's difficult to deny, and tickles both of us. How can it be avoided, since the memory works by association, except by external controls like suppression, organisation, ordering, censuring – I suppose, the artistry of a creating craftsman, like a novelist? And this is a life, not a fiction. And lives are not artistically ordered. They happen. They are, next they have been. We sometimes may try to make sense of or impose order upon them. Only, the various elements, strands, features – whatever you want to call them – are almost certainly not in any way related to each other, but disparate, separate, diverse, independent. Take my desk, for example. It has around me things I've recently looked at or been involved with: letters I've read and am keeping, notes I've made to help me in the future, spectacles, a tin for spare coins, pens, pencils, batteries, a camera, a musical instrument, glass of water, notebook, a few magazines and catalogues piled at one side, the brass 'dinner's ready' handbell inscribed 'Captain's table' I took as a souvenir from my mother's household effects, my mobile phone, a watch, a copy stand, glass of water and so on. It looks like untidiness; in a sense it is. I *could* put everything somewhere else overnight. Even then, I should struggle: some things just do not belong in any drawer, on any shelf or other storage place because they are just themselves, fitting into no category. The biggest folder in my *Documents,* with a similarly named one in *Pictures*, has usually been 'Miscellaneous'! Mysteriously, I also have one called 'Extra', another 'Temporary', a third 'Things in Transit' … need I go on?

'If I were you, I'd sort all that lot out,' my wife remarks; or less tolerantly, 'I couldn't *bear* to live like that. You're so messy!' Ah, but my dear: that's life! A few paragraphs ago I wrote about being 'transported with our small contingent' to what became a living sacrifice. What I was unable to record was *how* we travelled. The party was too small to warrant a City bus. The school had no vehicle of its own. Even if the lady teacher had had a car, there were too many of us to fit in it. I abandoned the search.

Overnight, between periods of sleep, it all came back in a couple of seconds, something I had emphatically not contemplated for over sixty years. I have never recounted the event before, certainly not written it down. It upset me at the time, but rapidly dematerialised into oblivion.

Our accompanying teacher walked us down Mary Street, then right up Edward Road to Alcester Road, where we boarded a bus (possibly the number 50). Red plastic tokens were given to the conductor to pay for us. We walked from the bus stop across the city centre to the imposing classical building.

How should that all have come back to me? It was put away such a long time ago. But it was still there. We could well wonder what else is dustily archived in our unlit remoter storage chambers! Maybe other things will be associatively brought out as I go further. Should anyone tremble?

I once spoke to a young man whose late teenage climbing accident had placed him in hospital for months and his remarkable recovery on some pages of a Sunday colour supplement. The week before his fall, a middle-aged man had plummeted to his death from the same spot. This younger survivor suffered multiple injuries: a shattered pelvis, broken limbs, broken ribs … his left arm and shoulder (his dominant side) were horribly sprained and dislocated. When he slipped, he did have some purchase with his ice axe, which after an agonising wrench and for a time held his whole body weight as he dangled before dislodging. He dropped hundreds of feet, skirting the rock face, lucky only in that he remained feet first, landing in deep, soft snow, the two circumstances that, with astounding specialist and intensive care, preserved him.

I mention this here because of what he added as a footnote. The comatose state in which he remained for several days was, he believed, a consequence of the enormous mental rush he had experienced in the five or six seconds he was falling, as (he claimed) *every experience in his entire life flashed by in a rewind or fast forward.* The resultant shock lightning-bolt-tasered him into mental paralysis. Who are we to contradict him? It is said that a drowning man's life passes before his eyes.

Is the current narration then, undertaken as I start my eighth decade in this sublunary dimension, the commencement of another final discharge?

*****

What did I take with me when I left St John's that Thursday afternoon, 1st July 1960? I walked home with a brown envelope containing my report, issued early before the end of the year on account of my departure, recording that I had remained first in the class. The single sheet, with brief handwritten comments and marks for each subject, held marks for recent tests and exams, apart from Reading, which was amusingly down as '98% (est)'. Mrs Knight had signed at the end, after a valedictory phrase. I had then an adequate foundation for literacy and numeracy. Though (I hope I'm not flattering myself!) sensitive and timid, certainly not a physical boy, I had in some areas gained confidence: I should stand a reasonable chance of staying safe some of the time if I worked obligingly and well. Somewhere on a slip of paper I had the handwritten address of my best friend, John Falkner, with whom I did exchange a few letters. He moved from Hallam Street to another area of the City shortly afterwards, but then we lost touch. In the following years I saw only two of my former classmates ever again, both at Sunday Mass, to which we were taken by my father: Treanor Stafford and Desmond McDonald. I did actually speak to Desmond.

Singing Together sessions (we actually used the radio broadcasts after Miss Strasse returned home) familiarised me with a fairly generous collection of songs: sea shanties, folk songs, even Lieder sung in translation.

> But skilful was the angler!
> With cruel delight,
> He sullied all the crystal water,
> And hid the fish from sight!
> Alas, by this deception,
> The fish the enticing bait sought out,
> And I was left lamenting
> The fate of that poor trout.

I have not seen that written down since leaving St John's, but hope that I have remembered it fairly well. The other verses have not remained. I could go on doing this sort of thing for several pages: words, words, words – absorbed through a few repetitions, now inked somewhere like tattoos.

Oh, and we were 'confirmed' when nine! I almost omitted to say! An even bigger fuss than our first confessions and Holy Communions, this (literally) visited upon us The Bishop. We were becoming 'soldiers of Christ' (even the girls?), had to choose a 'confirmation name' (Peter in my case, because I liked Peter Farrelly, who had started school the same day), have white shirts, learn special prayers and hymns, be instructed and lectured at, attend rehearsals. We memorised words and music to what they called the 'confirmation hymn' *Veni Creator Spiritus*. I found the fourth line particularly difficult to latch hold of:

> veni creator spiritus
> mentes tuorum visita
> imple superna gratia
> quae tu creasti pectora

Fitting 'creasti' to the Gregorian tune repeatedly caught me out. From later life, I can say I am grateful to have had in my early experience this music and poetry, not appreciating their historical interest and value then, nor suspecting I might one day be a member of an early music group, a thing utterly beyond my imagination in every possible way. Latin hymns, prayers, much of the ordinary of the Mass were all inputted into my retrieval system, by sheer repetition, much like the hypnopaedia in Huxley's *Brave New World*, the electronic voice whispering your destined tastes and axioms under your infant pillow as you sleep. As with their conditioning, there was no need for us to understand, merely absorb and remember for the time being, and then like good Catholics of every letter of the Greek alphabet to repeat when prompted:

salve regina
mater misericordiae
vita dulcedo
et spes notra salve
ad te clamamus
ad te suspiramus
gementes et flentes
in hac lacrimarum valle

Salve, Regina, Mater misericordiæ,
vita, dulcedo, et spes nostra, salve.
Ad te clamamus exsules filii Hevæ,
Ad te suspiramus, gementes et flentes
in hac lacrimarum valle.

I wrote out the first version as I have carried it around from the age of eight or nine, when I couldn't have translated it, but had also learned an English translation by heart. The lower version is what I have just looked up. I see I have omitted the second half of the third line there, although I have apparently versified it into half lines, probably fitting in with the tune I remember. Here follows, without looking anything up, the translation we memorised:

Hail, Holy Queen,
Mother of Mercy;
Hail, our life,
Our sweetness and our hope.
To Thee do we cry,
Poor banished children of Eve;
To Thee do we send up our sighs,
Morning and evening in this vale of tears etc

Not written out or seen on the page all this time either – but two things to observe: (i) I include a translation of the phrase I omitted 'exsules filli Hevae'; and (ii) the translation supplies 'morning and evening' to flesh out the meter.

Lastly, if your patience has not expired, I have just listened to a performance on YouTube, which proves I forgot the music for the three omitted words too! You can now play a private game and give your marks out of ten or whatever for the effectiveness of: (a) the conditioning; (b) my memory!

We never heard a quality *performance* of the piece; it was for us to *use* as part of the routine business of 'church'. The dominant voice that came our way from the altar, though, was far from musical: loud, foghorning, overloading the air, insensitive to musical phrase. It suited Father Burrett.

Whilst I never want to endure another voice like his again, I am deeply glad I learned those and other pieces, both original words and music. I wonder at their exquisite beauty, can place them in the traditions which produced them and other early religious lyrics and their settings. Equally, how useful this indoctrinated background has actually turned out to be. Increasingly over the years of my teaching career, I found pupils unsupplied with ideas and background I seemed to have known for ever. How can you begin to understand Blake's *A Poison Tree*, never mind a huge number of other 'garden' poems or references in our literature, if you have never heard the Genesis story of the Garden of Eden? Coaching a sixth former privately a couple of years ago, I quickly saw why she was so puzzled by Marlowe's *Dr Faustus*: she had absolutely no concept of the soul, Hell, temptation, eternity and many more essential notions. With what I knew, you would never want to name your newborn son *Cain*, though that is not unknown now, any more than you would *Adolf*! When you introduce teenagers to Chaucer (whether that's always a wise idea or not) you have to provide so much information before the true evils of the Summoner and Pardoner, for example, even begin to be comprehended. I could go on: Dante, Michelangelo's *Last Judgment*, Bach's sacred music, and many, many thousands of writings, paintings, compositions, and almost endlessly so on. *And muchel moore.*

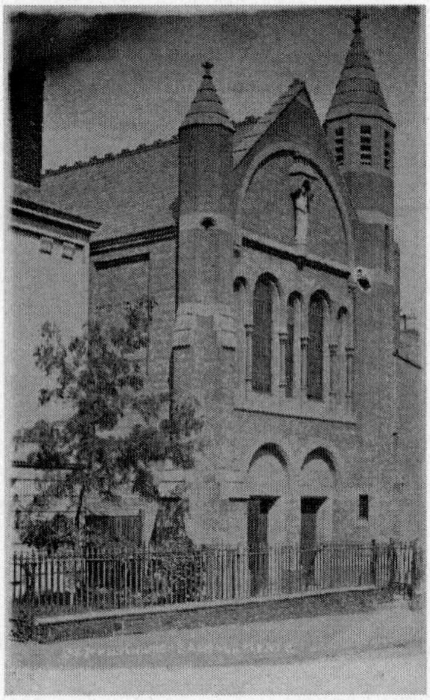

St John's Church, now Church of Saints John and Martin

Moving On

Something is pushing them
To the side of their own lives.

Philip Larkin, *Afternoons*

Hearne's First Law of Emotion states: *Everybody continues in a state of happiness that will go on forever unless someone else stops him or her from doing exactly what he or she wants.* This discovery is as important as Newton's Laws of Motion, which claim to have predated it. Newcomers to it, no matter how universal and eternal its actions and requirements, often struggle to accommodate the notion. 'Ah but,' they object, 'why does that boy allow himself to be pushed into studying medicine when he would much rather go to art school and do something suited to his interests and abilities? Or how is it that your very talented and apparently well intentioned Director of IT, who is forever holding lengthy discussion and planning meetings and drawing up compendious schemes for his aims and their methods of implication, never actually gets anything done? That poor woman down the road has such a miserable time with her dragon of a mother. The old monster just uses and abuses her. Can you explain it? If I were pushing forty and still single, I'd get a place of my own and move out. She should start looking for a man. Her time's almost run out.'

With all the forces operating on these three unhappy and suffering souls, the net force is what they choose to accept. It may be apparent stasis, but that is not necessarily happy equilibrium, rather imposed inertia. The reluctant medic respects his father too much, wishes to retain his approval and love, and intellectually can only acknowledge the power of the assumptions and arguments directing him where he looks like going. That infuriating computer man has a pathological need to punish himself because he is deeply persuaded that he is no good. He is more preoccupied with his headaches and the importance of his work if everyone depends upon him so much that the whole organisation's attention is concentrated on *him.* The daughter who is sacrificing her prospects of marital happiness has balanced her wishes against her strong sense of duty and her mother's emotional manipulation combined. Guess which side of the issue the scales grounded on! There was a tragically comic television series called *Sorry!* with Ronnie Corbett years ago on just this theme. I found it, though compelling, more painful than amusing.

Ah yes, but what if some other person or persons take over and compel an individual to suffer what he or she powerfully does not want, whatever it is? Some yobbo beats you up when you just want to walk peacefully down the street, or a national emergency obliges you to be conscripted, utterly against your wishes and inclination. The Law still operates under the special condition *if they are free to do so.*

The same authority's Second Law goes: *Actions are determined by thoughts* (or *ideas*, which for this purpose are the same thing). Zyklon B does not kill six million innocents, any more than the kitchen knife you cut your food with dispatches your mother-in-law. It is only when some demented human hellishly conceives the possibility of using an industrial pesticide to commit genocide that such heartbreaking outrages occur. If he had not accepted the *idea* that certain types of his fellow creatures should be got rid of, thanks to the crazed and inhumane notions of a twisted little man with bad breath, he would not even have bothered to devise that way. (I hastily clarify, for any literal-minded soul who cannot even detect the dark glass in front of him, let alone dimly discern something through or in it, that I am merely jesting about your wife's mother! If she is anywhere near as amazing as mine, 100 years on and going strong as I write, you will be daily showering her with roses and chocolates. But even though, unusually, I admit I am digressing, I shall not be prevented from adding that my asseveration does not in any way endorse the claims of those minded like the American Rifle Association to liberalise the availability of lethal weapons to more or less any adult: *Guns don't kill people. People kill people.* On this point I stand with Eddie Izzard, that the guns do help – rather too much! – when you allow them into the hands of thousands of unhinged folk who proceed through life believing that it is their right to assert themselves and ease their feelings as they wish, that is. Blast! Bang! Groan! Thud! Oh that's better! Gee goddam! I *needed* that! Of course, the Second Law still applies, overriding the Fifth Amendment.)

How did my mother take the single massive step from the comfort, affluence, social freedom and status that walking out forever from her home, family and job meant that weekday just before March 1948, into the poverty, hardship, drudgery and drabness of this new, circumscribed life? Explain to me, please, why my father started and ended in a completely uncongenial, sometimes shady, unreliable, dirty and really quite soul-destroying series of jobs, when he had no testosterone-fuelled drive to beat others in a tough, but lucrative game, but was a gentle being who loved listening to classical music, learning languages, reading contemporary books and articles about social theories and philosophy? I never heard him play the violin, though he had lessons for years and handed on to me his pile of pieces played through with his teacher accompanying him on piano: Beethoven's 'Spring Sonata', the better known Max Bruch Concerto (in G minor), the Brahms Concerto (perhaps the slow movement only), Bach's A minor and E major concertos, Bach sonatas, lollipops by Kreisler, short pieces by Elgar and so on. I played as much of them as would suit my instruments; I may be the only recorder player who can more or less get through a four movement Beethoven violin sonata, and from memory! He went often to concerts in Birmingham Town Hall: Albert Sammons, Yehudi Menuhin (as a teenager), other big names of the day. As well as Menuhin's he had Wilhelm Fürtwängler's autograph on a programme, adored Dr (before his knighthood) Adrian Boult, even (I think) heard Richard Strauss conduct live one or more of his own works. In my life the instrument almost never came out of its case.

He can have had only four years of French at school, but could still hold a reasonable conversation, for example with the old, black-habited French lady at church. When I was starting the language, he was a great help, likewise with Latin. Terms like 'ablative absolute', 'deponent verb' (and its definition), 'the passive voice' were all in my vocabulary and theoretical grasp before I learned any declension or conjugation. He still recalled all of those too, and could rattle them off and translate them, just as he could recite to you and explain several continuous lines of *Georgics IV* or sentences from Caesar's *De Bello Gallico*. Out of nowhere he would sometimes tell me some historical anecdote connected with a famous Roman writer or statesman, or some incident from Roman history, most likely from Livy. 'And that was why Hannibal was such a great general.' If an Italian film happened to be televised, he could follow the storyline fairly well, even without subtitles. When I was at university, in the early 70s, he joined evening sessions offered by a local Anglican curate, to learn New Testament Greek, acquiring from scratch the ability to read to me and translate parts of St John's Gospel.

Numerically, he was adept at converting and manipulating figures. When metrication came into his trade, he understood, mastered it and could tell you in a flash what an imperial weight was metrically, unlike others, both at his warehouse and generally in the business, who functioned only with tables kept on their desks or in their pockets and, to Dad's snorting scorn, pronounced the Continental *tonne* as *tunny*, to distinguish it from the *ton*. No one used a Vernier or micrometer more nimbly or speedily.

He enjoyed introducing me from pre-school days to model yachts and motorised boats. I had several yachts, the best a Triang '24', a small mass produced toy which even among the much bigger kit made or scratch built large expensive craft, the owners of which stood in the pond wearing waders and brandishing long handling poles with rubber tips, performed brilliantly on Bourneville model boating lake. The rudder was ingeniously linked, via a hooked metal tiller and an office rubber band, to the main sail. You had to let the sail out or bring it in according to the strength of the wind, and Dad knew just the right setting, so that, when the wind filled the sail, the rudder would immediately be turned by the link to steer the yacht into the wind. Other, usually small wooden ones off the shelf tended to go sideways or capsize. There was one glorious afternoon when my Uncle Ken, Dad and I went to the lake in Ken's open topped Morris 1000. The winds blew steadily and stiffly, enabling us to send the little green thing scudding keeled over at astounding speed to each other, back and forth across the whole lake. I should think that must have been forty or fifty yards each way.

Clockwork boats required special care. You needed to work out how long the spring lasted and judge what you could risk before power ran out and you lost drive. Either runs along a secant of the pond, taking the breeze into account, or a sufficiently tight circle were safe. Sometimes you had to lean out to arm's length to arrest the boat before it went on a second circle and so out of reach. On a calm day you then waited for minutes on end for the thing to drift its way to the side somewhere. To my horror, Uncle Ken once set the rudder straight and pointed my Triang FIRE boat (12s 6d) straight across the whole pond. As I had foreseen, it died right in the middle. I stood despondent for minutes on end. Finally, a kind young man borrowed a club member's waders and cautiously made his way across the lake to stage the recovery. It seemed he was in serious danger of toppling at several moments, from unexpected currents or invisible debris he stumbled or trod on. For the rest of the afternoon, I sailed only my electric launch.

My earliest dreams were about toys! Dad's boss, Mr Brearley, had passed down from his son a whole box of Dinky cars. He might as well have given me the Crown Jewels! Added to over several years, they were my inseparable and very best friends. Mom automatically fed my hunger for cars. I could identify all the makes and models we saw on the roads, and while Top Trumps had not been thought of, I had absorbed a readymade set of facts and opinions. Vauxhall were not reliable. Triumphs were quite high in the quality league, though Jaguar a little better. Grandad swore by Triumphs. Of course, Bentley and Rolls Royce took all the supreme glory. Austin 7 clutches were very fierce, Singers delightful to drive, and so on. In my nightly visions, the doors opened on my Dinky Austin Devon, allowing me to step inside, climb behind the steering wheel and drive off!

The boats Dad provided for me included a Sutcliffe submarine. You have to cork the winding hole tightly, because the propeller really did make it submerge! In a typical park pond it could only be a passing novelty, since for most of each trip you could see nothing after the dive but a circling ripple above its passage! You just hoped it would run out and float to the surface within reach of retrieval!

My largest and best boat ran on four Ever Ready U8 or equivalent batteries. Made by Victory Industries Ltd of Guildford, the RAF Vosper Crash Tender proved a steady performer, but promised more than it gave. The impressive twin brass propellers were disappointingly not powered by individual motors, but jointly and rather feebly via a drive band off a single, pulley-equipped motor. Yet again, and even more alarmingly in case it broke, a vital component was an ordinary rubber band! I used a new one for each outing. When I think of it, the same, in more ways than one flexible, item not only attached the wings to my balsa wood aircraft but also crucially powered them!

Dad enabled all these boyhood interests to exist and thrive, reading my mind before I knew it. He chose perfect presents. They must have reminded him of his own happy younger days. He still had his old stationary steam engine, kept at his mother's house. On some visits there he would steam it up and get the single piston to drive its flywheel. He was quite a daredevil with flame and fire. The combined smells and sound of steam, oil, and methylated spirits producing that accelerating whirring beat will ever cheer and thrill me.

With an unfailing touch and a leather whip he set wooden tops spinning furiously. His supreme skill, which I have never acquired, was flying kites. Though bought for me, and in turn for my sister and brother, they were in reality part of his surviving boyhood. Just a glance at a toyshop or seaside stall item would tell him if it would fly: 'Tail's too short' and 'Hopeless! You may as well make the frame out of stone!' As with many champions, he succeeded and failed with his greatest achievement. Some years later in Skegness, when I was fourteen, he bought 'us' a square 'Telstar' model. The lightweight wooden frame, six pieces in all, the four sides and north-south, east-west struts, had simply a durable polythene sheet, colourless apart from a red silhouette of the world-famous satellite, forming the body, with a long strip of polythene, weighted at intervals, for the tail. Instantly he saw it, he exclaimed, 'Ah!

That's a good 'un! You'll enjoy that!' Before the first flight he tied five or six sweet wrappers, twisted into butterflies, on to the tail. 'Extra stability; won't peck.'

He was right with all claims, though our pleasure and fun were largely at seeing how stupendously high he got it from the beach and even more his beaming excitement and joy. It really did fly well. Overnight, before the next day's scheduled lift off, he had bought an extra *three* balls of suitable twine from a hardware shop, and linked them all on. You could hardly get your hands round the resulting ball, which must have been six inches across. So, mid-morning, the four of us marched, over the dunes, to the beach, Mom left for an hour's peace in the caravan.

The offshore wind ruffled your jumper, flapped your trousers and startled your hair like an alarmed flock of birds taking off. As the eldest and tallest, it was my job to take the kite, straining like a greyhound, walk downwind with it, hold it above my head, and, on the signal, let go. I walked towards the sea.

'All right, Martin. Hold it up. That way a bit. Now just try it.'

A second launch was out of the question: it rocketed up! Within a second the unwound length of string was twanging taut. Dad unwound. And unwound. And unwound! Our Telstar became the merest dot, high above the waves. At the time we had not given a thought to aviation laws and maximum permitted heights. The urgent soaring just continued.

When the remaining thread was just a ping pong ball in his left hand, Dad paused in his unwinding to admire his work. It was a moment of fulfilment. The high-level cloud layer was screening the sun; the brilliance made your eyes water.

'Hey, kids! Look at that! Nearly three balls of string!' He was shaking with laughter. His chin and tummy wobbled.

That very instant there must have been an extra violent tug from all those yards up. He had the remnants of the ball in his weakened left hand; his strong right one had loosened momentarily to change grip.

The ball shot from his hands.

'I can't hold it! I can't hold it!' He was simultaneously proud and distressed.

We strained to follow it till it was lost in the heights. It did not take very long. We all went very quiet. I cannot remember who spoke first.

Years on, at unexpected moments, the memory would return.

'You remember that kite at Skegness? I just couldn't hold it. Wonder if it's still over the North Sea!'

*****

Apart from boating lakes, other places were weekly visited *en famille*, usually after Sunday lunch, which was always a roast. The Lickey Hills, the swings at Lickey End, Swanhurst Park, Cannon Hill Park (again!), and on bank holidays sometimes further afield, for a whole day out with picnic. We ran around, kicked balls, shot down slides. My sister picked buttercups and other wildflowers. In autumn, Mom looked for blackberries.

Sunday mornings were Church, with Mom inexplicably excused. She stayed at home, did 'things' and prepared the lunch. Dad liked variety in his worship, often asking as we put our coats on, 'Where shall we go to dinger-dongery?' He had his own, silly expressions for things. They tickled him. A few, conceived in a single thought one time, became linguistic habits, our family lingo. I think Bernstein calls it 'restrictive code'. *Bouquets on a boomerang* was one of his favourites, employed to spike the self-approval of those who, apparently praising others, are in truth shining their own halos! A few were crude. Whilst a passing lady's tight posterior might draw the under breath utterance *nut cracker*, another's much more generous gluteal provision would trigger *coconut cracker*! In truth very prudish – he never once uttered a syllable to me about sex before I was twenty-seven – he liked to think of himself as cheekily naughty.

Our home church was St John's, next to my school in Balsall Heath. Generally we alternated between there and The English Martyrs in Sparkhill. There were so many masses every Sunday, starting early in the morning and often continuing at hourly intervals until the final, midday mass. We often were taken to the eleven o'clock at Sparkhill. Unless we arrived a few minutes before it started, there were no seats or even standing places left in the main church. Overspill went into the Sacristy, fitted with backless benches, the door of which was left open. Words came out of a speaker, but you saw nothing. The adjacent Catholic school hall – or perhaps it was a gymnasium – was cleared for either another mass, going on simultaneously, or sometimes even for sound relays from the church. It was strange to be standing in the middle of hundreds of people, mostly men in (I think Co-op) two piece blue suits all standing, responding, kneeling, bowing their heads and so on in unison for the whole performance *without a conductor*! Before the Papal ban of it from 1963 onwards, most of each mass was said, sung or intoned in Latin. One learned by heart, just by listening, more or less all the words of the Ordinary (the sections that never change), but the variable sections, to which you fumblingly turned in your missal at the right moments, also were. Mysterious and captivating to listen to when well 'sung' (= chanted) in a sixteenth century setting, the gospel cannot have been readily understood by more than, at the best, one percent of the congregation. You could follow a parallel text if you managed to pick one up before they ran out.

For variety, Dad would sometimes make a last-minute decision, for example to take us to the Oratory in Edgbaston, which he had come to know when at grammar school. Glittering with gold, marbled, ornate and spacious, it could not fail to impress and awe you. After mass, Dad guided us round the shrine to St Philip Neri, telling us about the glass-cased fragments of his clothing and other salvaged morsels. Another regular venue was his old parish church, where he was married and I baptised, St Augustine's in Handsworth, Grandma's spiritual shopping market. We never saw her in the church. She went to an early mass. Calling in on her afterwards, of course, went without saying: a cup of tea for the adults and Co-op orange drink (half an inch from the bottle and water from the kitchen tap) for us. An alternative was St Teresa's in Perry Barr, round the corner from Grandma Elsie, whom we likewise dropped in on briefly before descending on Lil, less than two miles away.

Without ever giving reasons, Dad invariably attended church every Sunday, taking us from when toddlers onwards. He never spoke to us about religion or said a prayer with us. We just went to church, as naturally as going to bed every night. Of course, before I was lectured at by Grandma Lil or worse at St John's, I had no idea what was supposedly going on or what they expected me to do about it. Resistance or any kind of non-compliance was never imagined. You did not talk or play in church. You just went along, tried to do what older people did, watched things, and waited for it to end. Getting out through the throng was as hard as waiting for your birthday.

The greatest ecclesiastical tortures, however, were timetabled for Christmas Day and your annual seaside holiday. In mid-winter, you just longed to be back with your new presents, though one return journey from The English Martyrs afforded some accidental excitement. We had just garaged the car at the end of the road. As we walked along towards our house, Mr Firkin, the window cleaner, who lived on the opposite side, near the corner with Whitby Road, flung his front door open and hurled a blazing, fully dressed Christmas tree down the path towards the pavement. Like us in those times, he lit his highly inflammable tree with little candles held in sockets on metal clips. The next year, Dad bought a set of twelve electric bulbs, of different shapes and colours. They came out every year. If one bulb failed, they all went out as the circuit broke, a very regular occurrence.

Another conflagration, but in a warmer time of the year, also occurred after mass at The English Martyrs, quite immediately afterwards. We were just walking along Evelyn Road towards Stratford Road, with the chain link fencing of the school playground on our left. Little groups of church goers on their way home were stopping to chat to friends. About ten yards ahead of us, two West Indian families, startingly smart in their Sunday clothes. The men had shiny light blue and grey suits, the women stunning two-pieces in pastel colours, with matching hats. They could have been going to a wedding. The little boys, unlike me in weekday shirt and trousers, had full outfits: small suits, white shirts, bright ties. The smaller sister of one of them was standing next to her father. If anything, she was the most eye-catching in her flouncy, gauzy pink dress, the skirt of which fanned out its layers like a bird at display. I think she even had a huge satin bow tied round her waist at the back. As we approached, the father unconsciously put his right hand down from his mouth with his lit cigarette. Almost instantly, a flame flashed up from the skirts. We were two or three steps away. Dad dashed forward, raising his hand. With whatever he was holding, perhaps a church magazine, he knocked the flames out.

The father spun round. 'Hey, what do you think you're doing?' He began to move towards Dad.

Things could have got very nasty, but Dad hurriedly managed to explain what had happened. One glance at the dark brown ring on the skirt told the story. The mother shrieked and put her gloved hands to her cheeks. The father's frown became a happy beam. He lifted his trilby fedora hat and leaned forward. 'Oh my Lord! Thank you, sir!' We walked on.

The first thing you all did after the interminable drive to the caravan site near a new North Wales resort was not to stampede over the dunes to the beach, but to get back in the car in the late afternoon and drive into the town to check the whereabouts of the Catholic church. You waited simmering on the back seat while Dad strolled inside, carefully read the notice board to find out the next day's mass times, and then not infrequently had an unhurried chat with a stranger he had chanced to meet before rediscovering the car park. 'He's an interesting bloke,' he would cheerfully inform us twenty minutes or more later. 'Used to be in submarines. And *his* father was at Gallipolli. Did I ever tell you about the time my friend Ray Curly ...' More often than not he had.

The last evenings of holidays, the best of which gave us the happiest father we ever knew, as well as every Saturday in the football season after he had checked his pools results, he would at some moment lean back in his chair, sigh and with a sad smile remind himself and us:

'Ah well, kids! Back to work on Monday!'

*****

I am struggling to find a word. I need the right tweezers or instrument to probe and extract a thorn of frustration. *Irrational* is not it. Neither will *unrational*, in itself dubious, do. The territory, if even *that* is the right term, to explore has some precious things to find, I feel sure, but I have no survey or map to start me off.

Shakespeare perhaps refers to this *realm* (?) in *A Midsummer Night's Dream* with rational Theseus's comment:

> 'The lunatic, the lover, and the poet
> Are of imagination all compact.'

Somewhere in the workings of our minds or maybe even souls, as surely as our bones form from jelly and juice in our mothers, form our certainties, our private pieces of personal knowledge about the world and its nature, of what we live and die for, of what cannot – or at least should not if we can do anything about it – be changed. I am still struggling. I shall try again.

> 'He's not trying to change me, Mother. You can't change people, he say, you can only give them some love and hope they'll take it.' (Arnold Wesker, *Roots* – author's punctuation)

Some things in some people, maybe some things in all people, cannot be reasoned with. Dad's religion was one. You could not talk about it. I did not even try. I knew very well that he would if he could answer *informational* questions, e.g. What does 'Papal infallibility' mean? What is the Feast of the Assumption? But that would have been it. You went to church, did what you were supposed to do, and that was it. It was as incontestable as 'You'll do as you're told. I'm your father, and that's it. Now go to your room!'

I came to understand that this inflexible certainty that certain things must and must not be done, could and could not be spoken of, and just had to be accepted, extended to my parents' marriage. If the Church legislated that birth control was sinful and in all cases to be eschewed artificially, there could be no discussion. I do not for one moment suspect or wish to suggest that my father was bullying, unkind or domineering in the marriage. It was just that he would not discuss some matters with my mother. At first love, gratitude and admiration must have meant she did not notice anything amiss. The succession of reproductive failures and health emergencies she suffered after my birth probably did not diminish her urge and willingness to continue: she wanted another child or other children. She loved her husband. She loved looking after people. My sister's and brother's safe and healthy arrivals increased the very considerable physical demands upon her, but she did not at these times show, or therefore probably feel, particularly negative. She saw many other working class women around her at least no better off. With others, she had made it through the war. Her own mother had set her an example of unremitting toil as a wife and mother. My parents did not have an easy time in their early years. Mr mother put up with their hardships and hers.

The things that should have been considered and discussed remained unresolved, for example her working conditions, the state of the house and garden, my father's complete omission to lift a finger to help her, kind and loving as he was. Mom did it all. If we actually went away for just one week during the industrial fortnight that Dad was allowed, it was because she arranged it at the last minute, sometimes the very day before we went. There was one Friday evening when, on opening the front door, Dad met the news that he was taking us to a rented caravan the next day! I cannot remember the details. They are not relevant. Impulsive acts like that were well intentioned and usually turned out well.

To my knowledge, finance was never discussed. I have no idea why. That too does not actually matter. The outcome was that we were always scraping along. Again, to war survivors that probably was no novelty. Other neighbours and relatives, though, even lowlier factory workers professedly bringing home less a week, had smarter homes, more clothes – effective solutions to many material considerations. My father's daily indulgences were not, in the long run, to ensure his happiness. Any spare cash he might have gathered was frittered away. He would not or could not change. My mother spent what she was given as she received it, almost all of it on us, but some of it unnecessarily, for example, on luxuries and treats, like cream cakes from Mrs French, the on-the-premises baker round the corner, whose inflated face and figure, never mind the smile, advertised perhaps the irresistibleness of her produce along with its redundancy: money going to waist or waste? It did not matter. Every day was tough; you might as well brighten this one with a little treat or so.

The way they lived was as inexplicable to fathom as the erratic behaviour, swooning devotion or working genius of Shakespeare's madman, Romeo or – well! – the very

Bard himself. The love of Valerie May and Douglas Clifford was not actually changing either of them fundamentally, in mind or action.

In addition, Dad sometimes troubled me, when I was old enough to hear of these things, with his unshakeable faith in ghosts, visions and so on. He was sure that his boyhood home at 6 Nursery Road had been haunted. He swore he had woken in the early hours one morning to see the figure of a young woman standing by his bed, looking wild and troubled. Years later, he came across the story of the young man who, sleeping in that very attic room, had been woken in the early morning by his sister, who had asked him where his razor was. Still half asleep, he had indicated the washstand. Minutes later, coming round, he had felt alarm, leapt from his bed, discovered the cut throat missing from his shaving gear, and rushed frantically to find his teenage sister – too late. She had cut her own throat!

Though chilled by the story, which he told well, I was always sceptical. There must be a rational explanation. But Dad was (almost proudly) obdurate. 'No such thing? Ah! Well, just you wait and see. One day …'

In November 1980, just six months before he died, he was hospitalised with pneumonia. I drove up on the first available Saturday to see him in Walsall's Manor Hospital. Still weak, he was over the worst, able to receive visitors. He was clearly shaken. A priest had visited him to administer the last Sacrament, Extreme Unction. I hope no clerical gentleman ever tries that on with me! What with the fever of his infection, the drastic fluctuations in his blood sugar levels (he had been a Type 1 diabetic for some time) and perhaps the drugs used to treat him, his consciousness had been severely affected, frightening and confusing him.

He told me he had been flying over Coventry in a bomber. 'It was so real,' he said, more in distress to himself than to me. He probably still thought it actually had happened, but just could not understand. Then he snapped back for a moment.

'They're given me rat poison!' he declared, with angry disgust.

The Warfarin, which he would have to stay permanently on, was to prevent blood clots. 'Fancy that!' Then a sudden laugh. 'Do you know what I did one night? That chap over there and the others told me all about it. Well …'

At the height of the fever, he had in his delirium got out of bed and, dressed only in pyjamas, made his way out into the bitterness of the wet night, barefoot. I have no idea what was going on in his mind. He could remember nothing of it.

'It took *four* of them to get me back in bed,' he boasted, beaming, 'four of the buggers! I put up a real fight.'

I never knew how much of this was accurate. From my earliest years he had repeatedly told me of how, as that child sick with poliomyelitis in the Children's Hospital, it had taken four of the nursing staff to hold him still while the doctors performed a lumber puncture. It was always the strength of his resistance that he stressed, with a strange satisfaction at the relived memory. Had this new shocking drama somehow fused with distant events?

My attempts to demystify this and any other similar stories and claims never got me anywhere. He would not engage with reason. Perhaps he despaired that it could possibly avail. Likewise, he could or would not talk usefully about his religion, discuss and improve household economy, devise and agree with my mother ways of making her life and everyone's easier, take control of practical matters like repairs and structural maintenance. If it fell apart, that was it. If he did not ever get the place painted, he did not.

As we both aged, sudden waves of sadness for him would at times wash over me. Until we left Newport Road, we were happy enough.

*****

When Sylvia was four weeks off her fifth birthday and David just over twenty-seven months old, we left the first home I can ever remember. For some time my parents had been less happy there. The place needed things doing to it, modernising, decorating, repairing. Mom had never liked the Mawbys next door at number 58. She considered them rough. They almost certainly loathed our shabbiness and neglect. Maude Mawby played the piano in a public house; Albert was a deaf and sullen factory worker. Maude once shouted to her aged mother from the kitchen to the outside lavatory:

'Don't sit there straining, mother. Have some Milk of Magnesia!' She was common, low, no better than a barmaid. Perhaps ridiculous class-based prejudices were stronger then. Those who apparently had more of something were immediately marked as 'stuck up'. They *thought too much of themselves*. It probably irked Maude that Dad acquired a car, quickly replacing it twice with better ones. Albert never progressed beyond a bicycle. Before my recall starts, a Rolls Royce drew up outside 60 Newport Road. It signalled the temporary reconciliation between Linnaeus William and our family. Granddad appears to have softened at the thought of having his first grandchild. Perhaps as a way of apologising for not blessing his daughter's wedding he visited to give me presents, wonderful, lavish ones, far too costly for my parents even to dream of: a Mobo two-wheeler bike, with stablisers, a Vindec tricycle, a real, professional quality leather football for later, when I could walk. (It was never inflated and brought into use.) The most spectacularly outrageous expression of my progenitor's feelings was a magnificent pedal car, not the usual sort you could see in even the better toy shops, perhaps by Triang, but an Austin J40, in turquoise. Complete with a tan leather seat, inflatable tyres, working headlights, horn and handbrake, with an opening boot and authentic Austin radiator grill, the J (for 'Junior') Austin was based on the late 1940s Austin Devon and Somerset. He had paid £40 for it, bidding in an auction. For some weeks he displayed it in his showroom, perhaps as a novel way to attract customers. Predictably, it was, to say the least, out of place: too wide to fit between the front door frames, a nuisance to store in that room (there being nowhere else), requiring more cleared space to be used than our garden ever had … I was aware of its splendid presence in the corner of the unused front room, but by then the tyres and battery were flat. It might just have been put on a scrap heap. When I was eight, I decided to reclaim it. Dad replaced the perished inner tubes. I was then strong enough to take it outside and pedal it along the pavement. With my street friend,

Jeffrey Cartwright from over the road, I had a succession of glorious and increasingly furious hours belting along where neighbours walked.

One day, I rode to the corner, turned left into Kingswood Road and tried to see if I could pedal up the hill. I could! I was now *in nova terra.* It was easy to turn left again into Chestnut Road, as usefully flat as our own. That took me to another corner, where the turn for home opened up the wonders of Church Road – downhill! I lifted my feet off the pedals.

The speed I picked up was quite breathtaking. How I didn't meet a shopper stepping out from the newsagent's or chemist's just before the final corner I shall never know. The pedals were trilling on their own like an insect's wings. I had to put my feet down and pull the handbrake back as hard as possible to slow for the turn into our road. From then on, the new circuit was in constant use.

Eighteen months later, other fads had taken over. I longed for a camera. I was broke. With Mom's help I put a postcard in the newsagent's window offering the J40 for sale. Eventually it went to an Irish boy for £3, a Titanic loss, but it gave me the means to enter photography. My optician Uncle Ken, a keen cameraman, undertook to get me a good deal. In a few days I received my first instrument, a Kodak Brownie Flash B box camera.

But to return to the neighbours. While we looked down on Common Maude, Albert stolidly looked after their house and garden thoroughly and well, erecting a new fence, keeping the privet hedge well-trimmed, painting the outside woodwork regularly. He churlishly did not hesitate on one occasion just to walk uninvited through the gate and spend time on our side cutting his privet hedge, doubly insulting by his lack of manners and ostentatious display of attentive horticulture. And of course Maude looked down on our shabbiness. One hot summer afternoon she could contain her disgust no longer. She flung some loud voiced remark about the garden wall for my mother's benefit. Why did we not do something or other to smarten the place up?

Mom was quite a sensitive and nervous woman. She avoided conflict and appeased wherever possible. Besides, she was exhausted and at times running out of spirit with her arduous daily toils, increased hugely by this clinging, fretful new baby, not long walking. An explosive flash exchange of insults concluded with:

> Mrs Hearne: I don't speak to shit!
>
> Mrs Mawby: You're no lady! (*The door slammed*)

Mordre will oute in the end says Chaucer. So will true feelings. From then on a feud that was all the intenser for being wordless persisted - wordless, except for the futile solicitor's letter Dad wasted money on getting sent. If anything triggered our decision to live elsewhere, it was the poisonous cloud that hung over two terraced houses.

A 'For Sale' sign was posted by the agent Lee Shaw. We started looking around. The whole family went in the evenings and weekends to look at properties on the market. I remember several that would have been wonderful to move into. Eventually, 33 Rowan Way was settled on. My A-Z of the City tells me there are two roads of this name. This one is to be found still in modern B31, not far from the old Longbridge car works. A small, quiet, through suburban road of neat detached and semidetached houses, it enjoys leafy front hedged gardens and an unusual central landscaped area on an island, so that each side of the road is effectively a semicircle and the two sides generously separated. We loved it. We revisited. Through the agent Dad was to make an offer. When he came home from work the next day, he was smiling. His offer had been received.

Meanwhile, our well-worn home was struggling to attract a buyer. Originally offering at £1000, in the end Dad had to accept £850, from a gentleman named Sampuram Singh. The solicitors took over.

Mr Singh was in a hurry to move in. Through his solicitor he gave an absolute final date as an ultimatum. Our vendor needed six weeks' more time. Pressures built up. Before the countdown ended, Dad agreed, with his solicitor's reassurance, to exchange contracts on his sale before he could on the Rowan Way purchase. That settled one condition. The six weeks interim had to be dealt with.

Someone in the family had the bright idea of Auntie Annie, soon to be encountered. She lived on her own in a family house, admittedly outdated. If she was prepared to help, we might stay for the six weeks with her. Dad went to Lozells to see her. She agreed. As I explained at the very start, we left our Balsall Heath house one Saturday in early July 1960, cramming ourselves in on our own invitation to the eccentric old maiden's lady's home and life as unobtrusively as possible. From the first day we were plunged into a Dickensian misery of literal and spiritual gloom.

Early on in the six weeks, Dad came home white faced. Rowan Way had been taken off the market. The people were not moving. Neither were we.

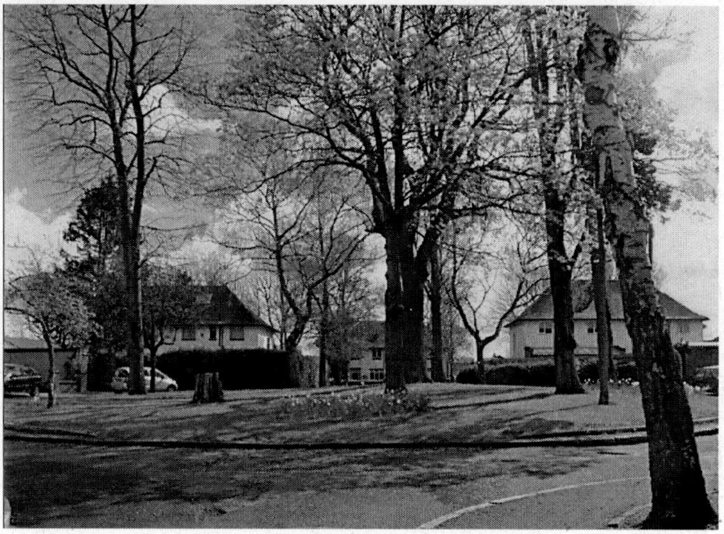

Leafy Rowan Way, Austin Village, Northfield

Interlude

So beautie on the waters stood
When Love had sever'd earth, from flood!
So when he parted ayre, from fire,
He did with concord all inspire!
And then a motion he them taught,
That elder than himselfe was thought,
Which thought was, yet, the child of earth,
For Love is elder than his birth.

Ben Jonson *Song* from *The Masque of Beauty*

Remembered ever since, it was, I think, only once that I heard the record. Dad and Uncle Gordon listened to it at Lil's one Sunday afternoon. I may have been four, perhaps three: Isobel Ballie on Columbia DX1103 *Shall Pales be the Last/Flocks in Pastures Green Abiding* at 78 rpm. As with other Bach arias, it was the obbligato parts (on flutes rather than recorders) that moved in to stay for ever. John Francis ('the Golden Breath') played one, A.Hedges the other, with John Moore on cello and brother Gerald on piano. *The Hebrides Overture* also featured in their after lunch sessions, if not then on another occasion.

I have had very little proper musical training, and no formal qualification till well into my sixties. Yet throughout my life since almost my earliest memories I know that I have always irresistibly listened with arrested attention to anyone playing or singing well: musical ideas and sonorities, the drama of performers and performance, charge circuits in me. I jump in shock if someone speaks to me when I am listening to a piece; I seethe and rage inwardly if an interruption prevents me from experiencing it to the end.

'But you've heard it before!' they say. Little do they understand.

I do not have perfect pitch. On the other hand, a random sound encountered will remind me of a piece in that key. Likewise, if I think of a work I know well, I can usually sing or play some of it in the right key. If I place my fingers on a wind instrument I play, I hear before I blow the note that will sound with each fingering. If I listen to someone else playing my main instrument, I can identify each note, probably by its individual sonority, which is perhaps surprising when you realise what variety of tone is produced by different makes of oboe, various reed scrapes, national styles, and individual players. In fact, though there are schools of playing, that every single player's sound is unique should not be surprising, since no two human beings have identical teeth and lip structures, or lung characteristics, or qualities of tonguing, and so on. Maybe other players are just the same. I wonder how many other people almost always have a piece playing in their heads. Is it most, if not all, of us? Just now, if you are wondering, I have the first movement of Symphony No 2 in D major by Brahms playing as my personal background.

I might have been aged 7 or 8 when my Uncle Brian made an unexpected call to Newport Road. Ever the salesman, he sold my father a 1930s HMV 102 portable clockwork record player for £2. The leather on the lid bore the outline of a hot pre-electric flat iron someone had thoughtlessly placed on it. Though scarred, it nevertheless played and was much better than nothing. Allowed access to the pile of 78 rpm records, I listened repeatedly to *The Road to the Isles/Bonnie Mary of Argyle*, sung by Robert Wilson; *Jolly Fellows* by a regiment of guards' band; *Serenade Basque* and *Serenade Espagnole* by Yovanovitch Bratza; *Sonata in D Major* by Handel, by Joseph Szigeti with Nikita da Magalov ... playing styles and fashions have greatly changed, as anyone who has listened to string playing over the history of recordings to the present day will know. I know only too well that Szigeti's Handel would these days be rejected as grossly inauthentic; nevertheless, it was – and still is, listened to sympathetically – powerful, moving and exciting violin playing. He must have had huge platform presence.

In short, I gradually worked my way through the stack of Dad's 78 records. Some even had chips out of their edges, and so could not be 'autorun'. In the fifties I experienced briefly some excitement at the latest commercial music. Of course I warmed to the Six-Five Special on Saturday afternoons. Was it partly because of railway associations? The only record that I asked for was Lonnie Donegan's *Last Train to San Fernando*, which began and ended with instrumental steam effects! I must have been 8 then. It did not take long for Dad's influence to work on me; once I became aware of the empty repetitiveness and mindless lyrics of the songs, they wore off. They were catchy numbers, but pretty silly when thought about. That does not mean I did not more or less instantly learn both music and words:

My friend, the witch doctor,
He told me what to do.
My friend, the witch doctor,
He told me what to say.
I know that you'll be mine
When I say this to you.

Refrain

He told me:
Oo ee, Oo ah ah,
Ting tang,
Walla walla bing bang. (*repeat*)

When our small valve radio went wrong, and I was about 9, we did not have a replacement mains model until a Prudential insurance policy in my mother's name matured, by which time I was 15. Grandma Elsie, though, passed on to us an early Pye portable, turquoise and cream. Still a valve set, it required a large peculiar dual-voltage battery, supplying 69 and 1½ volts, a luxurious consumable, since it cost twice my weekly pocket money of five shillings and lasted only a few hours, most probably the cause of its being so readily given away. I should say that, over the years, we bought only two or three batteries.

One Sunday evening when I was 12, I sneaked the set upstairs to my bedroom, to listen under the bedclothes to Alan Keith's *Your Hundred Best Tunes*. It must have been a track from the 1946 recording of Evelyn Rothwell playing the concerto arranged for her by husband, John, from a Corelli violin suite in F major, that utterly entranced me. I wanted to hear it again. Oh how I should love to play it! The first two bars of the second section of the Gavotte, such a perfect antithetical answer to the first section, filled with me joy and longing.

In our weekly single lesson of music at St Philip's, Mr Morgan, ran a few things past us. Apart from the obligatory sessions of learning hymns and other pieces to be sung in assemblies and in the Oratory, he spent some pointless lessons trying to impose plain chant on us, issuing some form of tutor and expecting us to sight sing from it. This was impossible enough chorally, but for anyone who was singled out for a solo attempt, inexpressible torture, though whether more imaginative sadism to the perpetrator or his audience might require the nicest judgment.

It would be Moran who alone could do it. The rest of us might just as well have been told to thread a small needle blindfold while wearing boxing gloves! Anthony, though, not only had the richest alto voice you could find in a twelve-year-old, but sang in a quality choir.

Otherwise, we listened to Alfred Della with another counter tenor singing *Sound the Trumpet* from Purcell's *Come, Ye Sons of Art*, the illustration to that composer, who (I think) was the first in the textbook we had of Great Composers. We heard some Handel and Bach too, Mr Morgan telling us that Bach's pieces, like *Jesu, Joy of Man's Desiring*, were better known for the instrumental 'extras' than for anything else. His own organ performance of the Toccata in D minor in Birmingham Town Hall at prizegiving stirred and held me sufficiently to make me resent having to stand up and exit before he had really got going. I realise now that I must somehow have already heard it as well as many other better known pieces in my early years.

With some of my thirteenth birthday money, I bought a plastic recorder, cost 6s 11d from Woolworth's in Walsall, teaching myself to play a few simple pieces by ear and gradually learning all the notes. I became fanatic about improving. At my new school, there was a recorder group, led by a teacher, including four different voices of the instrument. I suppose observing them in an assembly prompted me to become interested. We had, of course, during our lessons been taught the notes of the clef and the principles of notation. Understanding rhythms on my own took most persistence. Before I made many advances into that territory, I had reached the third form and my fourteenth birthday, to mark which I requested a treble instrument. The next Saturday, 6th October, Dad took me into Taylor's music shop in Walsall, where he bought me a Schott softwood instrument. I taught myself the new fingerings, or rather the different notes produced by the same ones. Soon I could make my way through *A Garland of Melodies* by Bernard Bramley, though the only other pieces of printed music I could find in the shop, some Mozart movements simplified and arranged by Walter Bergman for two decants and a treble, and some Handel duets (descant and treble) proved frustrating, since I had no one else to play them with. (To this day, I never have!)

Early in the autumn term of 1963, the Deputy Head announced in assembly that the county music department was providing the school with an oboe: anyone who was interested should see him. Along with, to start with, three others, I put my name forward.

Though this is anticipating my account of times at my new school, I should explain that this teacher, of whom more will follow, apart from his teaching and managerial roles, was a keen instrumental musician. His first instrument being the clarinet, he was also no mean amateur bassoonist, and gave weekly lessons on both these instruments, as well as on the flute. For some months, he even started beginners off on the trumpet and trombone, before a specialist brass player could join the small number of visiting staff.

The day arrived when I had to leave my lesson for another classroom. There, to begin with, I was shown how to assemble the oboe and issued with a reed. Each of our reeds was to be kept clipped to a backing card in a small box kept in the walk in cupboard, our initials being written above 'our' reed clips. A practice timetable assigned us one lunchtime session each, again in a classroom, as well as allowing us one evening a week to take the instrument home. Impressively shiny in its cherry-red lined case, it was to me wonder and riches, though as time passed I discovered its limitations. Since any oboist will know what I am talking about and no one else will be even faintly concerned, I shall merely say that it was more than good enough for a beginner to acquire the rudiments, and with the right following wind to incubate a desire for something better! But oh, how sharp third space C natural was!

In many ways I progressed swiftly through *A Tune A Day*, thoroughly absorbed and dedicated, obsessed I suppose. The many calls on a Deputy Head's time meant that that first year many scheduled lessons were cancelled at the last moment. Nevertheless, I moved on through the tutor to the end of Book 1. If forced to confess, I should have to admit that I probably somehow worked things so that I had the instrument at home for as much of the school holidays as I could, and certainly more than any of the other learners!

Strangely, the more frustrations I encountered, the more bloody minded I became to persevere: limited access to an instrument; few lessons, erratically spaced; a non-specialist teacher, who despite the best heart and intentions knew nothing beyond the bare essentials of playing the instrument, and apparently nothing at all about making or adjusting reeds; a basic, limited and limiting instrument; and that not even my own – all these obstacles and impediments might have made me throw it in. 'I had as lief have a partisan I could not heave as a reed that will do me no service,' might completely reverse what the Second Servant says in Act 2, Scene 7 of Shakespeare's *Antony and Cleopatra*, but the misquotation might pretty well have represented the feelings of an early seventeenth century hautboy player, at least a couple of them being required to make some sort of eerie noise beneath the actors later in that play: *Music of the hautboys as under the stage,* runs the stage direction just before the Act Four battle which goes so badly for Antony. Why the hautboy, the somewhat louder, more trumpet-like ancestor of the modern oboe (from French hautbois, of course, 'high wood'), should have been used like this has probably been commented on somewhere, but the sound would have given the audience a sense that something important, and almost certainly ill-omened, was about to befall someone important …

Reeds! At least one major professional has broken down in an orchestral rehearsal, complained that he did not 'have a bloody reed to play on' and been unable to work for some months on account of a mental breakdown. Graham Salter's encyclopaedic book *Understanding the Oboe Reed* runs to over 500 pages of small print. Fashions change. Schools of thought and practice come and go: this scrape, that scrape; minimal resistance, more body left; thin here, thicker there; short staple, standard staple; French cane, South American cane; wired, unwired; one shape, another shape; these and many other variables, almost endlessly. Instruments themselves differ and vary too, not just among makers, but over the years of a maker's output, reflecting the materials available, the variety of technicians, design modifications, the form and fitness for the work of the craftsman. (One anecdote maintains that a well-known firm of makers declined and failed as their instruments' quality deteriorated, their chief worker dropping his standards over the years, particularly after his increasingly liberal liquid lunches.) In short, each player, each instrument and each reed is not only very much itself, with unique qualities and characteristics, but also ages and changes with time. A man, Heraclitus might have claimed, cannot step into a river twice, because he will have aged at least slightly with each moment, and the actual water flowing along will have been replaced by other supplies! Change is the only constant. That, on top of all this, the student has to contend with the scornfully assertive temperament of every teacher he goes to, serves merely as the final unfairness. 'Just where did you get this reed from? Mrs Who? Charlie Which? She/he has got it all wrong! This is hopeless!' You walk away with something new to try, with an unfamiliar resistance … more long notes, more retreating to advance … Particularly when playing a long programme in an orchestra, say an overture, concerto and Romantic symphony, the concert hall heats up and the instrument rises in pitch at a greater rate than other wind instruments or the strings, although anyway, a reed normally becomes sharper with extended playing, especially when ageing …

Inevitably, in 'teaching' myself I formed some bad habits, particularly of posture and stance. Repetition and persistence can make the fingers and tongue function fairly well. Sight-reading improves with experience and practice. I just could not make the kinds of sound I heard coming from recordings and broadcasts. (I think I did not hear a professional playing live until I was sixteen.) I carried on. Over five decades later, I still do.

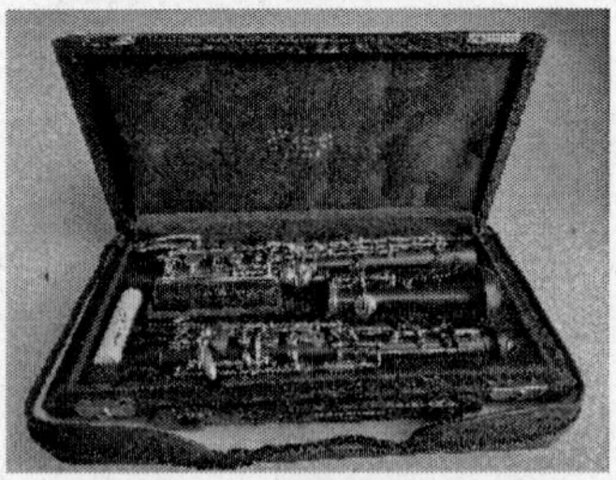

Burbury Street

Per me si va ne la città dolente,
per me si va ne l'etterno dolore,
per me si va tra la perduta gente

Dante, *Inferno*, Canto III

Ok everybody: can we start now? Come in a bit closer here. Could you just step on to the kerb, please sir? Don't want you run over. Thank you. Right. Let's begin.

Hello everyone! It's good to see you all. I hope you slept well in town. How was breakfast? All right? Who had the full English at the Crowne Plaza? Not you, madam? You dieting? Oh, too much for you. I see. Right … now.

My name is Publius, Publius Maro. Yes, I know that's weird. Blame my parents. You can call me Pub if you like. It's got better associations. I'm your guide for the morning. We're going to see some of Old Birmingham and visit a few sites, starting here. So welcome to Burbury Street in Lozells. These houses were built nearly 150 years ago, and as you can see they're very much lived in still. This is a busy area, with lots of families, all the races, all the religions: very diverse. Back in the late nineteenth century, Birmingham was already booming, with hundreds of businesses and workshops and factories. So these houses were for the workers, who would walk to places like Hockley and Aston or even up Soho Hill and over towards Handsworth, though that was more residential.

I'm standing in front of number 202 Burbury Street, a very typical house. Behind you, where your minibus set you down, is Graham Street. These streets are very typical of this area, which is right on the edge of all the activity that gave the city the title of 'the workshop of the world'. You didn't know that? Well, it was. You think of it, it was made within a mile or two of here: jewellery, silver, all kinds of small and large things that people wanted to buy, like cigarette cases, fire irons, tools, machines, almost anything. When they started to mass produce motor cars in the early twentieth century, firms made lots of components and spares for the trade: dynamos, small pressings for light clusters, carburettors, batteries, all kinds of things. You've heard the name Lucas? Their big factory was just down there. You'll be going to the jewellery quarter after a break for coffee. There you'll see a workshop in operation as it was all those years ago, with craftsmen and women making cuff links, bracelets, necklaces, brooches, tie pins – you don't know what a tie pin is? I'll show you some later. You can buy one in the gift shop.

We're going to go inside number 202 in a moment. What you'll see is as faithful a reconstruction of the house exactly as it was in 1960, sixty years ago. We wanted to show not just how one household was at that time, but also how different some things were from what we know today. We had to demodernise it, which seems rather daft, but the Historical Trust thought it would be a good way of preserving a little piece of the past. Since we opened to the public, we're had visitors from all over the country and the world, including some old people who used to live here years ago when they were kids. You should see their faces when they step back into their childhoods!

Just before we go inside, turn around and notice the corner shop. It's now a general store, which in itself is quite an old-fashioned thing since supermarkets and shopping centres started to appear in the middle 1960s. But they are still very much alive and thriving in some places, as you can see from this one. The locals love it. I'm told that if Mr Ghosh hasn't got something on the shelf or in his back room you either don't want it or he'll have it by tomorrow. If we have time later on you can pop inside and say hello to him. He'll sell you a bottle of water or something to nibble if you're hungry. Back in 1960, the premises were first owned by a family called Darby, who lived above and behind it. Mrs Darby was a hairdresser and ran her salon there. Otherwise, she looked after her son and daughter, Jon, who was 11, and his big sister, who was 18. She was called Jill, and by all accounts a very pretty girl with a great figure who made all the boys' hearts race when she went off on a Saturday hike in her shorts. It's ok, sir – you can turn back this way. You won't see her now, and anyway she must be nearly 80. When the Darbys left that year, the salon was turned into a general store, as it still is.

Number 202. The door. Just before I open it, I'll explain that this is as near as we could make it to what it looked like then. Same with the window frames and everything else. We used some old colour photographs of similar doors to match the colour, and chemicals to age it quickly. It took a few days for it to reach this stage. Anyone like to tell me what the original colour was? Grey? No. Natural wood? I wish! Light coffee? Afraid not. It was a rich, dark brown. Yes! That was a really fashionable colour, from Victorian times onwards, usually paired with cream. The smart coaches of the Great Western Railway over at Snow Hill had brown and cream for their livery from way back before 1900 till well after they came into the Western Region of British Railways in 1947, slightly different shades over the years, of course. From all the evidence we can find, this door had not been painted for decades in 1960, maybe not even since the 1930s. Yes, astounding. But that's why you see only this dull grey base layer behind a few traces of – how would you describe that? Milky coffee? Inside, it'll be a sadly similar story – no decorating of any of the rooms for ages. We had to use some very new techniques on the rugs and wallpaper to get everything back like this.

Japanese gentleman wants to know if masks are necessary. It's all right, sir. You won't catch anything, and it's not smelly. There are no fleas either. All right? Just step into the hall in a moment. There are some plastic covers for your shoes which I'll ask you to wear, so that we don't make things any more worn or grubby than they already are. You can give me them back at the end. Everybody ready? Here we go then.

I'm at the far end of the hall, facing the front door. If the last person can close the door, please. Thank you. What do you think? First impressions? Gloomy? Yep. Depressing? Right. One of our visitors said it was like sinking into a giant pot of cold molten horse glue. I must try that one day. Now, could you just turn behind you and close that curtain? Thanks. That heavy, dirty looking thing is a draft excluder. It was supposed to be a rich red velvet. Yes, really. And that's obviously where you could hang your hat and coat or check your hairdo before you went out. On my left, your right, is the front room, which we'll see at the end. So follow me into the first room. Watch the step down. Oh, and all the doors are dull brown too, aren't they?

This is the living room. Let's go round clockwise from where we came in. Treadle powered sewing machine on its iron stand. Singer made these from the 1890s onwards. This is quite an early one. We've reconditioned it, and it still works perfectly. The serial number on this one is from 1912. Yes – that old! Two-seater red vinyl sofa. That would have been quite new and fashionable in the poorer houses in 1960. Just the one window behind it looks out on to the yard and further down the garden. You don't get much light in because of the garden wall on the left and the kitchen on the right. Just to help, there's this grubby looking net curtain up to halfway – goodness knows why. There's no one able to look in from outside anyway. They must have thought it was pretty or something, a feminine touch. Yes, defeats me too. Further round, the door (brown naturally) down into the kitchen – just you wait! Then a single red armchair, the fireplace, with a home-made rug in front. Yep, it would have been pretty filthy, with all the stuff from the coal and the fire. First thing in the morning the missus of the house would clear out the grate, lay the fire and light it. She usually crumpled up pieces from an old newspaper, put strips of rough wood or sticks on top, got that going with a match, and then placed her smaller coals on the very top. You had to watch a fire all the time to make sure it was burning well enough. In the deadest part of a bad winter, this was the only place in the whole house that might be fairly warm. Of course, you roasted right next to it and shivered over there where you are standing, sir. You'll see there are fireplaces in both bedrooms and the front room we'll see last, but they would be lit very rarely, the downstairs one at Christmas maybe, when the family gathered, or upstairs when someone was ill or having a baby.

That side of the hearth - the other red chair, then the piano against the wall. That old black and white television on the top doesn't belong to the owner. It isn't used. I'll explain why later. The piano hasn't been played for over thirty years either. Before that, the folk would get together most weekends and make their own entertainment. Lots of even working-class people could strum along. Now in 1960 this is just an old brown waste of space, thought to be too valuable to get rid of but actually not worth much more than firewood and scrap metal.

Against the piano, the table, with its leaves folded down and this old worn velvet cloth on it, and two chairs under. You'll see the other two chairs in the bedrooms. So, what else? If I hadn't said 1960, what would you have guessed, apart from the tv and three-piece suite? Go on. 1880? Earlier? Before the War? Which one? Oh, both! Yes, I'd say the same. Well, if you think this is dingy and drab, wait till we go into the kitchen, which is through the door. Follow me. Watch the step down again. I'll go right to the end.

Now what year are we in? Or should I say what century? Who's seen a brown earthenware kitchen sink like this before? Look: one cold tap, scrubbed wooden draining board. Like it? What about the height? Yes, you'd have to bend down quite a long way. How tall are you, sir? Six feet how many? Have you ever had back trouble?

Yes? How would you like to do all your washing here – yourself, the baby, the crocks and dishes, your hand wash items? You'd send it to the laundry! Well, you could – if you had the money. Or maybe you could find some woman down the road who did extra washing and ironing for a few shillings. But you probably would want to save the money for food.

I want to tell you the story of 1960 in this house, about what was happening on July 4th of that year. First, the owner of the house is out at work. She's an unmarried woman of 57 called Annie Beatrice Hearne. She's lived here on her own since her stepmother, Ginny (that's not short for Virginia – her real name was Jane), died in 1954. Some time after the first Mrs Hearne died at the early age of 40, from a congenital kidney condition, Harry Hearne remarried to this lady, who by all accounts was remarkably kind and well loved by all the family she inherited. Annie had a brother Clifford – actually she had two, but one died in childhood, as I'll tell you later. Anyway, Ginny was such a lovely lady that even Clifford's three sons loved her every bit as much as they could a real grandmother. When she was widowed, some time after Clifford married and moved out with his wife, she looked after Annie devotedly. Annie thought the world of her in return. Back to Annie.

To put it straight to you, Annie Hearne wasn't very bright! After Ginny died, she managed to live a very basic life on her own. She had a simple, low skilled repetitive job in a Hockley Brook factory, did her shopping, had one or two friends, and looked after herself. Buying the red sofa and chairs in the room behind you was about the most daring thing she had done in six years. She had help from her factory worker friend Hetty and her husband, George. When the factory had its annual fortnight's holiday in the summer, she didn't even go away, but just stayed here. She had a few clothes, no hobbies, no interests that we can trace. She didn't read books or buy a newspaper. The funny looking dark brown dome shaped radio next door dates from the 1930s, and is still working in 1960, though Annie almost never turns it on. It's a mystery how she occupies herself at home on her own. There's no phone line here, of course. Only about two or three houses in the whole road had a private phone in those times. You can think about that one.

Let's look around. One small metal framed window with more tacky lace curtains, ancient boiler in the corner, early gas cooker from before the First World War, 1920s scrubbed table, 1920s kitchen dresser. Cupboard in corner with broom, bucket, ironing board (pre-World War 2), and a more recent – actually only 1950s – mangle or wringer. You don't know what a mangle is? This is an Acme Wringer Mangle, of which there were thousands up and down the country. To squeeze the water out of your washing before you hung it on the line outside, you lifted it out of the wash tub with big wooden tongs – because it was steaming hot – and with one hand fed it in between those padded rubber cylinders whilst you began to turn the handle with the other. That squashed a large amount of water out of the washing into the bucket you put underneath. Yes, it was all really hard work. Before you even got to this stage, you would have brought the tub in from the yard outside, filled it with water heated in the boiler, put your detergent and clothes in, and them bashed it around with the big copper sucker thing in the corner. Round here they called that a *posher* though it was really a posser or dolly. The earlier ones were all wood, with four big pegs, like teeth. You then kept lifting the washing out with your tongs and dunking it a few times before possing it around some more. When the water got too cloudy, you had to empty it all out and fill it again. Then some more empties and refills for rinsing. By the middle of Monday morning, the whole floor would be under water, and the steam would have wet all the walls and the windows. You'd have to have the back door and window fully open, even in the middle of winter. Primitive, don't you think? What, you'd keep on wearing your dirty things? I imagine you probably did get away with as many days as you could. We're much fussier now.

In some ways Annie Hearne wasn't too badly off. She had only herself to look after. So not much washing. But on 4th July 1960 it was a younger woman who stood dripping here while Annie was a mile away on the assembly line. We don't know the details, but for some reason a family of five – two parents and three children – had come to stay for a time. So, another Mrs Hearne, who had a crying baby trying to hang on her, was doing the washing. She probably did Annie's for her too. We've made the house as exactly as it was just after Annie's nephew Douglas came to stay with his family at the beginning of the month. We thought that would give you an idea of how they somehow managed to cram in so many folk in such a small and, by our standards, prehistorically old fashioned place then. As I said, we don't know the whole story. But let's go outside and check the garden and outside lavatory. What do you think of the walls here? Yes, just bare brick that was painted ages ago, but most of that has blistered off. How do you think the family washed themselves every day? Where did Douglas have his shave? Ok, can you open the back door, please, and lead us outside?

Not much to explain here really. Common blue-grey paving bricks for the yard. Back wall heavily covered in weed ivy. Garden just completely left to itself: uncut grass, self-sown weedy flowers, a bit of a rubbish mound at the bottom. The path is mostly covered with overgrowth. Those two posts at either end were for the washing line, where your clothes dried. If you walk down past the kitchen – look how worn away the brickwork is, all those hollows and gaps in the mortar too – you come to this door. In here was the only lavatory. No light. No heating. Nowhere to wash your hands. You had to go back into the kitchen to do that. What's that? How did you manage in winter? You made it quick and got a cold bum! At night? When it got dark, you'd have to feel your way around or bring a torch, or even a candle, as recently as then. Oh, at night you might well use a chamber pot in the bedroom. Douglas Hearne called it the 'guzzunda'. Why do you think that was? What, Italian? No! 'Yo doe talk Brum! Yo call it a *guzzunda* coz it *guzzunda* yer bed! Gorrit?' Yes, that's right. Can someone explain that to our Japanese friends, please? Thank you, madam. Oh, *you* are a Brummie – or were! You can translate for me then. Let's go back and take a look upstairs.

I'll just put the light on. Doesn't make much difference, but it helps a bit. That's a low wattage old bulb, very yellow. Makes the old wallpaper even dimmer. Yellowy now, with orange patches. They're to suggest patches of damp. These places were never warm or aired enough to dry out completely. It actually started off cream, would you believe. Please turn left at the top and go in the room facing you, not up the little staircase by the side.

I didn't take you into the attic because it's too tiny anyway and we haven't yet reinforced the stairs, which were suspect even in 1960. I hope the Hearne children were kept off them since our surveyor thinks they were probably structurally unsound then. Right, this is the second bedroom. Annie moved into it while her guests stayed. No surprises: old, shabby, cold, dingy, gloomy. Cold lino on the floor, dull and ancient. The chair from downstairs to put your clothes on. Dresser with shelves and mirror. Second-hand wardrobe from before World War 1. They didn't have much, did they? What always strikes me in these bedrooms is just how everything seems to have died a long time ago. Even when you were living here in 1960 it must have felt like being in an earlier age where time had simply given up in misery and stopped. Or am I just being imaginative? Can we turn round and go across the landing to the main bedroom now? You'll really have to squeeze in, I'm afraid.

The Hearne family bedroom! Double bed, two single beds, that green cot from the late 1940s. You can edge your ways sideways between the beds.

So how would this have worked? Bed the youngest down first? What about if the next one up disturbed him when she went to bed later? Or if he cried and woke her up? Then the oldest one has to creep in and undress, maybe in the dark, and get in bed without waking the other two. He definitely mustn't nudge their beds. Tricky! Anyone slept in a tent with the whole family? Great for the first half hour? That's funny! Probably true too. Snoring? Oh yes! And not to put too fine a point on it, it can't help your sex life, can it? I mean, if all the washing, feeding and other things haven't wiped you out in the day, you might not feel too amorous anyway. And what if one of the kids wakes up? Or throws up? That's going to happen one winter night for sure. Then they'll all catch it, and so will you. Packed like sardines and heaving your guts about all in your own time. You'd normally have to take the ferry to Calais for that sort of fun! I think we'd better move on!

Look: he's already out of the door! Hang on, please. Just one more thing before we leave this room. See that creamish thing in the small space between the two single beds and the double one? Know what that is? It's a Valor paraffin heater. Douglas Hearne couldn't let his family freeze in winter, could he? Yes, I know it's July right now, because of what will happen later in the year.

Anyone ever been in a room with a paraffin heater? It stinks! It's horrible to breathe. It makes your eyes sting. It uses up some of your oxygen and fills the air with water vapour. The windows and walls would be running wet all over after an hour. You might be warmer, but you're also choking. Would you want your children, never mind yourselves, to spend even a minute in that kind of atmosphere? Exactly! It was quite a fire risk too – knock that thing over and the room's ablaze in seconds. Same thing if there's a fuel leak or if you spill some paraffin and you're refilling it when it's still lit. Douglas could have done. How much room is there, or isn't there, to get past it? A few inches? If you were a child, you'd just be tall enough to give your bottom a nasty burn if you only brushed against the top. That's metal. It's where all the heat ascends to and radiates and conducts from. It's hot enough to set your nightdress on fire if it's not really flameproof. We don't have to think of things like that with central heating, and anyway only the cheapest pyjamas are not fire retardant. I'm sure you read the labels when you buy them for your grandchildren.

That's enough horrors. There's just one more room to see. Back downstairs, please. First door on your left. I'll see you there.

All right then. You're in the front room, the best room as I said to start with. It's almost never used, of course, on the good working-class principle that if it's good you save it for ever, or perhaps never! You want to keep it unspoiled. You've worked hard for it. It's got your best pieces of furniture in it and your treasures, the things you'd like other people to know you had. Maybe one or two things mean something to you because they've been passed down in the family. This is saved for special occasions and our VIP family guests. What do we see?

This fireplace is more decorative. The mantelpiece, which actually is marble, has old family photographs, probably of long dead loved and respected family members. That large framed photograph in the middle of the wall is a bit unusual. That's Annie four-year-old brother, Johnny. He's wearing his best shorts, shirt, tie and jacket for the photographer whose studio they've gone to. And this can't have been long before the little lad went down with diphtheria and passed away. Yes, sad, incredibly sad, but such things were shockingly common in those days. What? Well, I can actually tell you quite accurately: if we've got his age right as four, then this is 1909 or 1910. He's back there now where he was for years and where I suppose he belongs. Where did we get it? That's another story. When Annie left the house to go into a home, where she died, her nephew Ken had the job of clearing the place and selling it on. Most of the stuff went to the dump, but a few smaller items were taken upstairs and left behind in the attic. Even the new owner didn't ever clear it out. That's where some of the other things here, like the clock, pictures and ornaments came from too. It was one of the happy accidents that local historians just love. When we sent the photo to a restorer, to be cleaned, he took it apart and saw that someone had written Johnny's details – his name, birth and death dates – on a slip of paper behind the print. We have checked those against the records in the public office, and it's been confirmed as genuine. A great bit of amateur research.

Otherwise, the stuffed owl in a glass domed case on the sideboard, typically dark brown. That isn't the original piece of furniture, but the nearest thing we could find to match the drawers Ken must have left in the top floor room. What was brilliant about those was that they still had all their contents as Annie had left them for ages. She just put things away and didn't look at them again, for years. Of course, it was the paperwork that we were keenest to look at, the old bills and receipts. Best of all were twenty or so wage packets. These were given to factory workers at the end of every Friday, not for the week they'd just done, but the one before that. They called it 'working in hand.' The best day was when you left, because they'd have to give you two together. I've no idea why they did it that way. It might have ensured some continuity in the work force. Or more likely it gave the office time to work out what everyone was owed and for it to be put in these envelopes with all the details on a handwritten slip: how many hours worked at a particular rate, or sometimes how many articles turned out at so much a hundred or thousand. If you were on that, which was called 'piece work', it could work for or against you, depending on the rate on the job and how quickly you were able to work. If you were in a team, everybody was paid at the rate of the slowest person! I guess they all loved her! Even in a good week you didn't bring home much. Annie's envelopes had between five and ten pounds, mostly just reaching seven. Strangely enough, she hadn't even opened most of them, which were still sealed with the full amount inside of notes and coins. She almost certainly didn't have a bank account.

Best crockery and glasses in here. Old fashioned horsehair suite, better to look at than sit in. It's quite hard and the wooden back pretty uncomfortable. I've mentioned the more expensive and ornamental fireplace. That coloured surround is moulded iron and enamel. They loved blue and white. Prints of country scenes on the walls – they were cheaply mass produced. Better quality curtains, though you can't tell that anymore. The polished fire irons and coal scuttle, more for show than use. If they did have a fire going, they'd probably bring the coal in with a bucket. Just have a look around and soak it all in before you leave. You can put the shoe covers in the box by the door. I'll be on the pavement. We'll go next and see Mr Ghosh. Excuse me. Thank you.

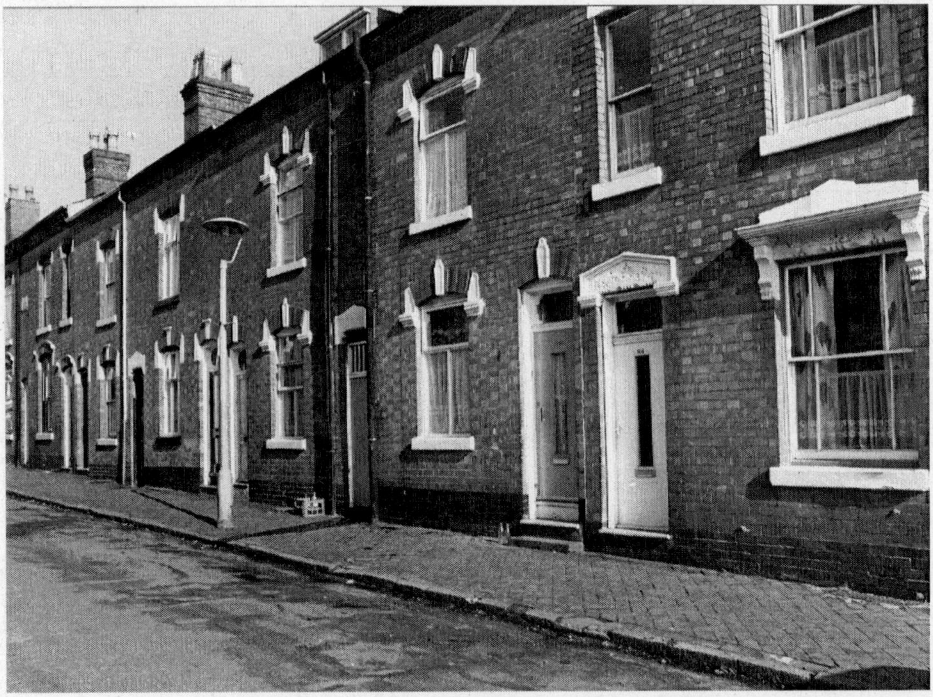

Well maintained Burbury Street houses in more recent times

Rondo Perpetuo

But al to litel, weylawey the whyle,
Lasteth swich joye, y-thonked be Fortune!

Geoffrey Chaucer, *Troilus and Criseyde, Prohemium to Book IV*

Where do I start now? When the roulette wheel spins on free and unbiased bearings, it can stop anywhere. Your chosen number has an equal chance of coming up with all the others. So your rational mind informs you. Superstitious sorts, gamblers and theorising statisticians may have other notions. I have always striven my very hardest not to be drafted into any of their ranks; a one in thirty-six chance of winning more than I have in my pocket will never tempt me to secure the thirty-five of giving it all away. I could buy myself a sandwich instead. Better still, I could wobble off into the kitchen and make my own for a fraction of the cost. I just love living on the edge.

But *faites vos jeux*! Just now it will not make the slightest difference where I place my pennyworth. Enough dithering: Auntie Annie! *J'ai fait mon pari. Mesdames, Messieurs! Les jeux sont faits. Rien ne va plus!*

Until we descended on Annie Hearne, she had not featured much in my life. She was at Sylvia's christening in 1955, as her Godmother. I am not even sure whether we exchanged Christmas cards. When the family mentioned her, the brothers among themselves, the thought of her provoked amusement: she was a bit funny, harmless, but still and always funny. Occupying her small gloomy junkstore of a dwelling, we tried to make as little impression on it as possible. The television was placed on top of the piano for storage, but never switched on. It might have worked quite well with a portable aerial. To a ten year old who turned the set on before 5 o'clock every afternoon and had learned the test card music by heart (movements from Handel's *Water Music*, a pyrotechnical piece of Liszt, the *Badinerie* from Bach's second Orchestral Suite, *La Primavera* from Vivaldi's *Quattro Stagioni* and so on) before the children's programmes commenced, watched Wimbledon and test matches in the summer, and had no need of *Radio Times* to check all the early evening and weekend evening broadcasts, this was a formidable mountain range blocking the desert, not manna. Annie was not interested in television. It might annoy her. (I might insert that I am sure my father paid all of the utility bills for the duration of our stay.)

My mother paid for Annie's food, cooked all her meals, washed and ironed her clothes, cleaned the house as well as anyone could. We tried to keep out of her way. In the evenings, Mom would take all three of us up to the bedroom, where we would lie on the beds and fall asleep according to our age. As soon as David was soundly breathing to himself, Sylvia, Mom and I would talk quietly about things. Mom was glad to rest and enjoyed being with us as much as she could anything at that time. As time wore on, we relieved the misery by mockery. It may not have shown gratitude for our hostess, but it made things a little more tolerable. Though she reached her fifth birthday over the summer holiday, Sylvia did not start school till the following January. Whether our parents did not get round to making the arrangement or perhaps believed we should be leaving so shortly that it did not matter for a few weeks, I cannot say. I must have shared some things about my days at the new school.

My father stayed downstairs, out of politeness, to keep his aunt company. That is, he endured her presence and the sights and sounds she presented to his senses.

According to Drummond of Hawthornden, who may have been inventing, Ben Jonson once, in a particularly wearied and probably tipsy moment, leaned forward to tap Lord Somebody on the chest and enquire firmly whether there was anyone within. My father showed more deference to his father's sister, leaving his feelings unrelieved. Annie's mind equalled her house and home admirably in drabness – or was it maybe the other way round? – being inexhaustibly furnished with junk. Her language briefly amused you with what you thought was its quaintness, quickly becoming irritating beyond endurance. She caught the *buzz* at least twice every day, not the *bus*. She was punctilious in informing you which one, at what time and how full it was. Since it was only ever the number 8, the Inner Circle, that had no value for even my bus spotter interests, though I confess to keeping in my blazer pocket at that time the Ian Allen ABC volume *Birmingham City Buses*, quite normal for a boy at the Age of Collecting. Annie registered surprise, often at the most routine comments (e.g. *It's raining*) with the phrase *Guy Squint* or its alternative *Guy Flip*. Occasionally observing some antics of my toddler brother, she might come out with, 'He's a right little nerker,' whatever that was, always without a smile. Trying to tell her a joke wasted breath and time. She paused to blink, but otherwise remained expressionless. The few surviving photographs capture her strange light, usually with her ventriloquist's dummy grin, but the eyes are elsewhere, disturbingly alert. Her lower lip, like a fish's or a dull red prawn, was a functioning slab, expressionless. You could never imagine that forty years before some inexperienced boy had leaned forward quivering to kiss her. She walked on her heels, with a thumping waddle. Her outdoor shoes and slippers invariably wore down or through at the back. She could never have achieved the fine handiwork of both my grandmothers, exquisite stitching from agile fingered needlewomen.

If you see or read Arnold Wesker's *Roots*, Beatie's mother, Mrs Bryant, bears some resemblance. She registers the passing of traffic:

> [*Off – as she hears lorry go* by] There go Danny Oakley to market.

later …

> [*on hearing a bus*]: There go the half-past eleven bus to Diss – blust, that's early.

The family, even the reforming Beatie sometimes, make the same inane comments every time they have strawberry ice cream.

BEATIE: This is good too – made from pink milk ent it?

[*Pause*]

JIMMY: Yearp! [*Pause*] Come from a pink cow!

They have no ideas.

Only, we can afford to be amused by Mrs Bryant and the others, safely distanced from us down there on the stage; spending every evening across the fireplace would be a different matter. Your brains would quickly boil dry.

While Sylvia and I were giggling upstairs with Mom, Dad maintained pointless, though no less brave, efforts. He used to pass her his copy of the *Birmingham Evening Mail*, perhaps in the hope that it would enliven her or at least occupy her for some moments. After a paper-bashing scan, lasting seconds rather than even minutes, it would be discarded: 'No news!' Sometimes, presumably through courtesy, this was elaborated to, 'No news then!' With a small amount of experience you could confidently translate that as: 'No reports of murder or rape.'

Whenever he could, Dad took us all out in the car, frequently house hunting without success, or in the better months to Handsworth Park or Perry Hall Playing Fields, to run about and kick a ball. On Saturdays, we might find ourselves enjoying crisps and lemonade in the car, parked at The Elms pub in Aldridge, perhaps at other places. We descended on both grandmothers, who were sympathetically generous with their welcome and hospitality. Though Lil had no television at this stage, Elsie rented the largest and most modern available. Towards the right time on Saturday afternoon she instructed me to turn the set on for the wrestling, after which we were allowed to watch what we liked till we had to leave to sleep in Lozells. Her roaring fires in winter lit everyone and everything. Even so, she would wrap herself in a fringed red plaid travel rug. 'Aren't I dreadful? At least there'll be one thing for me to look forward to in Hell!' Our dad really loved her, in a way he could not even his own mother, dear to him as she remained till her demise.

One aspect gave Dad some cheer: he was back, to within half a mile of his boyhood scenes, from birth till his teens. He relished driving us round the old haunts, telling us the tales.

'That's where Potty Potter lived. He was completely barmy. One day Gordon and I watched him mend his fence in the rain. He held the umbrella up over him while he picked up the next nail, put it down to knock it in the first bit, then picked it up again while he finished hammering it in. He did that all along the whole fence, all afternoon. He got absolutely drenched. Silly old sod!'

Some things had not changed. Though at least in his seventies and white haired, Dr Target was still based in Farm Street, having been joined in the practice by his son. He was the only GP I have ever come across qualified to be his own pharmacist, on one occasion dispensing medicine to us in the street from the boot of his car, a mushroom grey Morris Oxford. These days he would be instantly searched under the 1984 Police and Criminal Evidence Act! He worked in the area all his considerable career, starting well before the NHS. St Francis RC church inevitably had not moved. Dad's old first school, St Mary's RC, was no more – in name anyway, having been changed to St Francis's. Of course, Dad disapproved. So did the Headmaster, Tom O'Loughlin, who had been Dad's Head too, attended school with Clifford, Dad's father, and remembered Clifford's father, Harry Hearne. On Monday, 4th July, Dad took me to his old school in Wills Street. It was now my new one.

You heard the noise from a distance: boys, rioting or at war. Stepping through the single gate from the pavement onto the tarmaced playground for the first time was more astounding than entering an animated Brueghel painting. Boys, hundreds of them from 8 to 15, hurtling around in an enraged Bedlam of simultaneous games, mostly football. The oldest, Senior 4 as I was to discover, occupied the full length of the yard, breathless booting a full-size ball from the street wall we had just passed to the classroom wall, thirty to forty yards away. Other games criss-crossed them, with the side wall of the neighbouring house as one goal and the left hand, Junior 1 and 2, building, the other. All the classroom windows had dense, heavy duty protective grills permanently over them. If you knew no better, you would think it was a prison or psychiatric institution, even a concentration camp. The whole set of buildings from the air would have resembled an L shape. Just inside the right angle was the single-storey later addition, with its flat slabbed concrete roof. It was the Headmaster's Office, staffroom, medical room and secretaries' workplace.

Without ceasing to move or holding their fire, the numerous combatants in these battles somehow allowed us to make it across the warzone to the office door, where Dad knocked.

Tom O'Loughlin, filling the door frame.

'Doug!' A searchlight smile. 'Come in!'

Tom O'Loughlin: Broad frame, large head, blazing blue eyes, broad cheeks with sub-filigree red vein traceries, short slicked down hair, light-grey suit, creased wide trousers, smart, at once mature and youthful. Headmaster, magistrate, promoter of amateur boxing for Birmingham boys, sporting official, father of eight (four of each, from eighteen to five), Catholic club man. My boneless hand lost in his slabpaw clutch.

'Douglas Hearne! This one's yours then?' A five-beat chuckle. Raising his voice as if I'm ten yards away, 'So how are you – Martin, isn't it?' A powerful man!

I have just left St John's? Who was my teacher? Mr McCarthy? (More chuckles.) L.O.McCarthy! Little Old McCarthy! And what class was I in? Junior 4? Mr Woods! He'd take me there in a minute. Half an hour later, my father bestrid the doorstep, hand imprisoned. The family history lesson, not to mention other ancient matters, was not over, merely suspended.

To be personally conducted to my new classroom by this consular headmaster could have matched the Lord Major of London in full regalia striding across Guildhall Yard to the kitchens with the caterers' rawest recruit, perhaps a trainee dishwasher, trailing behind.

Junior 4 here turned out to be the equivalent of Junior 5 at St John's, that is the last class before the move to the senior school. Too shy to mention anything, I was to stay with older boys till a major change at Christmas. There is something else I must explain.

St Francis was in its last days – till the new term in 1961 – as what was called an 'Elementary School'. After the 11-plus selection test, you moved on to Senior 1 on the same site if you had not qualified to transfer to a grammar school or technical college. Relatively few cleared that hurdle, thereby merely changing classrooms and teachers every year till, at the end of Senior 4 when 15 years old, they ended their compulsory schooling and went on to employment or training. Apprenticeships were an option for some, as was night school. Some firms took on school leavers as trainees in their line of work. Otherwise, factory work or unskilled labouring, sometimes more or less the same thing, was your prospect. That explains why the playground was such a battlefield. The oldest boys were large, manly, muscular and vigorously physical, whilst my voice, never mind those of boys two or three years younger, was nowhere near breaking. I had always worn shorts. Moreover, at this school every possible freedom was allowed for boys to evolve into young men, the sporting (first!) and working warriors in the approaching Battle of Life. It was a daring, yet brilliant strategy. I doubt whether it could have succeeded in a mixed or all girls' school, but here it largely triumphed fairly resoundingly.

Discipline was supplied from various springs: from the Senior 4 prefects, vigilantly patrolling, whose very presence and alertness gave stability. Once triggered, their response was swift and literally hands on. The arresting hand would swoop on an offender's neck from behind, rather like stopping a cat in its tracks, so that the malefactor leaned forward, shoulders lifted and frozen. If he obeyed the warning to, e.g. 'pack it in and clear off', that was usually enough. Defiant resistance or a really foul action, for example, belting a smaller or weaker boy pitilessly, in such an extreme case might provoke, 'Right, we'll see what Tom says about that,' or something similar, the prisoner being briskly propelled at arm's length by the directest route across the playground to the office.

Teachers kept us in line with little punishment; we knew not to trifle with them. They could resort to the stick. Mr Hickey never did. Mr Woods ignited two or three times a term, but always sent out clear signals in time for you to retreat or take cover. Only Mr Davis, Senior 3, who conducted the choir for the 11 o'clock sung mass every Sunday as well as for our weekday school masses or Friday morning Benediction, ruled by terror. (I always looked forward to a pretty little setting of the 'Hosanna in excelsis', a solo sung by a boy treble called John Drinkwater.)

Davis took each class in turn for singing. We were accompanied by a crewcut pianist, Mr Duckworth, who occasionally played for us an astounding piece of Chopin or Liszt. Our sea shanties and other BBC *Singing Together* pieces and Catholic hymns in truth wasted his time, but I suppose he was grateful for a few extra pounds a month; at least he did not have to spend the entire time in total anxiety that Davis would snap at him. For the smallest thing or even no discernible reason he would with tight-lipped fury whip your hands beyond any imaginable threshold of pain. Slim, straight-backed, light-grey-suited and unsmiling, he belonged, I much later realised, to that subset of musicians who know something of their subject but share neither beauty nor joy from it with others, only anger. When Michael Brown, sitting next to me, once mimed along to a piano introduction, cheerfully air conducting, he was instantly caned on each hand. He sat next to me, writhing with the insupportable anguish, shaking our joint seat with his silent sobs.

I thought of this moment just over a decade later, on teaching practice. The Head of Music came into the staffroom at break, chuckling. When he had played an orchestral recording to a second form class, a boy had just got up and danced around the room, to the music and himself. For Mr Sutcliffe that was a Eureka moment; Davis would have executed the child.

With this one exception, the teachers were all right – tough, but fair. Wonderfully, so were the boys. Initially taken aback by their energy and physicality, I found both my classmates and even older boys either left me alone or treated me, like everyone, as well as I treated them.

One small incident can illustrate this. It was morning break. A group of us were playing some game. I did something underhand or uncalled for to a boy called Alfie Perry, smaller but nut hard, fierce, direct – a quick-living town boy. Maybe I pushed or tried to trip him, thinking he would not identify me in the melée.

He stopped in his tracks, faced me, eyes locked on mine.

'You do that again, Martin, and I'll …'

He did complete the ultimatum, but I am not sure what he said. It must have been something like ' … smack your head.' I understood. Having tidied that up, Alfie forgot all about my meanness and carried on with his morning. We always were on good terms from then on. It was very decent to give me the chance of a final warning at the same time as he took proper care of himself. Respect for others starts with respect for oneself, or should that be the other way round? In my case I just knew that he was prepared to like and accept me if I played fair. St Francis R.C. bred that kind of discipline without explicitly teaching it. It came down from the top.

Tom O'Loughlin was The Law. Everyone understood this so well that only the most outrageous instances of misconduct needed the full treatment in his office. In my short time at the school there can have been only a handful. I happened to be present at one. He was giving me a private session on cricket scoring (about which more later) when he broke off to glance at the clock. He asked me to go and sit on an empty chair in the corner whilst he saw a boy. I remembered that at registration someone had called out, 'Sir, So-and-so's got to see Tom.' Mr Woods would say nothing, but drew his breath through his teeth and raised his eyebrows.

Unlike McCarthy, Tom was not a thrasher. He could cane and occasionally would. I think you would be glad when you reached that stage. You knew you deserved it.

There was a knock at the door.

'Come in … You want to see me. Just stand there. You'd better tell me what this is all about. What do you want to say?'

Gravity, effortless authority, a constant blue-eyed look at the boy.

'Well then?'

There was not much more to it than that. The whole story came out. Without prompting, this Senior 2 boy, new to me, gave the whole account. He just said what he had done, that he knew it was completely wrong, and that he was sorry, sir. He would go and apologise to the lady and mend or pay for what he had messed up. He had been very stupid, etc.

'You know what most upsets me, don't you?' the Head asked.

'No, sir.'

'Well, you should. I have to tell you I am very upset. It troubles me you've let yourself down.'

He did not say much more. The boy would not be playing in the team on Saturday. He would come and help the caretaker for the morning.

After the door closed, he brought the scorebook back to the table. 'You know what *really* troubles me, don't you, Martin?'

'Sir?'

'He's their second-best bowler.'

Yet even justice hand in hand with wisdom can sometimes afford to be sporting, if not exactly jolly. In that final autumn term before the senior classes were moved to the new, purpose-built school in Hamstead, an ugly grudge developed between a Senior 4 prefect called Stuart and a very challenging Senior 3 boy, Alex. Fit, physical and fast with his fists, the younger, broad-shouldered lad stood two or three inches above the fair-haired, milder prefect. A show down with someone was inevitable. Alex was always pushing his luck. We were all excited and yet strangely worried.

The Head must have seen them together after some flare up. He no doubt spent some time listening to each in turn. He pronounced no verdict or sentence. He gave them the option of settling things in the ring if that was their wish. It was.

The next Friday afternoon. The annexe around the corner in Brougham Street. Single-storey building like a youth club. One large, main room normally divided into two classrooms by a removable partition, toilets and a cloakroom. Before we arrived there, the furniture had been stacked outside, the partition folded back, an elevated ring brought in and assembled centrally, and chairs arranged in rows around the four sides. All the Senior classes and as many of the Junior ones as could be fitted in occupied the seats. Patrick and I were about half-way back with a clear view.

Tom O'Loughlin sat with two priests in the front row to our right.

Gentlemen, boys, good afternoon and welcome. This is your Master of Ceremonies, Senior One's Mr Hickey.

Reverend Fathers … Headmaster … gentlemen and boys … This is a three rounds contest of three minutes each, to be decided by a knockdown and count out, withdrawal, or on points, between, on my right hand Stuart [surname], School Prefect of Senior 4, and Alex [surname] of Senior 3. Your judges are Father [name] and Father [name] of St Francis Church, and the Headmaster, Mr O'Loughlin. Your timekeeper is Mr [School caretaker] and your referee Mr Woods. Over to you, Mr Woods.

Our teacher, tie and jacket off, white shirt open at the collar, wearing cleaned white plimsolls. Calls both boys to the middle. Their heads bunch together. He straightens up and stands back a step. The boys touch gloves and turn to their corners. The handbell rings, the same one that the secretary uses when it's time to go inside for lessons.

It might be thrilling entertainment to some, offensive brutality to others, and disturbingly dangerous: young boys bashing each other around, trying to punch each other's heads. More boys boxed in schools and youth clubs in those days. At my second grammar school, we had a team in each school year, as for other sports.

Prefect Stuart looked at a natural disadvantage, being shorter and less developed. The younger Alex, whose natural dark curls had been cut for this match, had the broad shoulders of a swimmer and a longer reach.

I think nothing much happened in the early stages of the first round, for all our shouting. Facing each other, they moved around, guards up, seeking gaps, still keeping some distance. Now and then a glove went forward, merely padding or failing to make any substantial contact. Just before the bell, Alex landed one or two smart raps on his opponent's body, propelling him backwards.

The seconds in the corners were friends. Unlike the televised bouts, there were no buckets and spitting, no sodden sponges, no flapping towels. It was disappointing, though better than lessons. Each sat looking ahead, breathing heavily. We spectators had actually gone quiet. The timekeeper called 'Seconds Away. Round Two.' The bell clanged.

Alex raised his game from the start. He drove Stuart back on to the ropes, landing several blows. The younger boy was in control. People were shouting both ways, willing Blondie to find some reserves or yelling at Alex to finish him off. I kept quiet. Stuart had always looked all right to me, smart and measured, a mature citizen doing his job even-handedly; Curly Alex threw himself around noisily, wild even at playground football, flamboyant and demonstrative. I think for most of us the needle always flickered between 'Acceptable Cheering' and 'Gratuitous Gloating' when he celebrated scoring a goal. In my conformist and inhibited eyes, he was more a lout than a hero, the prefect a decent chap. And he was going down. His head was down between his two raised arms, the elbows down towards his stomach. Alex was whipping into him with both hands. I thought Woodsie was about to step in and stop it. I would have understood. If the first round had been a no-score draw, this one was going Alex's way. Then, in the last half minute or so before the bell, Stuart found something to unleash. He struck out, stood up more, lifted his head, went side on, left hand forward. In quick succession he surprised Alex a good few times: left-left-left-right; left-left-right, all the way into his own corner. Clang. Woodsie pulled him back by the right shoulder. Curly walked back across the diagonal, arms down by his sides.

Round three was a sustained exchange of blows, some landing heavily. It was going back and forth, but increasingly it seemed to me that Stuart's dominance was growing. For a smaller boy he had surprising energy and endurance. Perhaps being a few months older made a difference. Or did having more to lose fire his resolve? At the very end he was clearly on top, driving his man before him, picking him off without retaliation. The final bell.

Anyone on the street walking past the building must have wondered at the sustained uproar in what the large sign said was a Catholic school as we all shouted, a couple of hundred of us, waiting for the decision. The moment the fight ended, the two priests and the Headmaster stood up. They briefly turned towards us smiling, then went into a huddle. Mr Woods was standing in the middle of the ring, holding each fighter by a wrist.

The judges drew apart. The Head moved to the ropes. Mr Woods leaned nearer to him, then nodded and stepped back. He raised Stuart's left arm high above his head. We stamped and yelled for ages. It was amazing. No one got furious and ordered us to be quiet.

The Head climbed up into the ring and walked across, clapping. He held his two arms up for a long time before we settled down. Things were still being shouted out now and then.

Tom thanked everyone and said well done to both boys. He was proud of both of them. We all were. Alex looked a little rueful, but nevertheless was managing to smile. Both combatants were. Each put an arm around the other's shoulders as they stood and took our applause.

We were home early, bouncing with happiness.

It is only when I look back that I understand how well I was treated by this man and his school. The actual place was falling apart, with decaying buildings, rickety furniture, disintegrating textbooks, and roofless toilets so old and poor that no amount of cleaning could bring them back. The boys came, for the most part, from very humble homes, living in houses like Annie's, but not so neglected or behind the times. Their parents were generally not well off, but worked solidly for relatively little. Most of the time, the boys got on well with each other, and excelled when they united in an endeavour, particularly in the main games of football and cricket.

I could not join in with this because I was not good enough – I liked kicking a ball around with Uncle Gordon, or taking turns to bat and bowl with him, but I was otherwise simply inexperienced, whereas the St Francis boys had played together for years and developed skills. Realising this, the Head took me on one side and taught me to keep the team's cricket score book, so that I was as involved as I could be. I think he did this because he remembered my father fondly, as a kindness to me, and also practically because he thought I was able to learn and make a reasonable fist of it. I soon found myself travelling by bus, after school and on Saturday mornings, usually with one or two others, to various grounds and playing fields within a few miles of Lozells, to keep the score for our games.

An even bigger favour, which I still do not quite understand, was that Mr O'Loughlin chose me to be his assistant when he officiated as starter in some quite high level inter school and even inter county athletic events. On several occasions I stood next to him by the various starting lines at Birmingham's Alexander Stadium, the home of Birchfield Harriers, a stadium of Olympic quality where some very famous athletes have competed.

Tom had two starting pistols, identical six-shot weapons revolvers that fired .44 mm blanks. They had been converted from service weapons by the insertion of metal plugs into the ends of their shortened barrels, exhaust holes being drilled on the underside.

My job was to cart these around, keep them loaded, and pass them to the starter when they were needed.

These were real guns, heavy and serious, no mere cap pistols. The purpose made starting pistols used in schools where I have worked are not a patch on them, being not much more than toys that make a snapping sound you just about register from any distance. When a .44 Colt goes off, it detonates! If you were in the grandstand when Tom started the 220 yards from the other side of the track, you would see the orange-yellow flash of flame from under the barrel and a split second later hear – and feel – a very loud, weighty bang! The firework we called a banger had nothing on it.

I always silently prayed that, when there were only two blanks left unused, that was when the false start would occur. If it happened after the fifth blank, Tom still had the sixth to call the runners back. But … if he *started* a race with the *sixth* blank, then I had to stand very near him, holding up the second pistol, fully loaded, by the barrel, the handle extended to Tom, for the 'false start' second bang.

It was not the noise that I wanted to keep away from, but the blast of flame and hot powder that would flash around me at high velocity! You could not work out where to stand; the emergency shot had to be taken as soon as the gun could be grabbed, no matter where it was pointing. Several times sparks showered near me. Once or twice I felt some heat. I am still here. My pulse is beating. I have told the tale.

Health and Safety … Risk Assessments … Child Protection … None of these had yet been imagined, along with all the other policy and procedures documents. My 'schemes of work' literature when I started to teach in 1973 was one typed sheet of (in those days) foolscap. The first half listed the responsibilities of the Head of Department, slightly more than the next sixth those of his Number Two, and the remaining three or four lines told any curious reader that I would teach a Lower Fourth form and an Upper Fifth set English, be tried out on three-sixteenths of the A level English work, get on with the Latin teaching for myself, run the debating and help with cricket, the last proving a total fiction, and the penultimate the heartless dumping of a wearisome chore. 'Well, I had to do it for five years; now it's your ruddy turn! Want another half?' To terminate this aside, let us agree to blame or praise the rapid provision of computers and printers from the 1980s onwards; when you (more or less) have the means and some mastery over it there is nothing to prevent you from generating, in time no one has allowed you, all the handbooks, policies, procedures, brochures, prospectuses, schemes of work et cetera usqu'ad vaccas revocandas. Of course, I am only half serious. Nothing matters more than children's safety and wellbeing. Everyone involved must keep constantly alert for any possible threats or problems. Fussy as things have become, we must be better equipped and positioned to look after our charges. I should never want to put the clock back in that respect.

On the other hand … sixty years ago Tom O'Loughlin broke most of 2020's rules, and over time hundreds of us hugely benefited from it! When he could, he drove us to and from fixtures in his Bedford CA vehicle, an early minibus. Because this had a column gear stick, I often found myself in the middle of the front seat, on occasions with daughter Maureen, 18, at the wheel to give her father a rest. I would take an oath that the vehicle was not fitted with seat belts. The Head drove us both when he was starting at athletics meetings, chatting easily to me next to him. All the cricket team envied Michael Costello, not just for his wavy blond hair, but because on the return trip from some game I did not attend the second O'Loughlin daughter, Margaret, then 14 or 15, saw how tired he was from bowling all afternoon, and like any good big sister took him on her lap *and laid his head on her ... you know ... there!* He could not say the word 'breast'! He did not want the journey to end. She was to anyone's immediate glance a lovely, indeed unusually beautiful young woman, clear skinned and cleanly proportioned. Further acquaintance showed you her gentle nature too.

Saturday morning rides to games started at the O'Loughlin house on Hunters Road, a large, detached house in its own plot, with land all around. If the front door was not wide open, when you would simply shout 'hello' and walk in, you rang the bell to be shown into the lounge. If the Head was not yet there, you were invited to step through the open french windows into the garden, to join in the kick around. Long ago a family garden, the ground had been trodden and trampled into a more or less levelled exercise area, with neither tree nor single green blade or leaf to be seen. The enclosing walls were newly painted with goals and stumps. Every time I visited, which was at least once a week in fair or good weather, two or more of the four O'Loughlin boys and friends, from about five to fifteen, would be punting a ball around. The two older ones, Michael and William, were already skilled at their games. Particularly Michael, about 15, would coach the youngest boys, five-year-old little Tom and his seven-year-old brother, in batting technique.

The drab and limited life at Annie's continued. At least Dad could escape to work during the week. Mom dug in and toiled away heroically. We all were able to enjoy our meals. There being limited space at the table, I sat on the sofa, covered with a protective pink sheet, and ate from a tray on my lap. All this would have to happen when I was being particularly fussy over my food! Maybe the strain made me worse. They say that hair twisting – we called it 'twiddling' in the family – is a sign of neurosis. I had long been an inveterate twiddler, compulsive. I loved the feel of a bent around loop of hair you could stroke repeatedly with the pad of a finger, relishing the smoothness. I had refused to eat meat or fish since before I could remember. I must have existed on a vegetarian diet with eggs and dairy foods, which I loved. My mother had always encouraged me to eat raw vegetables, especially carrots. I had tried them all: potatoes, swedes, turnips, sprouts, cauliflower, cabbage for certain, even slices of Spanish onions. I probably drew the line at parsnips. The year's seasonal highpoint occurred when fresh peas were in the greengrocer's. Nothing, not all the sweets in the shop, could ever beat shelling a brown paper bag of peas into the colander and eating most of them there and then!

When the weather allowed, Sylvia, David and I escaped to Annie's garden, where I did my best to get them to kick the ball around with me. The clumps of wild, weedy flowers were gradually knocked down, leaving only coarse grasses, around which I practised dribbling the ball. I tried to make it as fast and fluently as I could from one end of the patch to the end, weaving around the remaining islands of growth, to where I could have a shot at goal, the undefended wall. A ball lofted 'over the bar' landed in a Carpenter's Road garden, ending the session. On summer evenings, I stayed outside, pummelling a ball around, until the heavier curtain of night obscured the dusk.

Family car trips to parks, grandmothers and house viewings recurred at intervals, like a theme or motif in a musical movement, but without the cheer that brings. None of the places we looked around was suitable or within our means. The three-bedroomed brand new small detached house by the canal in Walsall Wood seemed perfectly acceptable to me. We could just have afforded it. The surrounding area and tiny garden abutting the dirty-looking and potentially dangerous water decided against it. We roamed further and further in our search, considering remoter Black Country spots and villages I had never heard of or been near despite extensive travelling round accompanying Dad on afternoons as he visited various customers. There was usually an ice-cream at some moment.

The best, because longest, escape from Annie's was a week's holiday in Burnham-on-Sea, staying in a caravan that overlooked the vicarage garden. In the late evening you could see the vicar sitting at his desk, writing under his lamp. Not even my sore heel, quite badly cut by jagged glass in a rock pool, impeded my enjoyment or activity; each step along the lane to the local shop and post office jabbed sharply, but could not keep me inactive. Most extraordinarily Dad abandoned his white summer jacket and tie; a photograph shows him relaxed and smiling on the beach in a high-necked jumper, tan coloured, one of the few such articles he ever wore. The kite string is just discernible against a darker patch of sky; the breeze is lifting his hair on one side. Mom enjoyed Somerset food, especially thick cream, which could be relied upon to give her indigestion. But it was worth it, wasn't it, kids: *burrrp*?

That first day at St Francis I met Jon Darby, who lived opposite. Mr Woods told us we were neighbours. That started a friendship that even survived for some time his going to a boarding school and the family's house move to the country. In good weather, we played street football and cricket outside his house in Graham Street. We used his garden wall and the facing one, convenient because they ran the length of each house's garden, for our goals and wickets. When one evening Jon shot wild and hard, the ball completely penetrated the downstairs front window of an opposite house, leaving a perfectly circular hole.

On wet days Jon taught me card games and Monopoly, which we played in his bedroom or at the downstairs table. I suspect I still play Pontoon, Whist and Rummy to his rules! We also roamed around quite freely, up to the shops on the Lozells Road to buy things for Mrs Darby, or for Jon, who inclined to plumpness, to buy himself a cherry-topped Bakewell Tart. Having discovered a toyshop that sold Triang Trains, over several months I collected every penny I could to put towards the incremental purchase of a very basic layout. I have no idea where the idea came from, but I so missed my model railways that I formed the idea of buying individual items of track and a truck or two to make up everything bar the locomotive of a short goods train that would one day at least be able to chase its own tail round the track. I hoped that my Christmas present might be a cheap loco. Initially keen on the 0-6-0 'Jinty', I later set my sights on a similar engine, newer to the catalogue (and using the same chassis and mechanism), the R153 black Saddle Tank, numbered 748. Since that has probably lost most readers' interest, I shall offer no more detail, though I could still list the items I assembled over months, and their prices in the old money, but one parting fling: a R193 length of small curved track cost 1s 3d, and so a basic circle would set you back 16s 0d! As I built up my collection, I kept everything in their original item boxes, carefully packing those into an empty cardboard groceries box. I used to take it to my grandmothers' houses on weekend afternoons, to get everything out and just look at it, trying to believe that one day things might actually be moving.

On the afternoon of Christmas Day, at Grandma Lil's house, on the table she used for eating and ironing, a short train ran around at last, powered by three 4.5v batteries connected by an R40 power unit. This gave no speed control, just forwards, backwards and off! Still, it was hugely better than nothing. 'I say, look at this, Doug,' said Uncle Ken, squatting to bring his eyes level with the circling train. 'It looks just like the real thing!'

I cannot explain why that enthusiastic comment pleased me so much; even if we had known how crude and toylike those mass-produced attempts have come to be considered by today's makers and collectors, or indeed how much more authentic (and expensive!) 21st Century products are, that might still not have made much difference to me that day.

Also near me lived the Kelly twins, Pat and Mick, both superb footballers, little field terriers and ball wizards. They sometimes joined Jon and me. For the first time in my life I had several willing companions, like tall, chubby Dave Arrowsmith, who did voices, for example, the one in the Coco Pops advert. To him I owe the ability to produce a Donald Duck voice, the generation of which is easier to show than to tell. Novices attempting to acquire this dubious art invariably waste much time and energy trying to persuade their vocal chords to do the business, but they are left completely out of it; air is squeezed forward from the cheeks, not the lungs, into the mouth, usually on one side only, whilst varying the amount by which the oral cavity is opened. The lips and tongue attempt to make the consonants, achieving some approximation of intelligible sounds. It was the voice actor, Clarence Nash, who started this off, though others took over from him in Disney's animations. Since Nash is said to have continued representing the cheerfully irascible character to audiences until not long before his death at the age of 81, I may still have some time to entertain young people! Over the years I several times surprised or teased classes by turning on Donald in the middle of nothing in particular, either because my auditors were being plain unresponsive, or as a practical joke: wait until they are all working silently, with heads down. Stroll in front of the class, facing away from them. Call out 'What's the big deal?' or something else when they are not looking. Then spin round and pounce sternly with, 'Who said that?' One lot of eleven year olds fell for it for half a lesson in the 1980s.

Another companion for the walk home was Mike Hazelwood, who like any other keen amateur boxer had his dark hair cut short and neatly tidied. This was the moment for us all to discover what was on top of our heads. With me, it was Jon who started off the Age of the Comb. He raked his long hair up, back and to one side, with a ruler straight parting. When he let it flop forwards, it came to his chin. The hair cream must have left him with a heavy top load. He would stop in mid-step in front of a shop window, check himself, pat things a little, and then take his comb from the inside pocket and rake away. A prize-winning pony could not have been groomed so dutifully! My lighter, softer hair would not stay where I tried to put it for longer than a minute. How wasted those labours have turned out to be. I lost all of my top growth in my early twenties. It has never troubled me or seemed to matter. Nevertheless, when a slight friend or new acquaintance suddenly notices my capillary sparseness and cheerily discovers, 'You're really bald, aren't you?' I feel more disdain than gratitude. Do they actually think that, in nearly half a century, I have not somehow noticed? It would be mildly comforting to know that the photographer at my goddaughter cousin's wedding is still daily and even better nightly visited by the intestinal scorpion I wished on him for publicly referring to me as 'Baldy' as we adjusted our positions for the group photograph. Love all men.

Another classmate, Patrick Burns, introduced me to trainspotting. It must have been on a holiday weekday that we took a bus to the city centre, alighted in Lawley Street and entered the palatial building. The entrance and booking hall immediately awed you with its scale, the high glazed dome and lights creating an ecclesiastical or monumental feel which the booking hatches, surrounded by stone arch décor with an end-on gabled roof increased. For 3d you could buy a platform ticket which allowed you to wander around the platforms looking for new or exciting engines. Though we sometimes deviated, particularly on weekday evenings, by visiting New Street, for the London Midland Region engines, the ex-GWR machines were what I yearned for. The named classes of Kings, Castles, Halls, Manors and Granges, especially those hauling expresses like the Cornishman, had an old fashioned splendour. Even in these last years of steam, they were kept in beautiful condition, their dark green paintwork clean and gleaming, with copper and brass embellishments to their boiler fittings. As they rolled in clanking with steam shut off, to rest hissing at the end of the down platform, the whole ground vibrated wonderfully. Everything about this place was superior: the signs, the wrought iron, the scale and proportions of the buildings. The summer after I left St Francis and had seen Patrick for the last time (he was understood to be joining Cotton College, to train for the priesthood), I spent many Saturday afternoons at the station on my own, changing platforms via the subway to get as near as possible to the glamorous arrivals. That an eleven-year-old was entrusted to do this, travelling around without an adult, would hardly be believed today, though my parents simply had no worries. I never felt the slightest bit at risk.

One afternoon, I used some of the coins in my pocket to buy a return ticket to Shrewsbury, standing all the way there and back in the crowded corridor coach. We hurtled along behind a named locomotive, most probably a Castle, at an astounding speed, bumping and lurching. Even to take the slower non corridor branch line train the one stop from Snow Hill to Hockley was a 6d treat. Once alighted, Patrick and I would spend as much time as we could writing down numbers and watching the diesel shunter marshalling trains in the goods yard. This pleasure would be terminated when a British Railways employee told us to leave, which we did as lingeringly as we dared.

The months I spent in Lozells taught me valuable independence. Particularly, I learned to travel around on public transport, buses and trains. On my own I could get to places on time. Looking at an old A-Z of Birmingham, I realise that I walked appreciable distances too. I do recall one occasion, during the school's summer holiday, when Mom, Sylvia, David and I walked from Burbury Street to Grandma Elsie's in Perry Barr. I later walked that route, and further, with mates returning from cricket. It was at least 1½ miles between the two houses, and so the return walk, with Mom and me taking turns behind the push-chair, which could accommodate both my siblings certainly made us hungry for tea! When Uncle Gordon walked me to the Aston Villa ground one evening, the somewhat greater distance became more tiring on account of the swinging pace he kept up, fit practising sportsman that he was!

The strain of living at Annie's told on everyone, not least our hostess. I cannot remember exactly when, but the stress actually made her ill. She heard noises which she called 'the bumping'. She went a little stranger in her behaviour, though the details have left me. She made repeated visits to 'Dr Pinner', who was actually called Dr Pincent. Understandably, our prolonged presence was making her unsettled and unhappy. Eventually, she had to go away to a psychiatric ward for some weeks. None of us had wanted this sad development. My father visited her very regularly. The only incidental benefit was that our tension lowered when the unfortunate woman was in hospital. This must have been right towards the end of our stay, in 1961. On her return, she had become calmer. She went away for a holiday with friends. On return, she recommenced her work. Time passed.

For the autumn term of 1960 my class became Senior 1. This meant being with Hickey in the annexe, scene of the gladiatorial event already mentioned. For the first few weeks my place was on the far left of the room, which turned out to be the slow lane.

My partner, Michael Brown, treated me on many mornings with little presents, like a new rubber or pencil sharpener, evading my enquiries from where they had come with dismissive generosity. Besides, he knew a shop on the Lozells Road where all this stuff was cheap. When I later went there on my own and found that W.H.Smith had not reduced any of their prices I came to my own conclusions about what one of my father's headmasters referred to as 'purchasing items without paying for them.' I politely refused his presents, saying I had enough of whatever it was; he passed them to someone else.

As for work, we crawlers were on the orange maths text book, which was baby stuff, disappointing even. After several pages of red ticks, Mr Hickey put me on the blue book, which was a little more interesting, but still below the level I had reached at St John's. Maybe the cane did provide some sort of effective incentive! What clinched my immediate transfer from Lane 1 to Lane 5 was a composition I wrote entitled *The Memories of a Retired Railway Station*. Naturally, I jumped at the chance to do that one! Though I cannot believe it was anything out of the ordinary, it made Mr Hickey purr. He brought it in next day and, first thing, read it to the whole class. I had to leave Michael and take a place next to one of the Kelly twins.

Relatively few recollections remain of that term. We were collected by coach on the Tuesday and Thursday morning of each week. Woodwork was on the Thursday. That started a couple of weeks before Science on Tuesdays. The workshops were two rooms at a school not far from the gas works in a turning off Dartmouth Street. Under razor sharp, stick-enforced discipline, we were divided into the two groups to spend the whole morning learning how to use tools for marking and cutting: gauges, squares, marking knives. The old school woodwork and P.E. teachers were frequently notorious for their brutality, lack of humour and constitutional unpleasantness. They all seemed to foster a pathological misanthropy, reserving its highest intensity for boys. Perhaps they had somehow omitted that phase in their own lives. Or was it that, standing all day for five or perhaps six days a week in term, they all developed intolerable haemorrhoids in the early stages of their careers, which understandably inflamed their tempers? I resorted to my old technique of saintly silence and spaniel-like attentiveness. And I really liked learning to work with wood too! For registration after arrival in the morning, all fifty or so of us stood in a line along the long side of the massive main room. The crusty old senior called our names scarcely audibly while his junior strode up and down, in front of us and then back around us in a loop, swishing his cane every few steps.

The school for Science was off Summer Hill Road, in Goodman Street. I suppose if you taught in such a place and had a visiting class brought in every week as part of your timetable you might well be apprehensive about having four dozen unknown boys arrive for one morning a week in your laboratory, where strictness is essential for safety anyway. Bunsen burners and even the milder chemicals are not casual playthings either. And boys from Lozells? Even those used to getting by in inner city areas like Ladywood might find that prospect daunting. So, a fierce reception there too, a prison camp atmosphere of silent standing to attention, the abrupt on-the-spot caning of a boy who spoke a syllable. Short, basic lessons. A weekly test out of ten on what we did last time, mostly single word answers on slips of paper. What does heat do? Rise. Which bit of the Bunsen flame is hottest? The tip of the inner, blue part. What does more oxygen do? Make the flame roar.

The most amusing aspect of both these away mornings was that the coach driver was my grandmother's neighbour's son, and Mrs Horobin ('Mrs Horrible') herself the hatted, Coronation Street style old woman who stood in the aisle and kept an eye on us! I think it upset her to start with that I knew all about her part-time descent into such menial occupations and could tell Grandma Lil. We liked to keep up the pretence of being an independent lady of some private means!

The term passed. The season cooled, nights drew in, things continued much the same. Julian Foukes (pronounced with the vowel sound of 'sound' and 'found') was hospitalised with a brain tumour, I think his second. In the months I knew him his head was always shaved almost bare. Brian McKessie ('Messy'), another misplaced simpering soul, once or twice lived up – or should that be 'down' – to his sobriquet by soiling himself. Well before the time the four Senior classes left Wills Street for ever, to be pioneers at Hamstead, realisation had occurred that I was misplaced. In January I should join my rightful age group, back with Mr Woods.

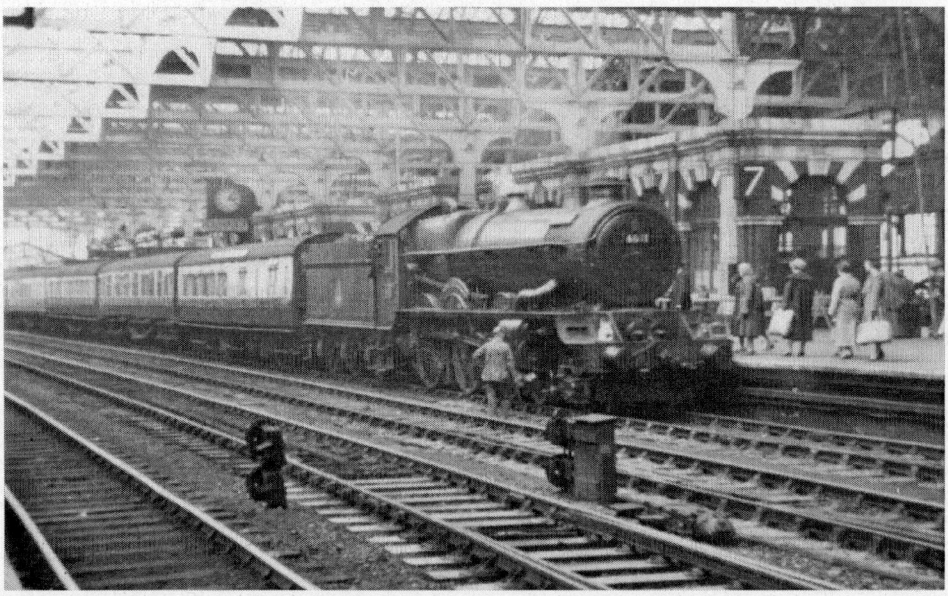

Ex-GWR 4-6-0 King James I at Snow Hill Station

A World Elsewhere

Come on, Sir. Now you set your foot on shore
In Novo Orbe*; here's the rich Peru,*
And there within, sir, are the golden mines,
Great Solomon's Ophir!
Ben Jonson, *The Alchemist*

Every beginning peels some old layers away. Morning, the new house, a child's first breath … For most of my life autumn has signified not the death of the year, but a hopeful, even joyful commencement: new clothes, books, rooms, maybe buildings, people, experiences, aspirations, possibilities … It may be mainly that, for six-plus decades, September has brought the next school year; but it is assuredly a sensuous celebration too. Those colours in gardens, grounds and parks; the thrilling coolness of the air; the blended scents distilling from summer … In just over nine weeks from today, I shall, quite unexpectedly and incredibly, be rewalking the paths I first trod forty-seven years ago to the day, when I started my first teaching job. I had just started living in a peculiar, single-storey flat 200 or so years old, a conversion of workmen's or stable boys' storage rooms. The shortcut to the school buildings was through some woods and shrubberies, past formal flower beds and lawns … This time, I shall take a long walk round from the car park on the other side of the fifty-seven acre estate in order to climb what is more or less the same path to my first meeting with what will be my pupils for only one term, while their regular teacher is away on maternity leave. Apart from the wry thought that it was my wife who took the first ever such permitted absence, under the new legislation, in 1981, I shall be savouring those few minutes in which I hope to recapture the memories and feelings of that wonderful beginning, the more yellowing light, the morning crispness, fragrance of wet, trodden grass and woodland musks …

After the Seniors moved to their separate facilities, St Francis became a Junior School, with more space for us in every sense. Though it was to be our eleven-plus year, we felt, without saying it, liberated: the oldest class in a blink. Mr Woods was more relaxed too. He smiled and joked. Only the fiery Irish lady teacher who moved next door to us sounded unhappy.

At the start of the year we sat practice papers, which must have been for the teachers to have some idea of how we were likely to fare, because they were never returned or commented on. The weeks passed, relatively untroubled. The only incident I recall was when, towards the end of one lunch break, Michael Nelson was led across the playground to the office, his whole head covered in blood! We feared the most terrible of outcomes. Would we ever see him again?

Twenty minutes later, he was in the lesson with us looking perfectly fine! Mr Woods invited him to tell the tale.

Since he lived just around the corner, Michael went with a near neighbour to have lunch at their homes every day. As they were returning, they jogged along dribbling an old tennis ball and passing it across the pavement to each other. When the other boy gave Michael a pass, he accidentally fired a gravel chipping from the pavement with the ball. Catching him right in the middle of the forehead, it had caused the tiniest wound. It did not even require a plaster when everything was cleaned up. Mr Woods explained that, in the right – or perhaps wrong – place a small cut can cause quite dramatic blood flow, and that a very little blood went a long, long way too! I am not sure whether that made us feel better or worse; I have certainly never since then seen such a sight.

Singing lessons suddenly became fun. With spiteful Mr Davis elsewhere, our sessions were led from the piano by virtuoso Mr Duckworth, who turned out to be both affable and cheerful. More than once he walked in, sat at the old upright without removing his raincoat and played some nineteenth century showpiece to us. I actually recognised Hungarian Rhapsody No 2 by Liszt; I had played Dad's orchestral version on our old wind up record player! It took both sides of the disk. To hear and see one man, straight off the street, do all that with just his hands left me speechless. Mr Duckworth did not have to ask for silence or wait for Mr Woods to settle us down; he started to play and we listened without a peep until the final chords, when we clapped our heads off for him. Sing another sea shanty from the BBC book or listen to something like that? Hmm! Tricky choice!

There was the time, perhaps during the previous year, when the Headmaster came into our singing lesson after a few minutes. He simply took over and said he was going to teach us a song. He fastened the song sheet to the board with some sticky stuff, gave a book to the pianist and taught us this:

Oh, the sons of the Prophet are hardy and grim
And quite unaccustomed to fear
But none were so reckless of life or of limb
As Abdulla Bulbul Ameer.
When they wanted a man to encourage the van
Or to harass the foe in the rear
Or to take a redoubt they would always send out
For Abdulla Bulbul Ameer.

There are heroes in plenty, and well known to fame
In the ranks that were led by the Czar,
But the bravest of all was a man by the name
Of Ivan Potschjinski Skidar.
He could imitate Toole, play Euchre and Pool
And perform on the Spanish guitar.
In fact quite the cream of the Muscovite team
Was Ivan Potschjinski Skidar.

One morning the Russian had shouldered his gun
And assumed his most truculent sneer
And was walking down town when he happened to run

Into Abdulla Bulbul Ameer.
"Young man," says Bulbul, "can your life be so dull
That you're anxious to end your career?—
For, infidel, know—you have trod on the toe
Of Abdulla Bulbul Ameer".

"Take your ultimate look upon sunshine and brook,
Make your latest remarks on the war;
Which I mean to imply you're going to die,
Mr. Count Cask-o-whisky Cigar."
Said the Russian, "My friend, my remarks in the end
Would avail you but little, I fear,
For you'll never survive to repeat them alive,
Mr. Abdulla Bulbul Ameer."

Then the bold Mameluke drew his trusty chiboque
And shouted "Il Allah Akbar"
And being intent upon slaughter, he went
For Ivan Potschjinski Skidar.
But just as his knife had abstracted his life
(In fact he was shouting "Huzza!")
He felt himself struck by that subtle Calmuck,
Count Ivan Potschjinski Skidar.

The Consul drove up in his red-crested fly
To give the survivor a cheer,
He arrived just in time to exchange a goodbye
With Abdulla Bulbul Ameer.
And Skobeleff, Gourko and Gorsechekoff too
Drove up on the Emperor's car
But all they could do was cry "och-whilliloo!"
With Ivan Potschjinski Skidar.

There's a grave where the waves of the Blue Danube roll,
And on it engraven so clear
Is: "Comrade, remember to pray for the soul
Of Abdulla Bulbul Ameer."
There the Muscovite maiden her vigil doth keep
By the light of the true lover's star
And the name that she murmurs so sadly in sleep
Is Ivan Potschjinski Skidar.

I understand that there are variant wordings to this Victorian music hall song, but I have been able to alter those of only the first and last stanzas to what we learned. I shall never have a certain idea why Tom O'Loughlin chose to do this. Possibly he wanted a good sing-song, or to show us that you could have harmless, rollicking fun together. I thought then that he and his friends most likely sang this sort of thing in the Catholic Men's Club with their beers! I have never forgotten the melody.

Eventually, the eleven-plus test day arrived. I think there were two papers, in booklets to be completed. When I began to read the questions, I understood why Mr Woods had not gone over the practice papers: they were the same ones! Presumably Birmingham Education Committee used their test papers repeatedly year in, year out; or perhaps they had a bank of a few, e.g. A, B, C, D, which they rotated. Otherwise, St Francis somehow had sufficient spare copies in advance to us to have our unmarked dummy run, which of course gave our teachers some idea of how we were going to perform. It was at least a dubious way to handle important, indeed life-changing assessment instruments, but I do not believe it can have made much, if any, difference. My classmate Stephen and I were the only ones who seemed to notice anyway. The one unexpected and puzzling section for me was right at the end, on the blank back page of the booklet, after all the test questions. It simply asked you what you thought of the examination. How could I offer them anything to impress or interest them? I politely reassured them that, in my experience, it had been a fair and reasonable business, with no dirty tricks, though probably not in those particular words.

These days, especially in private schools, it would be different. The carelessly or shamefully leaked public examination paper is published – or even sold or perhaps peddled – on the internet or via social media within minutes of release. Even before our technology, mothers grilled their sons and daughters on entrance examination questions as soon as they had them in the car, writing down as much as they could glean to pass on to younger siblings or their best friends. Thousands of tutors and businesses offer a legal equivalent, gathering as much of whatever they can from specimen papers and their own research, before giving sessions to assist the passage of little Sam or Samantha to the chosen Big School. My pennyworth, after over thirty years' involvement in the admissions assessment business, across the age range from seven years to sixth form, is that that the more you have to do to assist applicants, the worse you are likely to be making their future lives. Raw ability will always reflect the light just as the opposite must dully absorb it. Experienced teachers are usually very skilled at identifying intelligence and potential, particular in their specialist subjects. The essay one fourteen-year-old girl wrote for us in the 1970s entrance exam had one or two technical flaws or slips, but more noticeably an originality and individuality of ideas and expression that made me smile 'oh yes!' to myself. The same girl, a few months later, had to spend an extra hour after school in detention one Friday, having fallen foul of a grumpy female colleague. Her punishment? To do the very thing she loved and excelled at: write! Wandering around the room, I glanced at her desk, instantly seeing the priceless observation, 'It must be so boring being a clock.' She has gone on to a long and successful career as a journalist and biographer, regularly appearing on television.

Some weeks later, a letter arrived to inform my parents that I had qualified to go to a grammar school. They had to choose three from a list of Birmingham schools, in order. I did not know any better than my parents and the prejudices of my Catholic education so far, and so St Philip's in Edgbaston, my father's and uncles' old school, was placed first, with King Edward's second, and Handsworth Grammar third. Many years later I learned that my new school fared quite well in the Eleven-plus Stakes, with six of us offered grammar school places and three the chance to attend technical colleges. Only two at the most from St John's in Balsall Heath cleared the hurdle, for all the flogging and praying. All six of us accepted the default option, St Philip's first. After more waiting, Alan Cherrington, Stephen Rice and I learned that we had made it. Dad bought me a Triang Track Cleaning Car, R344 price 9s 6d, as a reward.

My teachers were pleased; Dad was delighted! He had so many fond memories of his own school days and friends. I could already retell several of his stories about colourful or eccentric pupils and masters … the fourth year boy who wore plus-fours and rode his motor cycle at speed around the crowded playground, as near to the walls of the enclosing buildings as he could, the French teacher (Benny Barratt? Jack 'Hambone' Hamnet?) who could not suppress his chuckles when he strode into the room to see a huge and very recognisable cartoon caricature of his colleague the chemistry teacher 'Bladder' Fitzgerald in chalk on the board: 'Who did that? Ha, ha, ha, ha, ha! Rub it off immediately! Ha, ha, ha! 'Creamy' Kiernan, history teacher, author of a book on Lawrence of Arabia, whom he had known … 'Tell us how you won the war, sir – and he did! It was much more interesting than the Tudors and Stuarts!' Most affectionately, he reminisced about his first Head, Fr Vincent Reade, nephew (?) of Charles, author of *The Cloister and the Hearth*, Arthur Conan Doyle's favourite book. Dad's nickname for Father Vincent was 'Twink', though I have encountered the more credible 'Vink', which may have been earlier.

Principal from 1920 to 1937, Twink or Vink appears to have been an excellent Headmaster, yet again illustrating the significance of that office. The man or woman in charge makes – or breaks – a school. Dad's emphatic claim was that everyone was happy under this diminutive man of the cloth, one of the Oratory Fathers, who was succeeded halfway through Dad's time by Terence Larkin, a lay headmaster. Dad had no polite term for him! He upset people and spoiled the place. Petty and pointless-seeming rules were suddenly introduced in numbers. The masters hated being forced to wear their gowns throughout the day, for example. One story told how a respected classroom veteran, on a boiling July afternoon, after fidgeting and trying to scratch between his shoulder blades repeatedly, pulled the item off and flung it into the corner of the room exclaiming at the top of his voice, 'I'm not wearing this blasted thing a moment longer. Another damned silly idea!' His liberating outburst accidentally coincided with Larkin's putting his head around the classroom door: laughter and sustained cheers from 4X. Twink had tolerated benignly, leaving everyone at their ease; you fully appreciated his humanity, his saintly, if at times amusing, love of people. Could his successor have been as appalling as Dad insisted?

Terence Larkin would still be in post when I joined the school in September 1961!

One afternoon that summer Dad took the afternoon off work for us to attend the information meeting. We sat down in the large hall with Mr Morris ('Moggy'), Deputy Head. He had taught Dad English. English Literature, eventually my specialism, was the only School Certificate subject Dad failed!

In the late 1930s there were two forms per school year, X and Y. My intake was to make up Form 1, 1X, 1Y and 1Z, in that order of ability. I was to be in Form 1, with Stephen Rice. Alan Cherrington would be separated from us into 1Z. In his droning drawl (What? English teacher?) Moggy told us that I had fared well in the exam. Before we left for home, Dad walked me round some of the old buildings, the ones he had known, pointing out the exact spots this and that had happened: ' … oh, and do you know, one day when it was absolutely tipping it down, a hoarse whisper came from the back of the room, "Horse on the roof!".' I had rarely known him so voluble and animated. He could not have been happier. He had no inkling about the numb dread silently swelling its icy masses within me, an Arctic vastness of three-dimensional expansion.

One Saturday in August the whole family accompanied me to the uniform supplier, Dunne and Company at Five Ways: blazer, badge, cap, grey socks, maroon sports jersey (for 'my' House, St Thomas More's), white football shorts with green banded tops. What properly interested and excited me was my first pair of football boots, bought that afternoon from one of several shoe shops on the Lozells Road: the standard pair of 'knockers', hard toe-capped leather articles with six wicked nail and leather studs. The basic model, all dull buff, retailed at 19s 11d – structurally and functionally identical to the deluxe version, shiny black with white synthetic lace hole strips which set you back 29s 11d. Please do not squander any of your finite allocation of earthly time resolving which I chose!

The summer holiday passed, hot days of street games, trips to parks, bus rides to railway stations, solitary roamings, weekly walks to the Handsworth public library on Soho Road, Wednesday afternoon trips on the number 11 to Uncle Ken, newly married, living with Veronica above and behind his first optician's practice on Oxhill Road, just around the corner from his mother in Windermere Road. (He took the afternoon off mid-week, and would indulge me, for example, by taking me to Handsworth Park to fly a superb balsa wood glider I had made from a half-a-crown kit and painted royal blue. One afternoon, it made numerous perfect circular flights around a whole field, returning sedately to the launch point.)

One Wednesday, Ken was painting the outside of the house, which gave me the important role of ladder stabiliser … while Uncle ascended to the first floor window, I planted one foot on the second rung up, holding both sides with my hands, theoretically steadying everything.

Uncle Ken had made himself a wire handle for the large pot of white gloss paint, looping it around the top and under the fold-over metal rim, tightened and secured by twisting the two ends of the wire round a couple of times: neat handiwork, he thought.

The best thing was that the almost full tin did not hit me directly. My exact central position under the painter's feet and legs allowed just the tight clearance for a serious head injury to be dodged.

A heavy tin of white gloss coming to an abrupt rest from a height of about twelve feet and arriving perfectly bottom down makes a curious combined sound of a simultaneous thud and heavy liquid slop. The impact speed, simple physics tells us, is just under 20 mph. Suppose a half gallon pot of paint is almost full, perhaps substituting the weight of the metal can for the amount of paint used, that is probably something between 5lb and 6lb. So, we arrive at an approximate answer of 1200 foot pounds or 1626 joules of kinetic energy.

That's an appreciable amount. It has to do something, go somewhere, be converted into another form of energy. In case you were ever thinking of disposing of some energy, just remember you cannot destroy it, only change it into another form ...

Some of those accumulated joules went into sound energy, with no apparent damage to anyone or anything. Most of the rest was transferred, in one or more shock waves, to the mass of white gloss paint, which had little time to decide what to do with this unexpected gift. Creditably rapidly, it had a brainwave: let's run a little experiment. See how far we can travel on a few hundred bonus joules!

Considerable amounts of the stuff shot joyfully up from the ground to give my best – my only – pair of grey, school shorts a hug. I stood there, cold, dripping gloopily.

'Well, blow me!' Uncle Ken said, descending. 'That was a brand-new tin as well!'

He then looked at me. And laughed. Aunt Veronica, who had heard the noise, opened the kitchen door, screamed briefly, and then caught Ken's roar. She laughed till she had to bring up her apron to dry her eyes.

When Dad collected me in the car, I was wearing Ken's tennis shorts, waist size 36 inches. My waist was probably about 22 inches. I have yet to see the funny side of the experience.

The summer weeks passed. I think we had another week in Somerset.

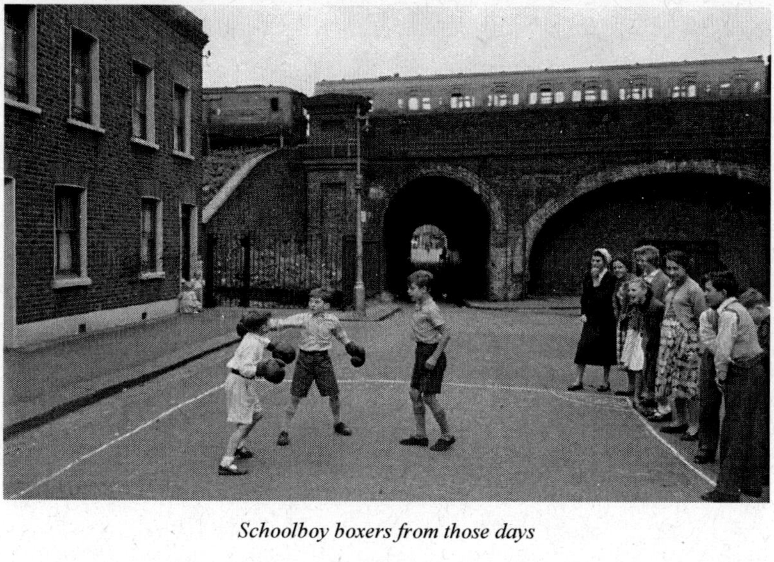

Schoolboy boxers from those days

Induction

I am the one
Who sounds loudest in my head.

Edwin Brock, *Song of the Battery Hen* (1977)

Put your bag and anything else you're holding on any desk and stand behind it. Hurry up. Don't talk. Last boy, close the door.

Stand perfectly still. I said, 'Still'!

This is your form room, Form 1. I am Mr Jones, your form master. You will come to this room when the bell rings at ten to nine every morning and wait for me. When I walk in, you will all stand up and stay silent until I tell you to sit down.

You will sit in alphabetical order by surname, starting at this front right hand corner of the room. So, come to the desk I give you when I call your name:

Abbott, Bailey, Brennan … come up here, Brennan … , Caffrey, Casey, Colling, Culwick … at the back, the *back* desk, Culwick …

… next row, from the back: Doherty, Ellis, Foley, Gannon, Goodwin, Hay – front desk, Hay … row three, from the front: Hayes, Hearne, Higgins, Hope, Hussey, Lunn … from the back again: Malpas, McCormack, McKewan, Milne, Moran … how do you say that – Mor*an*? ... oh, *Mor*an, Nevil ……[other Catholic-sounding names] …….. last row: Pegg, Rankin, Rice … and Williams. That's thirty-five. Interesting number. All numbers are interesting, as you will find out. I shall be teaching you mathematics.

Sit in silence while I complete the register. Leave your bags alone. Don't open the desks.

These little notebooks I'm giving you … pass these back … come on - hurry up! … are your homework diaries. Write your name and 'Form 1' on the front where it tells you to. Then copy your timetable from the board behind me *exactly as I've written it* (I'll explain what it means later) into the page at the beginning, which has a table for it. Underneath, for each day of the week, you will write down your homeworks, copying them from the book *exactly* as I've done it, three every evening until the weekend, when you will have five. You will take at least twenty to thirty minutes on each piece of work and write the time you took in the column on the right of the section for each day. Do that as soon as you've finished the work, or you'll forget.

At the weekend, you must ask your mother or father to sign the book for the week and hand it in to my desk on Monday morning at registration. In our form period first lesson on Friday afternoon I shall slipper any boy who fails to meet either of those requirements, or whose homework diary is incomplete or messy. Don't worry: there will be at least one every week.

Any master – or prefect – can, and will, hit you at any time for any reason, or (in the case of a sixth form prefect) just because he doesn't like the way you're looking at him – or not looking at him – or he's just having a bit of fun in front of his mates.

You, Culwick, are correctly seated, according to alphabetical order, at the back. But after a few weeks, you will swap places with Bailey and sit in the front desk but one. This will upset my orderly mathematical way of looking at life, but by then our experience of your failure to understand and follow instructions will have forced us to read the file from your primary school, where we'll find that you were born totally deaf in your left ear. So you're going to be a nuisance. Even after we've moved you, Mr Walker, your French teacher, will smack you really hard several times across the left side of your head for not answering his abrupt French question, when he's repeated it in your face, and you have feebly informed him, 'I don't understand, sir.'

Ellis, you will prove much less able than we have expected you to be, and so in a few weeks I'll put you down into IX, to be replaced by that curly-haired blond chap from Poland, Mickiewicz. None of us masters will ever learn how to say *Mitts-key-ay-vitch*, even though the class tells us every lesson, and so we'll all, as an educated joke relished by graduates, have a cheerful laugh every single time and call him *Micky Witch*.

As first formers, you're all fags, of course. That means we'll give you a hard time and you'll do what we tell you. That's everyone – teachers and boys. Everyone will instantly know you're a fag because you're the only lot wearing short trousers. Anyway, you all will look worried most of the time.

You'll queue up to go into lunch along the north Oratory wall in the playground, but only after every other year in the School has gone first. As you wait, usually for over half an hour, various older boys, especially second formers who've already eaten and that fat boy from the fourth form, will wander up and down the line, thumping you on the shoulders where it hurts, scragging you by the lapels of your new blazers against the wall and trying to knee you in the balls – if you've got any yet. It's because you're new.

You'll all try at all times not to be given the Blue Goldfish, but one of the beauties of this fine tradition is that it can be celebrated at any moment, in anyone's honour. I'd better explain. The idea is that any group of older boys will just decide to grab one of you, carry him off to the bogs, hold his head down in the bowl of one of them, and pull the chain. It makes you all laugh.

Sandwich eaters, you have to sit at the *very, very* end of the hall with all ages of boys. All the bigger ones will entertain you every day with their elbows, knees and fists while you try to eat your sandwiches. They'll grab those off you too, of course, and either eat them to save you the bother, or speed things up for you by chucking them in the disgusting waste bin. Sometimes they may increase the enjoyment of your food by squashing it all as flat as they can. Sliced white bread is especially good for this. Remember at all times: your KitKats, Wagon Wheels, chocolate digestives, crisps, apples or any other little extras put in your lunch bag or box by your mothers are actually meant for the older boys, who don't need to ask for them.

Water is provided for everyone. It's probably best if you let the second formers spit in your glass or pour its contents over the fly area of your shorts, so everyone can shout and laugh at you for pissing yourself.

If any of us catches any one of you eating your sandwiches anywhere apart from in the hall, you'll be slippered or caned.

This is a great school, a wonderful Catholic school. You've done very well to get here and to have made it into my form, which is the top one. We're all going to have real fun with you.

I imagine you just can't wait till you meet Itchy Green!

So, a warm welcome to St Philip's Grammar School!

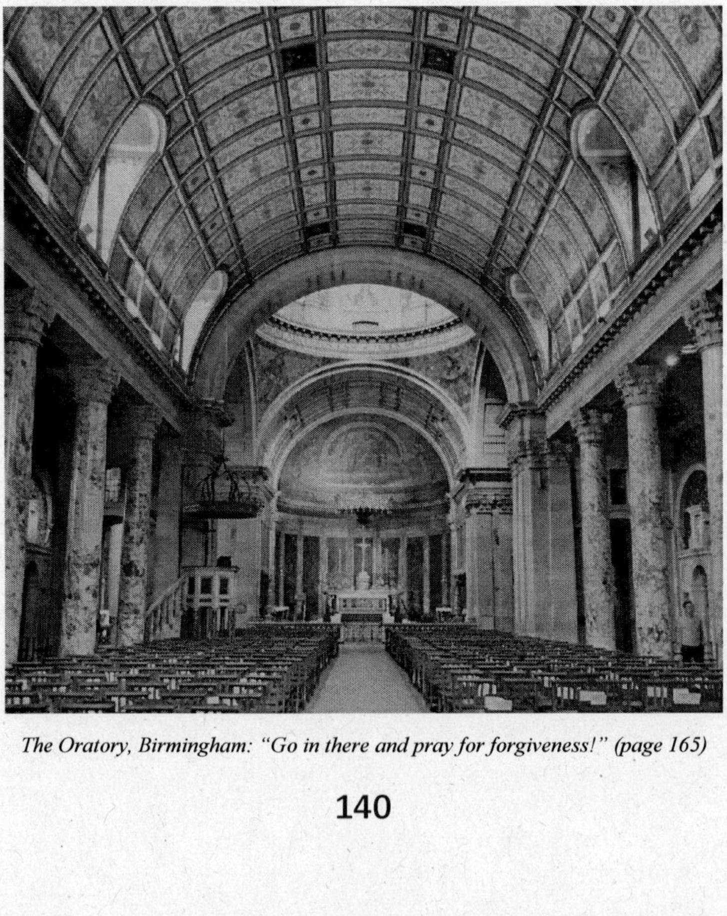

The Oratory, Birmingham: "Go in there and pray for forgiveness!" (page 165)

Fagged In

But words came halting out, wanting Invention's stay;
Invention, Nature's child, fled stepdame Study's blows;
And others feet still seem'd but strangers in my way.
Thus, great with child to speak, and helpless in my throes,
Biting my truand pen, beating myself for spite,
'Fool,' said my Muse to me, 'look in thy heart and write.'

Sir Philip Sidney, *Astrophel and Stella, 1*

For almost three weeks I have stalled. I have been trying to think of ways or perhaps a way to avoid being predictable, routine and potentially dull. Generations of my pupils might well have been tempted to risk the 'b' word at this point, standing well back of course …

The novelistic idea, of writing a prose dramatisation of an imaginary social gathering of the school staff either just before or perhaps a week after the start of the autumn term, discussing the new pupils, revealing their own characters etc fought for breath for a day or so after delivery, but then arrested and panted no more.

The fabricated letter home to his mother, from a student teacher telling of his first week at the school, kicked and yelled with some show of lustiness before suffering the parental rejection of a Roman citizen disdaining to pick up the infant laid at his feet on the grounds that it was illegitimate. In short, I was deviating to indulge myself.

I began to question myself on what I was doing and why. For what reason does anyone attempt to write an account of his or her life? Has one's experience been so unusual or extraordinary that a number of others might be illuminated or informed by it? Are there lessons or warnings that could be useful or necessary to share?

What are simple ways to be intolerably tedious? No doubt we all could supply some answers to that. Just as (Lansdowne's Law) we all boil at different degrees, so our *Nervus Irritabilis Individualis* twitches to its own trigger stimuli.

I react badly to whatever is predictable, already known, commonplace, humdrum, mundane, unvaried, repetitious, dull, ill or thoughtlessly expressed, cliché-blown, obvious, self-evident, inefficient, clumsy, ugly, laboured, lazy, to suggest a few sensitivities. There no doubt are others, many of them variants of these. It is not just word or idea choice, but structure and construction that I am squeamish about. Evil be indeed to the writer who makes every sentence a compound one, or who offers us the word *preprepare* or *preplan. Preprepare* does deserve special consideration. Since the Latin root *paro* meant 'get ready' you could think our derivative *prepare* had already added a note of anxiety before the more recent *overkill* of *preprepare*. But I digress. What do I suppose myself to be at? What do I wish to set down? Surely I must squeeze and shake it out, mindless of the form or substance, hoping that the inventive reader will perhaps think of something to do with it?

As I think back across fifty-eight years, it seems fair to state that the boys in Form 1 with me proved sociable, accommodating, able, accepting, harmless and good company. We did not bully amongst ourselves. In the other three first year forms, I recall but one boy, name lost, who threw his weight around, at least in the early stages, only himself to suffer a dreadful and very worrying accident towards the end of the year. One Monday afternoon in May, when we were distributed around the playing fields in separate games of cricket, while fielding at mid-on (without teacher supervision) this boy was hit in the eye by a firmly struck ball. Going immediately unconscious, he was carried limp from the field in the arms of the games master to where the ambulance would collect him. Of course, he should not have been moved. For weeks we heard nothing of him. Then, one day he returned, still wearing an eye patch, shaky and subdued. The old loud, boisterous, overbearing self had been succeeded by a quiet mildness.

To all of the older boys, we were sport and playthings. Since they had been through it, they made sure we had our share. Our caps and other things were snatched from us and hurled around. We were pushed and tripped. The fat fellow from the fourth form wandered around manhandling us. A thin-faced whippet of a prefect slapped one of our heads in the cloakrooms now and then. A boy in 1X, a very ordinary inoffensive sort, received the Blue Goldfish one lunchtime.

This perpetual out-of-lessons insecurity had a number of effects on me. After a few days I privately decided not to endure the threats and pummellings of the lunch queue and dining room tables. I stayed out of that part of things completely. For several weeks I just threw my carefully prepared sandwiches away – two rounds on sliced bread, wrapped in greaseproof paper and placed in a greaseproof bag, usually with an apple. Perhaps I found a remote corner to dispatch the apple in, or ate it at morning break, when such consumption was not prohibited. We understood very clearly, from our form master and on-high announcements in assemblies, that we were not to eat sandwiches anywhere except in the dining hall, and would be seriously punished if we were caught so doing. That could mean only one thing – or perhaps two: the cane or slipper. So I went hungry. Later in the year, practical furtiveness asserted itself; I wandered to the far side of the site, behind some terrapins near the multi-storey science building, and ate my sandwiches around the corners of workmen's sheds. That was some time after, in his end-of-term letter to parents, Mr Larkin mentioned the 'beautifully prepared and wrapped' food regularly found thrown in the litter baskets. My mother asked if I had been doing that. Of course I denied it. This is the first time I have confessed. The regime had made me secretive, dishonest.

Gradually, it also toughened me. I started to push back, to yell and thump – always choosing my skirmishes shrewdly. On one occasion, when that weasel prefect came bothering us in the cloakroom at the end of school, shouting at us and shoving us around, he went too far. He had already forced his way past me and down the central aisle between the rows of pegs when I picked up my school bag, weighty with as many books as it could hold, and with both arms hurled it as hard as I could at his retreating back. The jolt certainly shocked him. He stumbled forward, half turned round, failed to identify his assailant, and speedily continued forward, on his way out. I must have frightened him.

I should think our form master, R.M. (Richard?) Jones took a 14½" inch shirt and weighed little if anything above ten stones, which at his likely height of 5'9" made him light and slight. Already thin-faced, his verticality was emphasised by his aspiring curly hair, but his species for everyone and eternally was confirmed by his protruding crossed teeth and bounding manner: rabbit! Whether initiating us into Lowest Common Multiples and Highest Common Factors, starting us on trigonometry or slippering us in Form Master period on Friday afternoons (untidiness, lateness, omission to have homework diary signed etc), he sustained unrelievedly a twitchy chirpiness, with ever fidgeting lips and tongue. He evinced that mysterious joy in their subject mathematicians share, and still taught with enthusiasm. If I have a criticism, it is that, like many of his specialism and profession, he could not imagine that anyone might not instantly follow his lines of thought. He twitted me in my first ever algebra lesson when my search for an answer got me counting my way through the letters of the alphabet, but then most of the others had received some exposure to the topic in their feeder schools and – more to the point – he had offered no explanation of how things worked, just thrown the problem at us. Maybe that was legitimate – I certainly cottoned on fairly swiftly.

I think he ran the School Scouts.

My most cherished memory of our time with Richard Jones concerns his weekly readings of instalments from *The Hobbit*. With his salivary excitement, the Gollum portions delighted me powerfully. But why did he not tell us that J.R.R.Tolkien himself had briefly attended the school, before transferring to King Edward's? Perhaps he did not know, or forgot to mention it.

I am indebted to Mr Sutherland, 'Sarky', for the most invaluable grounding he gave us in grammar. His two secret weapons, NIPPAVAC and SOOCI, established for life the Parts of Speech and the functions of a noun or pronoun (in a sentence). I have used them in my teaching. Clearly in his sixties (or older), Mr Sutherland employed a deliberately phrased, half-voiced delivery, almost husky. Perhaps he had throat problems; he never shouted. When he smacked a boy's head mid-sentence with the volume he was holding, he kept his finger between the pages at his place. Nothing changed in the pace or pitch of his uninterrupted spoken delivery.

We were fed fairly dull fare: *The Lost World of the Kalahari*, *An Elegy on the Death of a Mad Dog*, *A Tragic Story* (Thackeray), *John Gilpin* … the only chosen reader that worked for me was *King Solomon's Mines*.

The syllabus content of History also remained vapid, fobbing us off with generalised material about Egyptians and Greeks. Mr Needham seemed as bored with it and us as he was angry with something. Most of the time he spoke whilst looking out of the window, hand in pocket, occasionally lashing out from nowhere with a furious slap at someone who (also) was not looking.

Apparently as an experiment, our form alone was to learn French in a different way from the other forms. Mr Walker, middling in respects of height, build and age, briskly told us on Day 1 that he would not be speaking any English after that first lesson. From Day 2 onwards, he impressed everyone, including himself, horribly well by implementing that threat. When increasingly irate repetitions failed, he would resort to sharp verbal prods of *hein*, accompanied by even sharper manual jabs. To assist our stumbling progress in these linguistic shadows, he issued us with a cloth-bound primer which alternated simple 'learning to read' style text and line drawings with phonetics. That is, the first double page had the foreign language in its everyday normal style: *le rat est noir, le chat est gris* and the following double page reprinted the illustration with the text rendered in international phonetics: ɭ̥ɘ ɾɑ ɛ ɳɯɑ, ɭ̥ɘ ʃɦɑ ɛ ɡɾɨ. (I am not sure whether I have remembered these accurately.) I believe the theory held that, if we used this sounds-alphabet from the start in speaking the language, we should make a better job of it. Meanwhile, the other forms moved ahead more swiftly in acquiring grammar and vocabulary.

I wanted to learn French. My father's knowledge of and excitement over the language encouraged me. I gave myself the same kind of practice repetition that an instrumentalist uses in learning scales and exercises. Do it over and over again, in all possible ways, until you have a ready facility. So, I rattled through the conjugations of all the verbs we learned in the positive, the interrogative, the negative and the interrogative negative. I went over and over the practice sentences in the exercises until I could do them at sight and up to speed :

> Marie donne du poisson (not *poison*, you idiot !) au chat.
>
> Pourquoi pleurez-vous, mon pauvre enfant? N'avez-vous pas un bon gâteau?

The phonetics nonsense mysteriously went away without acknowledgement. Walker even lapsed into English now and again. His explosive temper remained. Some time after he had been moved to the front of the room on account of his deafness in one ear, Martin Culwick (lamb-harmless, gentle, compliant) stared bewildered in shock when Walker spun round to him at the end of an interrogative torrent: *hein, Culwick*?

- Boy nonplussed. No response.
- Question loudly repeated, from three inches' distance, into boy's face.
- Boy, paralysed: *I don't know, sir!*
- Master delivers four resounding, swinging hits, open-palmed, to the near side of boy's head.
- The deaf side.

One November, Malcolm Rankin, who sat next to the windows on the left, idly doodled in the condensation. Soon after Period 1 started, Mr Pichler, our elderly Austrian Geography teacher, halted in mid-sentence. 'Who did that?' he demanded, with a break in his voice. 'Tell me: who did that!'

Rankin stood up. We were unsure what to expect. Mr Pichler walked towards the window, arm extended, finger trembling: a Swastika.

Raised Jewish, Mr Pichler had somehow become a Catholic. More moved than cross, he told us never to do a thing like that again. If we only understood what it meant …

As decent as he was thoughtless, Rankin freely spoke up to apologise:

> 'I'm very sorry, sir. I didn't do it against you, sir. I was just being very silly.'

This was the tallest boy in the form, later to prove our most elegant batsman. Mr Pichler told him to sit down. 'Yes, boys are silly sometimes,' he said, turned away from us.

He gave me double twenty for my project on *The Chiltern Hills*, which involved much meticulous copying (in turquoise *Quink*) from library books, and copious inappropriate quoting from Housman's *A Shropshire Lad*.

Practical Maths turned out to provide all the nastiness of my former woodwork lessons without any of the tools and wood. Mr Sutcliffe fear-taught us the kind of block writing used in technical drawings. We had to buy two 2H Venus pencils and a blade sharpener (from a stationer's at the top of Ludgate Street, opposite Snow Hill Station). Having cut the wood back to expose about 3/16th of an inch of lead, we rubbed the point on a strip of sandpaper to produce the right sort of tip. Sutcliffe's beastly unpleasantness, a sadistic relish in exacting a perfect preciseness in everything he did and demanded, may have been its own reward. I remember the man himself as offensively smug and humourless. Perhaps he too merely gave us first years an austere time as a matter of course, and allowed himself to melt a little as we aged; I left the school before that could be tested.

By contrast, 'Bushy' Bennett, the black-bearded biology master we visited at the top of the science block for a double lesson on Friday mornings, sat calmly engowned before us, talking us through elementary matters like the Characteristics of Living Things, the principles of Darwinian evolution, the structure of the cell, the amoeba and other genuinely engaging matters. His relaxed chats informed and enriched us without our realising it. We were free to put up a hand and ask about whatever occurred to us … the time zipped by. The only moment I noticed him falter was when a puzzled boy pressed him on *where* the *male* sperm emerged from and *how* it got to fertilise the *female* ovum … Moran and I shot our hands up, offering to help: *please, sir!*

'Ah! I see you know,' he said to us, and turned slightly red. 'Well,' waving our hands down, 'we'd better wait till everyone's ready.'

We copied a huge drawing of a house fly into our exercise books, and labelled its anatomy.

Often a prey to laziness: *42%* was Father Hamish's entry on my Christmas report. Tall, bony, so fair as to be approaching an albino, this teaching priest, like Father John Challenor, Head of R.E. and (as mentioned) form master of 1Z in 1961, was to establish some reputation in religious and intellectual circles. If the reader is curious about Father John, 'the priest who took a wife,' a résumé and appreciation of his life and career may be found at https://www.ccc4vat2.org.uk/ccc25/news-comment/news/129-an-uncompromising-christian-or-just-another-turbulent-priest His son's obituary for him appeared in the national press: https://www.theguardian.com/theguardian/2014/jun/04/john-challenor-obituary

Hamish Swanston was still in his twenties when he taught us. From what I have later learned of him, he earned respect as an intellectual, becoming one of the first Roman Catholic Professors of Theology, in his case at the University of Kent. Whilst the ex-priest John Challenor married an opera singer, Hamish Swanston published, amongst various largely theological works, books about the art and its exponents: *In Defence of Opera* (1978) and *Handel (Outstanding English Thinkers)*(1990). New to both the priesthood and teaching in 1961, this to-be-distinguished cleric and scholar taught twelve year olds rather poorly, showed off in front of them, did not appear to be particularly interested in such small fry but developed and exercised his eccentricity. With his black academic gown *over* his priest's black suit, he would stand towering before us at the front of the platform, arms outstretched in crucifixion pose, and woefully exclaim, like some Dickensian actor hamming the part of a ghost, 'Ooooh, my children!' We were not sure how to react. Michael Higgins entertained us afterwards with a plausible take-off.

Fr Hamish marked all our work out of twelve, 'because of the twelve apostles'. No one was ever given more than eleven and a half: 'God alone is perfect.' He set us comprehension exercises from a two-inches thick Catechism text book. Unlike in English, where I could usually score full marks or thereabouts, I fared dismally, on one occasion scoring three out of the holy dozen.

Question	What is a revelation?
MH (aged 12)	A revelation is a revealing.
Fr Hamish	Tautology! 0 marks!!

He offered no explanation of what tautology was, though I learned it from that moment. He completely failed to see that, for a child of that age, it was not an altogether brainless answer, since *revelation* was a less common word whilst *reveal* should be known to all. Of course, he wanted something religious about God's making himself known to man by some means, fires in clouds, burning bushes, blinding flashes and challenging voices on the road to Damascus and all that. I suppose I failed to oblige in that department because it all seemed rather phony and creepy anyway; I did not want to play his *God* game.

My father could do no better. When I drew an absolute blank about the homework task: *Write an explanation of* The Lord's Prayer *phrase by phrase*, he generously dictated one and half sides of his best ideas straight into my exercise book. After all, he had gained a Distinction in School Certificate Religious Studies! But *like son, like father* if I may tailor the expression to suit this occasion: Dad's homework was valued at five out of twelve!

Quirky and yet somehow fascinating, Fr Hamish is the one master from that year I should like to have engaged with when older and better able to question ideas. He strikes me in retrospect as a talented clown with a brilliant mind.

We had little contact with the Art department. Our regular teacher, Mr Bell-Foster, encouraged us to think of and experiment with texture and design. Approaching retirement, silver-haired and gently calm, he contrasted with his fiery colleague, the smock-wearing younger man who spent most of his time with the sixth form. When occasionally he had to cover our lessons, his impatience and ratty temper became the business of the afternoon.

I have left the real horror to the end: Mr Green. 'Itchy' Green. P.E. and Games.

A prize brute.

I left St Philip's after one year because that man made me so unhappy. There were other factors too, as will emerge. I earnestly vowed, on leaving, that if ever I were to set eyes on him again when I had become a man, I should punch his nose. This pledge even had a sequel, but not till I was twenty-seven. I recall the place and date: Swansea, Tuesday 26th July 1973. (If my intentions are realised, I shall not mention that occasion until the end of Volume 2 or the start of Volume 3 of my reminiscing!)

I do not hesitate from declaring that I was not the most physical of boys. I did not relish, certainly strove not to seek, rough and tumbles. I had learned to get by at St Francis' and had no problems with my peers at St Philip's even. But I was no street or playground fighter. In no way was I uninterested in or desirous of avoiding sport, games or physical activity; on the contrary, I hugely regretted that my father, of course owing to his boyhood polio, did not resemble his brother, Uncle Gordon. From when I was about eight onwards, at every opportunity he and I would make for the nearest park or playing field and spend as much of the evening as we could at ball games, often until it was too dark to see properly. I joined in every single playground game, according to the season, that I could. I always had a ball in my pocket or school bag for break times.

As I see him now, Green was nothing more than a bad-tempered bully, small of soul, vicious, uncompassionate. Like others of his kind, he could never have questioned himself. For him, a doubt would have presented an intolerable weakness. Had his impact not been so seriously and unnecessarily unpleasant, it would have been simple to see him as a comical caricature: the stereotypical hard thug of the gym and field, obtuse and truculent.

He was not so simply reducible. In his late fifties or very early sixties, perhaps 5'10" tall, straight-backed, virtually bald save for some silver flashes, he might have been a P.T. instructing sergeant in the Army: gladiatorially rugged of face, with dark cheek hollows and thin lips, shaved so close as to gleam, but with pronounced eyebrow feathers, he had a perpetual hawk-hatchet glare. Abrupt and fierce, he never smiled.

Green told us in Week 1 what we were to do. For Thursday's P.E. lesson, we were to wear nothing but our white plimsolls and white shorts. Even in the coldest part of winter, our tops were bare. Having stripped completely and donned our three permitted items (two pieces of footwear and the shorts), we had to run between the buildings, from the changing room to the lesson. We were allowed a certain time from when the lesson-change bell rang till when we must be in the gym, just an exact number of minutes by the clock on the wall. When, on one or two occasions only, a boy was a few seconds late (Milne? Ellis?), Hell's Furies were released, in the form of long-distance, full-lunged male screams, and red-faced rage that advanced at speed down the length of the room to the boy, to yell at full power in his face from close quarters. The offender was energetically informed of his nature and status: useless, slow, sloppy, spineless etc. Some punishment was imposed, perhaps a lunchtime detention in the gym. This would involve standing to attention for a defined period, e.g. 20 or 30 minutes, facing the wall and close to it. Green would be busying himself around the place, alert to any sound or movement, which would be instantly responded to with spleen.

At the start of each lesson, our kit was inspected. Plimsolls had to be whitened stiff. I used Meltonian 'Easy White', which came in a tube or bottle. It did the trick, but instantly dissolved in rain, leaving white traces where I walked. I retain the smell of the stuff. To ensure we were not wearing anything under our shorts, Green would sometimes pull the elastic away from a boy's waist and peer down. Underpants when exercising were unhealthy.

Lessons were never skills based, nor did they ever progress to the enjoyment of a game, like indoor soccer or basketball. Usually we stood in lines, separate from everyone else, and did exercises on the spot: standing to attention, then at ease, running on the spot, hopping, feet astride jumps and so on. At the end of several minutes of fast activity, we would be ordered to stand at attention, perfectly still. The eyes raked up and down the lines, scanning avidly to detect the smallest movement. You could hear the accelerated breathing, on winter mornings see the steam rising from bodies and mouths. If anyone flicked away a trickling bead of sweat, the blood-thickening roar 'Doan't scraatch, lad!' would ring around the whole room. That was how he earned his nickname of 'Itchy' Green. The accent came from South Wales. The nearest thing we got to a game was a buffeting session of British Bulldog or something similar where we were required to bash into each other or knock people clattering to the wooden floor.

Swimming took place first thing on Tuesday afternoons. After release by our form master, we had to make our way as quickly as we could – at a run – to the public baths in Monument Road, I suppose about a quarter or a mile away. On one occasion, I followed everyone else down the new road almost directly opposite the school gate. Still very much under construction, the housing development allowed us to cut a few yards off our route. The new road was not even yet open to traffic. The cambered road, gutters and drains had been made, and the kerb stones laid, but the paving slabs for pedestrians were still stacked up, ready to be laid. In single file, we ran along the kerb stones …

When I lost my footing and fell, the inside of my right knee, going right round for six inches, was cut open by the sharp edge of the stone. In fact, there were two gashes, the full length one, revealing a quarter-inch wide strip of white flesh, and a shorter, deeper one that bled more at the inner top end of the wound. Of course, it stung and looked a mess. Helped by a couple of classmates, I hobbled the rest of the way to where we waited, silently in two lines, outside the swimming baths. I had to hold my towel over the cut, to mop up the blood.

When he came out, someone told Green that I had had an accident. He took a brief look, tutted and told me to make my way back to the school office. No one came with me. Once in the buildings, I had to find the secretary, who I assumed (rightly!) would dispense first aid. She put a large dressing over the wound and all around my leg. By rights I should have been taken to hospital for stitches, at least for the shorter, deeper part of the injury. Healing took weeks. Since it was winter and we wore shorts, any contact, for example being caught there by a plastic football or just accidentally brushing against the leg of a desk or table, hurt furiously. The scar is with me still.

It was, however, early summer when the critical Green incident occurred. By then some major things had changed in my life, mostly for the better. I was beginning even to find ways of surviving in this new school environment. Then one event tipped the scales the other way, and I left St Philip's to start the next school year elsewhere.

First, momentous things awaited.

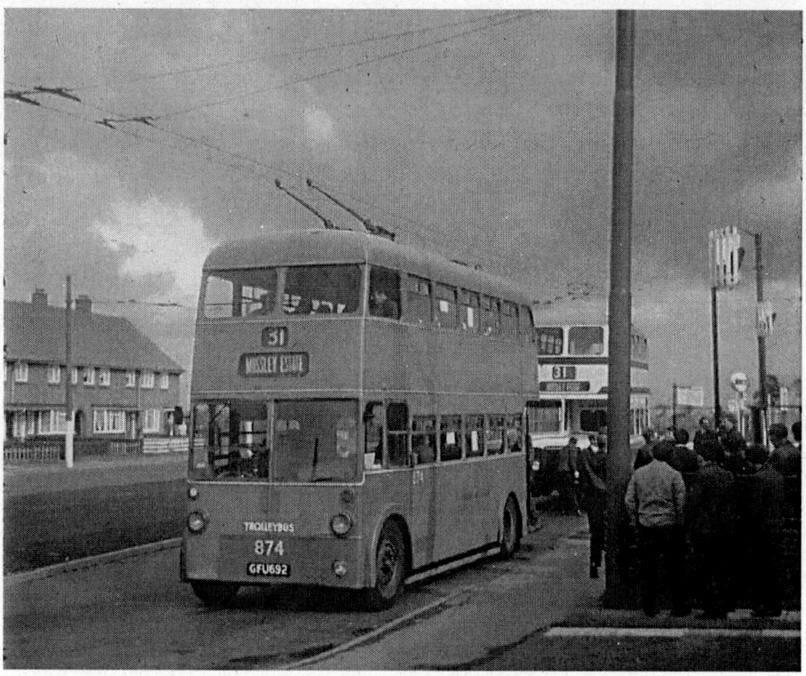

... trolleybuses, flat-faced cans of people [photo David Hillas]

Flight

And arrived at evening, not a moment too soon
Finding the place; it was (you may say) satisfactory.

T.S.Eliot *Journey of the Magi*

It was a Wednesday. That morning, probably at about a quarter past eight, I said goodbye to my parents, walked for the last time out of 202 Burbury Street, then down the hill to Nursery Road, which I crossed to catch the number 8 Inner Circle bus.

I have concluded that it was a cold, but initially dry day in Birmingham on 6th December 1961. I cannot forget that date, since it came to have a recurring significance, as will emerge. I would have been wearing my conventional navy-blue belted raincoat and the still oversize brown leather gloves my father had bought me the previous winter for 11s 3d, an adult pair I would grow into over the next three or so years.

Am I alone in cherishing certain solo journeys?

I do not recall how the day passed. Shortly after four o'clock, on exiting the school gates, I turned not left, to travel back to Lozells, but right, to walk to a different bus stop on the Hagley Road. Wide, busy, broadly pavemented, this respectable main thoroughfare conducted vehicles westwards out of the City. But I was going *into* it, via nearby Five Ways, along Broad Street, leading to the monumental gilded statues of distinguished former citizens, Matthew Boulton, James Watt, and William Murdoch, and some elegant neo classical buildings.

From where I alighted, possibly near the old Town Hall, I had to walk across town to, was it Corporation Street, opposite large, illuminated department stores, Christmas decked but not unduly swarming midweek, to walk along the line of sheltered bus stops for my Midland Red, the 118 to Walsall, via Great Barr. The pavements were full, the bus stands thronged, the ground shining wet. The shoppers and homegoing work people had no idea. Just an ordinary schoolboy, going home.

I could have directed the driver along his route, I already knew the streets and roads so well from travelling around in Dad's black Morris. The 118 even passed through Perry Barr, very near to Grandma Elsie's road. I always strained to see it. Before that, the cinema's neon sign, mauvely shining. Odeon. Then through the traffic lights, the Crown and Cushion pub on the left, past Perry Barr station, the dog track, and along the dual carriageway passing a mile or two of housing, mostly semi-detached family homes. Later, the curious pre-fabs on Great Barr's outskirts, squat shoeboxes of dwellings, surely too restricting for conceivable living. So, past the small parade of shops, steam blossoming from the laundrette, swiftly drifting to dissipate. Another cinema, the Horns and Queslett traffic lights, more shops, thinning out, and houses, the University of Birmingham athletics ground. The road widened. Snow was falling. In the vehicles' headlights, on the green verges, white patches gathered. Larger detached houses, set back, open plan, hedgeless front gardens. As always, I sought the upstairs grand piano, lid permanently propped high, in the futuristic glasshouse home of some musician. Both the huge first floor music room and the matching ground floor lounge beneath it were invisible walled, entirely glass, Venetian blinds being variously lowered, sometimes shuttered, at others louvred. At night the whole house usually blazed light, otherwise glowing like a giant's Chinese lantern.

After the Broadway roundabout, we continued north for the last mile or more, into Walsall town. I watched more attentively, nearing my stop, unfamiliar with this unknown stretch. Dad always turned right before this part. Early evening traffic in the narrowing streets, shops pressing brightly in on us from both sides. Our progress slowed: vehicles, crossings, pedestrians … Finally, a loop of streets to the terminus. The Midland Red stand, next to the buildings and arcade.

Walsall had trolleybuses, flat-faced blue cans of people. Men with huge hooked poles switched the overhead collector arms across the lines of their separate bays. Ordinary diesel vehicles, visibly pensionable, rattled throbbingly to and from the other bays, each with its line of three or four stands, straggling lines of people stretching beyond their area to mingle and mill with the one behind.

Soft snowflakes were swirling in the yellow headlights, melting on impact with the shining blackness beneath.

I had gone back in time: strange old buses, yesteryear's workmen, in their grey raincoats and flat caps, shabby, shapeless female forms with handfuls of floppy shopping bags, cigarette-smoking, trailing, drab, inconsolate children.

'Is this for the Pelsall bus, please?' Eight or nine heads turned towards my unfamiliar sounds.

'If it ay, we'm in fer a lung walk um, ay we?' came a man's voice from behind me. Some people laughed.

'Yo'm awright, sun. Next un's the twelve,' a matronly factory worker, headscarfed, assured me. I shrank along the line to the end of the queue.

Threading our way out of town, we passed the swimming baths. Behind the glass wall, the young man steadied on the high diving board, balancing, swaying … rising on his toes, he leapt upwards to jack-knife and spear vertically down out of sight.

Past the Arboretum, its dark giants looming above the high brick wall. Along the straight road to take the left fork at some shops. A curving road of houses. The snow flurried more thickly all around, muffling sounds, squishing under the tyres. The window opposite mirrored the passengers either side of me. I must be nearing my stop.

This ancient blue bus had no bell push to request a stop. A single leather cord ran in eyelets along the centre of the downstairs ceiling. I watched people pull it down a couple of times to release it snapping against the painted surface above. You heard nothing other than the flip of leather against metal, no metallic ping. Presumably the driver knew. Maybe something tinged in his cab. Guessing, I rose from my sideways-on seat near the rear platform, and pulled the cord down, letting it whip back. Would anything happen?

We had stopped one stage too early. I had to step off. I had alighted just short of the peculiar, hazardous, hump-backed road bridge over the railway. Curving narrowly leftwards, a relic of the previous century, it brought about (as I was to find) many motoring mishaps. The filling station behind me stood out illuminated like a cruise ship against the flake-swirled blackness.

So, cross the road. Follow the pavement briskly, steeply over the bridge and down, out of Pelsall Lane into a new road. Three pairs of new semi-detached houses shortly ahead on this side. Rapidly, nearly running up the short path to the door of the fourth, Plot 4, Walsall Road, Heath End, Pelsall, Staffordshire.

Our new home.

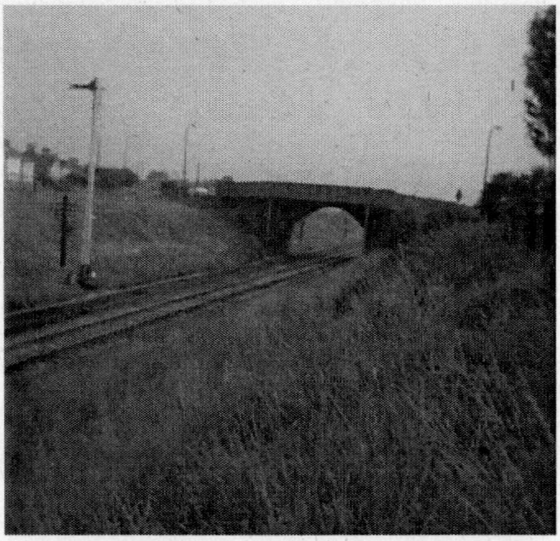

Looking right from our garden ... [photo David Hearne]

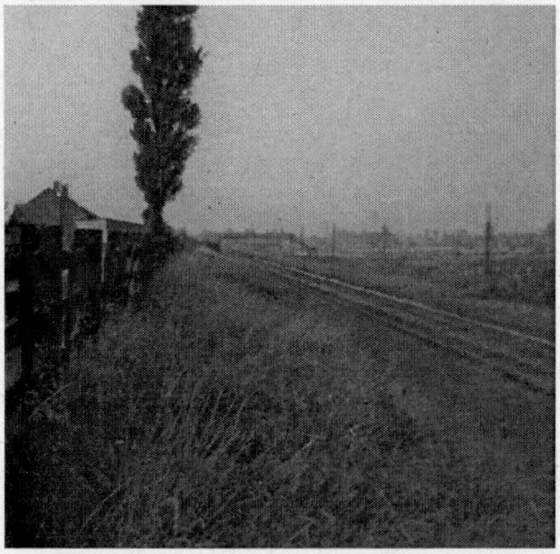

... and looking left, towards Pelsall [photo David Hearne]

New World

When first I came here I had hope,
Hope for I knew not what.

Edward Thomas, *When First*

The village water pump looked new. When I asked our guide, Sunil, he told me they had had it for ten years. Smiling boys waved and giggled as we walked, unhurried, along the unmade sandy tracks.

The blacksmith squatted in his compound. His furnace, a small intense fire in the hollowed ground, was fanned by his elderly wife, sitting cross-legged in her loose, draping clothes. A few feet from him, younger than her husband but at least in her seventies, she unendingly turned the improvised device with alternate hands. The bicycle wheel, mounted on a frame from some adapted front forks fixed to a stable base, was cranked to rotate, the belt around its tyreless rim descending to spin the smaller flywheel of the encased fan directed from inches away at the roaring fire in the earth. Scarlet intensity seared beneath its low mound of coals. Even in the pressing morning sun of October, you felt the heat from fifteen feet away.

After some minutes, the man gripped the rag-covered handles of his home-made tongs, lifted the red-hot axe head from the mound and hammer shaped it on his anvil further towards completion. It would clearly become a master crafted perfect artefact and tool.

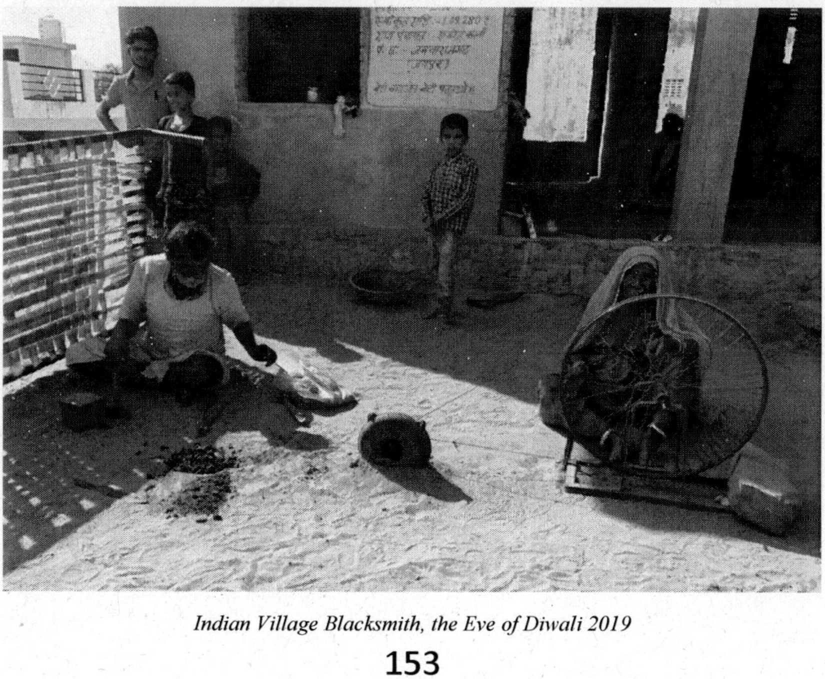

Indian Village Blacksmith, the Eve of Diwali 2019

Ten yards to the right, before another part of the building behind, a very old woman, colourfully clothed, moved on all fours, resurfacing the floor of their outside kitchen. She took the mixture of animal dung and cement from a large plastic bucket in a double-handed scoop, swung it round her body, placed it down in front of her, levelling and smoothing it with her palms in gliding sweeps.

It was the eve of Diwali, the air tremulous with excitement and happiness. The annual renewals and tidying, spring cleaning combined with Christmas, bonfire night and preparations for everyone's birthday rolled into one, were well down the launch ramp.

The house had a door frame but no door, window frames but no glass or other apparent means of sealing the rectangle from the outside. Someone's bed, a platform of interlaced flat-stripped material, remained outside, presumably where he was currently sleeping in the open. Festooned fairy lights were illuminated. Periodically, the crack of a hand-thrown cracker, detonated by being thrown against a hard surface, usually the ground, made a girl squeal and some boys laugh.

After our walkabout village tour, the coach took us back to our hotel, a few minutes away. Our group was occupying a former maharajah's hunting lodge. For a few nights we slept in enormous beds, larger in all dimensions than Super King size, on their six inch platforms that nearly broke your neck during your nocturnal bathroom sortie. At least forty by twenty-five feet, and perhaps twelve feet high, the magnificent room could have served as bedroom, lounge and study for any prince, being expensively furnished and with luxurious curtains and upholstery. The central windowed doors swung open onto a wide balcony, with lush fields expanding level to grey-blue rolling distant hills. You could imagine a newly crowned or married monarch emerging to smile and wave to the cheering crowds of happy subjects below such a grand feature.

In the 21st Century, India remains a country of contrasts and extremes. The hundreds of maharajahs ('great kings', from Indo-European roots) regional rulers of great power and wealth, though formally deprived of their status in the second half of the twentieth century, still enjoy considerable riches, influence and the musical pleasure of words like 'lord' and 'highness'.

Plot 4, later number 9, Walsall Road, Heath End, contrasted almost as sharply with Annie's Burbury Street place. Six decades on, and considerably altered and improved, it remains a very small, semi-detached house, with three bedrooms, a bathroom, kitchen, lounge and dining area, all bijou. Realistically, it would by modern standards suit a young couple as a starter home; for a family of four or more, it would be unsatisfactory: scant of space and storage, unsoundproofed, claustrophobic.

That cold December day in 1961 it was the happiest place on earth.

By the time I stepped from the softly snowing darkness into the bright interior, the others had been there for some hours. The painter, Mom said, had just been finishing off upstairs when they arrived. Cardboard boxes, stacked all around, some opened.

The dining table and chairs at the other end. A paraffin stove already burning. Black, curtainless windows. The new gas cooker not arriving until the next day, my father had bought a Pifco electric boiling ring, on which my mother heated Heinz tomato soup, served with sliced white bread.

The fireplace, showroom new, empty, cold. Clean, dark Marley tiles throughout downstairs, shining, unmarked. Bare, clean, whitewashed stairs. White floorboards, narrow and modern style, upstairs, Cold cleanness and freshness everywhere. Smells of wood, paint, plaster.

I was to have bedroom two, overlooking the back garden. Completely unmade, only roughly levelled, presumably by the builder's machines, the standard strip, twenty-five feet wide, perhaps less, extended for fifty to sixty feet to our boundary chainlink fence, two feet beyond which was the wooden fence before the railway embankment, sloping down. Wonder of wonders! Glory of glories! The Trent Valley line ran past our garden, our house, my bedroom!

Somewhere in the unheated bedroom: boxes, some containing my electric train and other things put into storage eighteen months before. Strictly instructed not to start getting things out, I tore the sealing tape away, disembowelling my possessions all around. My breath steamed upwards.

The first three nights we slept without curtains. Mom somehow draped sheets or other cloths over the window handles, more as a gesture than for any other reason. It was properly dark before any of us went to bed, remaining so till well after we rose. On Saturday, Dad bought some Swish curtain rails, fibre Rawlplugs and a Rawlplug tool, a curious and scarcely effective aid you hammered into the wall, twisting every couple of taps, to make a hole somehow for the plug. Easy enough through the new, soft plaster, it did little to the underlying masonry. Even a hand drill would have been useful. On account of his polio, I did the fixing, just about adequately. From then on, in the practical sense, I was the man about the house for DIY, and quite pleased about it. I did the repairs – or tried to! Without suitable tools or knowledge, I was out of my depth, but usually, more or less, I got there, as will follow. That first weekend we discovered the Heath End corner shop and Post Office, run by the Chandlers for years. Mom would shop there every day, having no refrigerator, or at the butcher's, a little further down the road. Both shops were end-of-terrace conversions of houses, the Chandlers' having a corner entrance and display windows on two elevations. The vacant side next to the butcher's was rough ground, perhaps a former building's site. Once a week, animals were unloaded here from a lorry to the side entrance to the yard 'round the back' for slaughter. On one occasion a couple of years later, an extraordinarily unwilling bull delayed his demise by breaking loose and running panicked around the area. For about half an hour men's shouts mingled with squeals of women and children, looking down from upstairs windows. Traffic was stopped and pedestrians kept well back until finally the snorting beast was somehow got into the gated yard, soon to be dispatched the way of marketed bovine flesh.

Before you reached Edna Chandler's, you passed, first the yard, and then the corner house and office of Nailer Loveridge, the coal merchant. Another task that befell me that first Saturday, setting the pattern for many winter weekends, was to buy a hundredweight of coal from Nailer, a small, gaunt, elderly man engrained all over, body and clothing, from his ancient flat cap to his scraping creased boots, with the grime and dust of his trade. After I had placed the ten shillings note in his discoloured palm, he forked, with a peculiar large, curved-tined tool, the coal from his staithe into a nearby large scoop on a balance scale, counterweighted to 112 pounds by four iron castings with 28 lb on one face, until, gently rising, the weights began to float. He always then threw one last coal in with his left hand. 'Just fer yer mom then.'

He nodded for me to bring my borrowed wheelbarrow forward so that he could tip the scoop on its pivot, tumble dumping its contents chuddering down to my weightening barrow. The dust swarm settled. I said thank you, at which Nailer touched his cap, turned and hobbled stiffly off, telling me over his shoulder, 'Yo cun put the barrer back when yo've done.'

Instead of a coal cellar, the new house had a store. Halfway down the side passage between our house and the neighbours', a wooden door opened on to a concrete floored cavity, wedge-shaped because the stairs were above its ceiling. Here I upended the barrow before returning it as bidden.

That first Christmas, just over a fortnight later, was a modest one. We still had a tree, presents and a generous roast turkey dinner. Some of Dad's Johnny Walker gift from his boss went on firing the pudding. Having been asked for restraint in my requests, I received the cheapest Triang loco in their current catalogue, blue 'Nellie'. Using the same 0-4-0 mechanism as the secondhand steeple cab I had been bought for my birthday, it cost ten shillings more, at £1 9s 10d. Prone to wheelslip under a heavy load, Nellie never failed, proving responsive and unrealistically nippy. At a full 12 volts, her scale speed must have been at least 150 mph. I was, we all were, wonderfully happy.

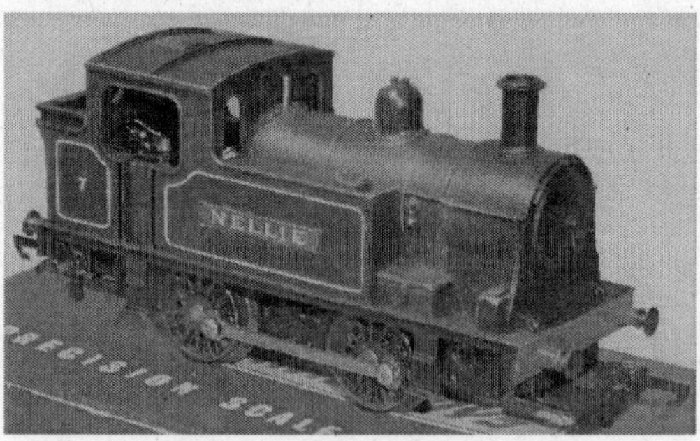

Changing Tracks

'I think he is capable of better.'

Terence Larkin, Headmaster, St Philip's Grammar School

My Christmas report, the conventional single foolscap sheet printed form, summed me up in numbers (age in years and months, starting and ending weights and heights, in stones and pounds, feet and inches, term and exam marks), supplying the handwritten pithy one-liners of my teachers, form-master and headmaster, blew no trumpets, banged no drums. Out of thirty-five boys, I was (I think) twenty-third in exams and twenty-fifth by term marks. It could have been, should have been very different; I can understand and explain it now. My parents did not seem to mind that I had come down dramatically. Whatever he privately felt, Dad satisfied himself and assured me by exercising his constitutional contempt for that [anagram of *hits*] Larkin and his ways. I was probably quite down, but then assumed that was just how things were. I had been put with a good number of cleverer boys. Maybe I should never again do that well at school. I had been top of the class for a couple of years at St John's. Though he made light of it, Dad had been first in his form *every year* at St Philip's, with the exception of one subject good at everything, excellent in French and Latin.

My journeys to and from St Philip's increasingly occupied my interest. On many days, Dad was able to drop me off at the school gates on his way to work, further down the Hagley Road. Otherwise, I was discovering exciting possible variations.

The least adventurous method of journey involved the three-buses taken on 6th December between Hagley Road and Heath End. However, I soon worked out that, instead of going into the City to catch the Midland Red 118, I could intercept it via the Inner Circle number 8 in Lozells, near where we had been living.

Much more cheering was to walk from the City centre, across St Martin's Square, to New Street, for the next Walsall train. I must have returned frequently by this route, since I can still rattle off the stations in less than a breath: Aston, Witton, Perry Barr, Great Barr, Bescot, Walsall! Most times I had all or almost all of a diesel car to myself. We steam enthusiasts scoffed at Yammers (diesel multiple units), but they throbbed along efficiently, skimming us on their gently dipping suspension past familiar sites and scenes: the station near Grandma Elsie's and Alexander Stadium, the expansive playing fields where Uncle Gordon and I had bashed balls around, the cricket field where he himself had top-scored with 37 not out for his works team. So, either three buses, with an optional alternative, or two buses and a train. Or …

… Pelsall had a station! An early walk or car lift could lead to a ride behind an early morning steam locomotive, usually a Standard Class 2-6-2 sidetank, or, rarely, the tender Class 2 2-6-0 'Mickey Mouse', an engine of irresistible charm to a smitten schoolboy.

Released from school at 4 pm, I set myself a return arrival time of 5.30 pm. This allowed me not only to vary the route, but (if I made the three-bus decision) enough spare time to look around Birmingham City centre, learning more streets and sights. Permitted and enjoying considerable freedom and personal responsibility, I never once was or felt threatened as I deviated and roamed, was never late home or suffered any mishap.

Over the weeks and months, we settled more and more into Pelsall. Heath End lies just under a mile from the village itself, to reach which we simply turned right from our short drive and continued along Walsall Road. After you had passed the shops, houses and three public houses, the buildings thinned out, opening on to the common, first on your left only, then from just before the dangerous crossroads onwards on both sides. In my years at Pelsall, this considerable expanse of green space gave the place its major advantage and attraction, the grass being of fair, lush quality, not the tussocky scrub otherwise seen around outlying areas of Staffordshire. I suspect it is still the same.

Some things have changed. The Common cross-roads, for many years an accident black spot, for decades has been policed by traffic lights, preventing vehicles from the compass's four directions speeding to beat each other, too often with predictable outcomes. Likewise, the village and indeed wider area no longer are postally or administratively part of Staffordshire, but West Midlands. Birmingham's cream and navy buses, the rarest foreign visitors in the 1960s, have become completely integrated. Two of the pubs went even before Nailer's yard. Houses fill their former sites and previous wasteland gaps.

Though when we lived there we did not consider ourselves to be Black Country folk, Pelsall is listed on the display in the museum at Dudley as among the area's principal constituent settlements. The pit (coat mine) ceased working in the nineteenth century, but not before the disaster which claimed the lives of twenty-two men in 1872.

That year, on 14th November, water began to leak into the working, rapidly becoming an overwhelming torrent and inundating ingress. Anyone curious to read the well written but harrowing account may go to www.pelsalltimes.co.uk. Altogether twenty-two bodies were recovered more than a week later, one never being confidently identified. The inquest the following month determined the deaths to have been accidentally caused by natural means, and by no human error or negligence. The 'long procession of doleful mourners, headed by the band of The Bloxwich Volunteers, playing the Dead March in *Saul*' would have passed along the very road by which our new house stood. Some eleven years later, the ill-fated colliery suffered a widespread fire, to be abandoned in 1890.

One Sunday morning, before Dad took the three of us to mass in Shelfield, an Irishman knocked on the door. He asked if we had any job to be done. As only she could do it, Mom had a flash brainwave. By the time we returned around midday, Paddy had almost finished digging over our unmade back garden. His suit jacket removed to lie over the fence, he paused to wipe the back of his hand across his beaded brow. It must have been a fine day in late February. When he finished, he knocked on the back door. He returned Mom the empty glass which she had several times refilled with water. Dad paid him £3. He left our spade and fork sticking in the ground, now releasing earthy smells, picked up his jacket and walked away down the passage. We never saw or heard of him again.

The hard ground having been broken up into turned over clods, I took over that very day after lunch, beginning to extract the weeds, mostly couch grass (which we called 'squitch'), to pile them on a quickly growing mound by the end fence. Starting at that far end, I worked my way backwards, eventually more or less clearing the whole area in a few days. Perhaps it was half term that week. We boasted only the tools that Paddy had used, but before very long I acquired a rake, allowing a finer finish to a cleared space. The soil was light, clay free to at least a spit, easy enough to work.

My plan – the whole design was my own, with input from sister Sylvia, still only seven: a more or less central path, with flowers to both sides from less than halfway from the house towards the railway fence. I would take the left-hand side, Sylvia the right for 'our' gardens. Not to be excluded, David (4) was apportioned a small patch, perhaps a metre square, at the extreme bottom, next to the mound. The area from the house to the flower beds would be grassed.

We bought seeds. A packet commonly cost sixpence. The village hardware shop, Owen's, had a rotating stand. I soon discovered the extensive gardening section on the first floor of Woolworth's, in both Birmingham and Walsall. Whenever I could spare a few pence, I called in between buses on my way home, to see what I could find.

My first purchase was a packet of Russell lupin seeds, which I sowed in a line across my patch, marking each end of the drill with stuck in twigs. Then, at intervals just wide enough to step between, followed French marigolds, nasturtiums, blue cornflowers, clarkia, pansies, Virginian stock, night-scented stock and other annuals, all planted in military-style ranks, later to be planted out suitably spaced. Not understanding what 'thinning out' meant, I nearly lost some seedlings, which wilted alarmingly after being moved, but with nervously generous daily waterings, almost all picked up and grew on. The thrill of detecting the first seed leaves, impatience when the early buds exposed just a hint of colour, before the fulfilment of the first floral opening and displays have remained with me throughout life, though never experienced as fully or intensely as in late spring 1962.

I bought a few alyssum and lobelia plants from Woolworth's for the border. In May, my pocket money provided three rose plants over a number of weeks, a dark crimson one, then a pink Margaret McGrady, finally a pure white Virgo. At Easter, Grandma Lily gave me *The Encyclopedia of Modern Gardening* (N.P.Harvey, Spring Books), which set her back 12s 6d. I read and referred to it constantly, retaining stretches verbatim to this day. In my late teen years, when my mother gave the book to Uncle Gordon, typically without asking me, I missed it sorely, even though by then I had ceased opening it several times a week. Well into my sixties, I obtained a used copy, still with the original dust jacket, through the internet. The cheap paper, total absence of colour photographs or illustrations and the dated line drawings came as a shock and disappointment; but I still treasure the volume.

By the summer we had flowers. I weeded and watered after school and at weekends. Dad strolled in the garden in the evenings, mingling his pipe smoke (St Bruno flake) with the stocks and alyssum. He loved pansies. At every opportunity I picked flowers for my mother's vases.

The postage stamp front garden, open plan with the pavement and council grass verge, succeeded less. The builders had left me more of their red sand than topsoil, so that grass grew poorly, sparsely from seed. The standard blue and white lobelia/alyssum border plants made a better gesture. Against the house wall, painted rendering up to the windowsill, I grew a line of clarkia, variously pink against the whitened pebbledash.

All this juvenile horticulture went towards expressing the joyful hopes we all had for our new home. Realistically, it was rather too much for a young boy and his even younger sister. Our intentions could never be realised or the drive sustained. We faltered during the school summer holidays. I had planned to lay a brick path down the middle of the back garden, with almost no materials and even less knowledge of how to proceed. A few house bricks, left over from the build, picked or dug up, had been laid to one side by Paddy. With enormous effort I used them, first as edging stones, then started laying a path, back from the fence towards the house. After two days, all the bricks were used up, with only about one yard of path down.

We would scavenge for bricks! The other side of the railway line was a rough, abandoned or just unused stretch of land, loosely referred to as 'the field'. Pedestrians used it as a short cut from Pelsall Lane to Shelfield. Across the far side, before you descended the slope to the concrete bridge across the brook (a polluted industrial flow that came to take the life of one hapless man who public spiritedly spent a Bank Holiday weekend attempting to clear a stretch of it and so improve the area … he died from some poison absorbed through his skin!). But between the field and the slope, where the branch line to Aldridge had been lifted, rails and sleepers, my source of bricks lay embedded in the summer-hardened dusty ground. Sylvia and I laboriously worked them out, carrying back home as many as would fit in our galvanised bucket. This we sustained morning and afternoon over several days, until our enthusiasm and energy finally deserted us. Our amateur path, without foundation, crude, unpointed, uneven, petered out after perhaps three yards, remaining like that for two decades.

As for other household jobs, I did my best. I had to. For Dad it was either impossible or unthinkable to hire a workman, perhaps both: 'they all diddle you.' An early exception was the fitting of an immersion heater to the hot water cylinder. One Sunday morning shortly after Christmas 1961, Pat Waltire, a friend of my uncles, came over from Handsworth, supposedly doing the job cheaply for a friend and fellow Catholic. Before that, we were able to have hot water from the kitchen kettle or after the coal fire had been burning for a time. Copper piping had been built into the brickwork behind the back of the fire grate; heat conducted from the coal fire to the water in the pipes, gravity fed from the first floor; the water in turn rose to the cylinder, to be replaced by colder water, and so on. Simplicity itself, this crude system actually worked very effectively and reliably, except that there was no means of preventing a boil over when the fire had sustained a high output sufficiently long to boil the water in the tank! That stage, which for a few seconds was heralded by an alarming roaring rush like a mighty extractor fan starting up until the scalding water discharged via the safety pipe into the hot water feed tank above the cylinder in the loft, allowed the cylinder to be refilled with colder water and so settle down again for a time.

For the cold months of the year, the coal fire occupied a central part in our family times at home, not just because through necessity we all got as near to it as we could, but also on account of the attention it demanded: fetching coal from Nailer, filling the scuttle from the coal hole, removing the cold ashes and clearing up, laying the new fire (crumpled and folded newspaper, scrap wood, small coals …), getting it going with oxygen (mouth blowing, using bellows, using a draw sheet or tin, throwing on fat, oil, sugar, maybe even paraffin …). Dad took prodigious daredevil risks, with the occasional flare up, though suffered nothing more than a fright. The sweep's visits were dreaded by Mom, for the filthy mess they always left, no matter how elaborately he sheeted up the room. Each visit removed astounding amounts of the fine, silky, foul powder. Despite the sweep's services, our chimney occasionally caught fire, when the caked carbon at the top end of the flue ignited. You stood outside in the cold and watched the flames dragon licking at the sky until everything died down. We understood that the pipes behind the fire had been put there to allow for solid fuel, or even gas fired, central heating, but that would have required inconceivable expenditure. So we roasted or shivered, too near or too far from the coals, drank hot paraffin fumes into our lungs, shivered violently upstairs, breathed on iced bedroom windows to make a clear porthole to spy the day's weather.

One Saturday morning, my brother David, perhaps four, rode fast up the slight slope towards our front door, jumping off at the last moment before impact to allow his scooter to continue through its momentum. The reeded lower glass pane of the door shattered theatrically. At that period, no regulation required safety glass in household doors and partitions. (A few months later, a classmate told me the horror story of his neighbour's child, a young girl who had stumbled through a similar glass panel at home, so severely lacerating one arm that it subsequently dangled uselessly.)

This was disaster enough. Unusually, Dad took action. After I had helped him to remove the broken remains and measure the rectangular space left – I should say it was about 18" x 21" – he drove to the village and bought a covering piece of board. It may have been only hardboard, though I suspect it was plywood. He set to hammering the replacement overlay panel in place, using his only percussion tool, a 4-ounce pin hammer, and ¾" panel pins.

He was kneeling down with his back towards me, tapping at a pin. After one firm final clout to one of them, he cried sharply, bent right over to the porch floor, his hands over his right eye. The pin had flown backwards and inflicted a stinging blow to his eyeball. For minutes he could not even open his eye for Mom to examine. She brought a cold wet flannel. At length, he could lift his hand from the watery, red socket. Looking down, he forced the lids apart, quickly shut them tight together again. When Mom finally managed to hold his head back enough for her to look, she saw the red wound in the white of the eye. Hospital. Shortly, the two drove off, I assume to Walsall A&E, leaving me to care for Sylvia and David as well as to finish the repair. I pinned the board tightly in place around all four sides.

A few days later, Dad brought home a tiny pot (a quarter of a pint?) of black paint, no primer. It must have been the cheapest he could find. It was actually cellulose paint, with its own touch up brush fastened inside the screw on lid. Though I managed to cover the whole panel, it turned out appallingly patchy and streaked, an eyesore in the figurative sense this time. Before long a form of mercy descended. When the board became so weather warped that water seeped in, the decision was made to reglaze.

Of course, I had no experience of fitting a glass panel, though the principles were self-evident: measure the frame, have the glass cut and buy some putty. Hardware shop man weighed out a sufficiency from his lidded bucket, double wrapped it in some resistant paper, then went backstage to cut my pane of glass.

How was I to know you not only measured with the precision of a neural surgeon interfering with a VIP's spine but also deducted a fitting allowance?

It wouldn't go into the recess! My measuring had not been too bad; I had probably got to within a millimetre one way or the other. But I had not left the necessary margin. Something had to be done. I had no woodworking tool, not even a chisel, to make more space …

… No one ever knew this, but I hacked away with a screwdriver on two of the rebates until, somehow, the pane would just slip in. I knew nothing about lining the rebate with putty; when that rigid sheet with its viciously sharp edges finally, after maybe half an hour's anxiously sweating hacking, hoping no one like our handymen neighbours would see, slipped in, it was coming come out no more! With just my fingers, I puttied all around …

Wonderfully, though I could not exactly join the glorious ranks of that little Dutch chap who saved the town by digitally plugging an incipient dyke leak, this juvenile bodge did the trick. Of course, it could have looked better – especially if the putty had not been left white for a couple of years, until I was given a tin of (again) cheap paint, a poisonously unnatural and emetic green this time. I suppose it has turned out to be of some use that perforce I was required to attempt tasks like these before my time, being incidentally allowed to learn by making mistakes. Practice makes something and all that.

Over the years, my teenage filling and painting, as the house settled in, cracking inside as it dried out and flaking outside under the elements, continued dutifully, keeping things going a little longer, with the quality of the finish in inverse proportion to my enthusiasm.

Life improved in many respects during the rest of my first year at St Philip's. It was only later that I understood how I had toughened up. There was some enjoyment to be found, especially in the better weather with playground cricket. In some subjects, I could feel my way better … My summer report placed me eleventh by term marks and actually eighth in the exams!

Despite the improving weather, as winter gave way to spring and summer, the daily travelling, something between 12 and 15 miles each way, became less exciting, then dull, finally a tedious use of time. My parents firmly maintaining the greatest belief in the supremacy of St Philip's, more local schools began to be considered, though not seriously. Aldridge Grammar School was well thought of, I heard them once saying, but the topic was not resumed.

One Monday in the summer term, after I been absent from school the previous Friday with a brief stomach upset that in more than one sense was passing through my classmates, we took ourselves to Ravenhurst, the school's playing field, for our Monday games afternoon. I was looking forward to some more cricket in the sunshine. I might mention that, to get to the sports ground in Knightlow Road, perhaps just over a mile from the school on the Hagley Road, we caught a bus, unescorted by any member of staff, from across the busy road. Earlier in the day, our form master would have given us two standard Birmingham City Transport red plastic bus tokens, for the journey each way. It was some walk from the bus stop to Ravenhurst itself, but we carried both our ordinary school bag and our sports bags, running encumbered for stretches in apprehension lest we arrive late.

We expected Itchy Green's mood to be foul. It had to be; he was made that way. This particular Monday, he scarcely raised his voice when he emerged from the changing room hut to motion us in. We had already frozen and fallen silent. We remained so as we changed, sensing something.

'Sit down!'

We did so, on the slatted seats underneath the clothes pegs. He disappeared into the masters' changing cubicle. We waited, still and soundless.

After perhaps two more minutes, he appeared and stood motionless for a time.

'Quiet!' His voice rang needlessly round the walls. We had made no sound.

'Listen!' Another pointless command. A pause, then, at a slower than usual pace: 'If you came to the athletic sports on Saturday afternoon, stand up and go outside. You will be with Mr Webster.'

Perhaps a third of the year group of 140 boys made their escape. He told the last boy to close the door.

I do not know how long he took to express his fury at our non-attendance. It seemed ages. Time has intensity as well as length. A summary might be that we had been disgracefully, shamefully at fault. We should have been there even if not competing – which meant almost all of us – to give our support to the runners and jumpers, the masters who so generously gave up their time to provide these opportunities for us, the House officers who felt let down, the good name of the School, the staff and Headmaster etc etc. He might as well have chuffed on to include the Bishop, Pope and maybe our Almighty Father; there was enough steam in his boiler.

'So, you won't be playing cricket this afternoon. You'll get some of the exercise you need. You'll be running. All afternoon. Get outside to the track. You missed the athletic sports; you can catch up now.'

I should have just ambled round at an effortless jog, of course. But I was scared. I ran quite fast. For a lap or so it was not too bad. Before long, though, I was suffering – desperate to stop and terrified to do so. If we slowed anywhere on the 440 yards oval, the furious voice would come hurtling over the field to us. 'Doan't stop, lad! Keep running!' The nearby local residents must have been able to hear every word. I became quite seriously out of breath. My sides ached. My legs were at once on fire and turning to jelly. I suppose I was on the way to what the medics might call 'physical distress'. When Itchy had made *his* point, many times over in my case, we were told to stop. I wanted to drop to the ground. Instead we lined up and stood to attention, facing him. Another full-voiced group denunciation, Ciceronian in its damning contempt if not in its oratorical quality.

What little there was left of the afternoon was spent waiting for dismissal. He actively ignored us, wasting our time as he accused us of wasting his.

By the time we had to walk back to the main road for the bus, my muscles had seized. My legs hurt all the way up and down, with every movement, If I straightened my upper body, a creasing pain shot across my midriff.

At home, I must immediately have spilled my distress – how worn out, how aching, I was; how upset at the brutal treatment. Dad wrote a letter to Mr Green.

In the intervening decades, many clouds have condensed and dissolved. Memories gather, fade, recede, disappear into air. It may well be a common habit to glamorise, ennoble or in some other way amplify our remote experiences, their triumphs and hardships … 'when I were a lad, we didn't 'ave this or that you modern softies 'ave; we med do wi' nowt' and so on; and (usually) 'it were grand!' What a child feels and thinks centres immovably on him: the pain of a fall, the joy of a present, the devastation of punishment or an adult's monstrous anger temporarily inundate our whole inner landscape. Later, as a parent, he sees only his child's uniqueness, its perfection, instinctively protective, protesting at any threats, real or imagined. Arctic terns nest on the ground. Trespass too near, and you risk painful, even blood-drawing pecks from screamingly enraged plunging father birds. As with those feathery furies, so elsewhere through nature. My father's letter must have taken the facts of my case to be exactly what I had so woefully related, presented them with elegant, even flourishing indignation and (almost certainly) implied contempt for the entire race of ignorant PE brutes.

My personal brute shocked and shook me by the rapidity and ferocity of his response. He saw things every bit from *his* own point of view as my father and I had done, only with much more emotional violence. He came to find me at morning break the day dad's letter arrived. He led me away from everybody else, to a small empty room. He was wearing his navy-blue blazer, blindingly white shirt, some sporting club or perhaps regimental tie. His red face shone from the morning's shave; I smelt his shaving soap when, bending down, he brought it to within six inches of mine.

The hot breath heated my face during his quivering, level-toned, sustained venting of fury. I cannot remember the words; probably I did not hear them. In short, I was to understand something along the lines that he was completely right, my father utterly wrong, and I everything totally worthless: lying, feeble, spineless, useless, stupid, despicable, and so on. Those were possibly not the words, but assuredly the essence. I compared most unfavourably with his own son, of whom he was (straightening up) extremely proud, and who at my age would have beaten me up most manfully and deservedly. I was to come and find him at the end of the morning at the gym.

By one o'clock, he must have distilled the rest of his bile into the blue-black ink applied in broad-nibbed fountain pen to both sides of five sheets of small blue Basildon Bond which he sealed in an envelope, addressing it to my father while I watched. When I reached out to take it from him, he bent down again and held on to tell me in my eyes to go straight into the Oratory that very moment and pray for forgiveness. Since he did not just then specify any particular transgression, it most probably was for my own personal portion of original sin, or perhaps for just being me.

Dad discarded the letter, after a few contemptuous snorts and lofty comments, onto the coffee table. Later he set fire to it. The summer term continued. I moved up to eleventh by term marks and actually eighth in the exams. I later understood Mr Jones was thinking of me for the Form Progress Prize, one of only two annually awarded to each form at Prize Giving in Birmingham Town Hall.

I never received it. Over the summer holidays, my parents arranged for me to leave St Philip's and transfer to a school nearer home. Aldridge Grammar was fairly new and well thought of. It sounded very suitable. We drove past the site several times in the evenings. I became increasingly eager about the place. I never went there.

A few days after Itchy's onslaught, I heard that a classmate had been treated even more brutally, again after a protest letter. His father had also written to complain, but for a different reason: if his son was expected to swim for the school in the evening, would Mr Green ensure that he had not been unnecessarily exhausted a few hours earlier?

This boy was definitely the best swimmer in the form, possibly in the whole year. Whilst a good number of us foundered or trundled, he would slice up and down lengths of the baths at racing speed, switching strokes at the turn. Once, when he had surged back past us, rising on the dolphin stroke, to touch and finish in the shallow end, we all stood up and clapped.

The story among us was that Itchy had taken David into the gym, bolted the doors shut from inside, backed him up against the wall bars, bellowed in his face, and felled him with a sideways smack to the head. Though only hearsay, it was entirely credible. Another Itchy tale that ran through the whole school was that, one cataclysmically wet afternoon when football was impossible, he had sat in a classroom while a fifth form got on with written work. At some point, he called out a small boy called Doherty, clearly to victimise him, verbally or physically. Reputedly, the rest of the form, all thirty-plus of them aged fifteen or sixteen, stood up and told Itchy to leave Doherty alone. A few fortunates did escape from Colditz.

Perhaps my best memory of St Philip's also involves the fifth form. One afternoon late in the summer term, we were excused lessons to go to Warwickshire's cricket ground at Edgbaston, to see our Under Sixteens contest the final of the Docker Shield. In the St Philip's innings, my ex-Headmaster's son, Tony O'Loughlin, looked like turning the tide in the School's favour, batting with elegance and effect. He reached 22 in little time, before being run out by his woeful captain, Smallwood.

I do not suppose that Itchy Green even realised, or could care less if he did, that he had sent me away before I really got into my stroke.

Service and Courage[1]

Oh, wonder!
How many goodly creatures are there here!
How beauteous mankind is! O brave new world,
That has such people in't!

Shakespeare, *The Tempest 5,i*

Shire Oak Grammar School and I started our second years the same day. Unlike me, it would appear to have completely resisted time's tides and currents, at least that is the case with the marginally under 250 pupils, 18 teachers, 1 secretary, 6 dinner ladies, 1 caretaker and 1 caretaker's wife of 1962 I am contemplating: eternally arrested, facing forwards, smart and attentive all, many bearing their names still – in my recollection. You might think so anyway, if you looked at the website of Brownhills Bob and saw his posting of the panoramic whole school photograph of that year, taken on the undeveloped land just beyond the rectangular ashphalt recreation ground. David Hughes (my year, I think, not my form) sent it from across the Atlantic.

New throughout, the buildings were pure 1960s functionality, reasonably practical but with no architectural beauty or excitement whatever. Though it amused me in my youth to hear my father rail against Victorian architects, who he said just should never have been trusted with a pile of bricks, as I grew older I came to think otherwise, noticing more and more distinguished public buildings and some splendid private houses, though there could never be an argument about the disgracefully poor accommodation sometimes provided for industrial workers. Funnily enough, and despite his socialist politics, Dad was not protesting about the latter!

I digress. Clean, fresh and new, the place provided all that was necessary. As one brilliantly wacky Headmaster I later worked for once remarked, a good teacher needs only a shed! This was much better than that.

My year was the first full one. The part year groups above us had transferred from other schools, presumably because of where they lived. My new form 2A was the top one of three, 2 Alpha being next door and 2 Beta, 13+ entrants and so as new as I was, further along the corridor. Before I left, pupil numbers had grown to well over 500, necessarily adding more teachers to the staff, one or two extra subjects to the curriculum.

There were girls! They always sat in the rows of single desks on the windows side of every room. Being sixth alphabetically by surname, I was told to sit sixth from the

---

[1] Our school motto, embroidered under the badge, as sewn onto our blazers. Deft use of needlework scissors rendered it more appropriate to the heraldic depiction of a standing black clad warrior, with battle axe, shield and (possibly) spear: *Vice and Rage*! Strangely, those were the very responses provoked by our modifications, official rage at our vice! I had already witnessed similar platform fulminations from Terence Larkin at St Philip's, though why he objected so vehemently to our homely transforming of *Pietas* to *Peas* ever mystified us.

front desk in the first row, not just by the wall but even in the back right corner facing forward: Birch, Bullock, Coleman, Eustace, Fletcher, Hearne … Or did that come the following year? In any case, I am certain I was always by the wall at the back of the room.

When in the first few minutes my new form-teacher, Miss Langley, asked me some routine organisational question, I stood up on reflex. Just as automatically, the form roared. I should have to learn other ways. Miss Langley smiled. 'You don't need to stand up.'

In the core subjects of English, maths and French, I had covered more ground, and so felt comfortable. German and physics were new to everyone. In fact, since in history, geography, biology, and music there were no unfamiliar techniques or axiomatic principles to employ, the transition proved painless. Always a dabber rather than a dab hand in art, I should not have been any different if St Philip's had leapt ahead of Shire Oak or trailed behind out of sight; my efforts at drawing and painting did not reach even the level of 'primitive'.

Why were woodwork and P.E. teachers always unnecessarily fierce and strict? I enjoyed woodwork, despite the touchpaper discipline, after my start at St Francis'. P.E lessons, on the other hand, not least because of the scars left by Itchy Green, were on the timetable only to be endured. Though never one of the sporting skilled or fanatic, I probably was not the least physically able either. In one basketball game, when I took a chance pot shot from just inside the halfway line, it went clean in. 'Fluke!' called Mr Gorman, turning dismissively away from me. A few minutes later, from about the same spot, I managed a repeat performance. Unlike lightning, total luck can strike twice. Mr Gorman's whistle dropped from his mouth, wide open like his eyes when he turned back at me. I do not think he said anything. Perhaps I upset him.

He assuredly troubled me a term or so later, in early summer, preparing us for athletics. Sequential movements, even to music, mystify me. A compliant dog would be a more competent ballroom dancer. The triple jump proved completely beyond my motor understanding. Perhaps on my own, given time, I could have worked it out; by walking the sequence through deliberately and repeatedly, I might have internalised it. (After all, I had been able to ride a bike since before my memory commences, picking that up by simply riding around the garden with stabilisers fitted to the cream and red Mobo child's bike. When Dad saw me scuttling around, he just removed the stabilisers, telling me later that it would have been more dangerous to leave them on.) But under the glare of an angry, quick moving young sports master, my self-possession fluttered everywhere. The more I was told, in louder and slower tones each time, what to do, the more I messed it up. This inspired Mr Gorman. He bent down, held my take off leg behind by the ankle, and slapped the lower part sharply six or seven times, so that it really stung. 'That will remind you which leg to take off on,' he triumphed. It did not. He snorted and gave up. So did I. So far in my life, I have encountered no emergency which vitally required the manoeuvre. Another fluke, perhaps.

Unlike my two all-boys' schools, Shire Oak allowed no untimetabled ball games. Though referred to as a *playground*, the pitch-sized tarmac area where we spent our mid-morning and lunchtime breaks saw us do little other than stand around and talk. On Monday afternoons, a double-decker 'Special' would reverse down the main drive and park by the art room. At the end of the lunch period, we climbed aboard, boys upstairs with two maths teachers, girls downstairs with Miss Langley and the girls' P.E. teacher. In time, Shire Oak would have its own playing and games fields on site, but for years the land, extending considerably far, in one direction towards the operational Walsall Wood colliery, remained unseeded, though roughly levelled by contractors. Until that day, years ahead, we were transported to Pelsall, where the football and cricket clubs' joint ground lay behind some houses on Walsall Road, just next to the Bush Inn.

Happy memories! For two terms of the year, we would play football here. Over time, we even adopted positions. Though not left-footed, I could use that foot to some extent. After a few weeks at left back, I went a rank forward, to left half, which seemed best to suit me. I was never much of a running dribbler, or stood a chance of being selected for the school team, but in our weekly games could on most occasions take the ball off an opponent coming towards me, and pass it on to one of our team. On one occasion when we were playing downhill towards the railway line, I saw a gap and booted the ball high over everyone's heads. It was not in any way a graceful shot, and no player thoroughly drilled in the grammar and practices of the game would have thought of it. From thirty or forty yards out, the leather sphere, stone heavy with absorbed moisture, described its inevitable parabola while everyone watched with upturned heads – including the goalkeeper! He was standing about ten feet off his line. Apart from looking upwards to track the ball's flight, he did not move. Goal!

Mr Seccombe, turned to his boss, Mr Roberts, Head of the Maths Department, and wrote off my effort: 'Toe budge!' Whatever that meant, he was probably right.

I was one of the fortunate few who lived near enough to the sports ground to be allowed, after producing a parental letter, to walk home at the end of these afternoons, extending my freedom.

Life became easier. The school bus, initially a blue Walsall Corporation double decker bus, later one of three and then four or perhaps five contract coaches, collected me every morning from the bus stop less than forty yards from our front door. Staffordshire funded our transport, issuing passes every term, saving our parents expense. From door to door now took under twenty instead of ninety minutes.

Perfect - only, there was Boz, in the year above. He threw his weight about, leading a small group from his year, requisitioning the rear seat. 'Yo'm in ma place!' Whether this was the case or not, he and his micro gang scragged and thumped several younger boys in turn over the days and weeks, the paralysing heavy punch to the top of the arm being a standard measure. In the morning, Boz and Co would have already boarded; I could sit nearer the front, away from them, preferably in a window seat, so that as they bulldozed their way out on arrival I would not be within clumping reach.

Going home presented more dangers. After a day of classroom confinement, the transport mafia let themselves go with unrestrained cheer. Let them get on first. Window seat. Look out of the window. Keep quiet. Don't look round at them.

Such tensions persisted for at least two years. Gradually, the bunch mellowed or lost interest. I worked at being, if not invisible, at least outwardly approving of them. The right comment, later even a joke, could make them laugh. Though several other boys were reduced by their treatment to tears, I somehow eluded the pummellings and humiliation. Were my fears unfounded or exaggerated?

Generally, no culture of bullying existed at Shire Oak. It is true there were skirmishes and, rarely, a serious fight. So life continued relatively peacefully. I suspect that being completely co-educational made a difference: girls generally induce calmness, gentleness … Brand new, the school cast no darkness of history or tradition; the plain openness and cleanness of the architecture and layout allowed for no lurking horrors. In my early days, I amazingly found that I was tougher than many others. When one lunchtime we were waiting to be allowed into the dining room (I always took my own lunch), another second form boy saw my packed sandwiches in my blazer pocket and gave them a squashing thump. In retaliation, I rounded on him to belt his shoulder in fine St Philip's style. To my instant regret, he started to cry. That in the sixth form he became the captain of rugby should suggest he was no constitutional weakling; I had been brutalised. Both by my conscious decision and the softening effects of being lastingly untroubled, I relaxed, could drop my guard.

Looking at the 1962 photograph brings many people back to life as they were then. I could fill pages with anecdotes, comments, and thoughts about them. This is not the place. Besides, the juicier memory morsels might be objected to by surviving contemporaries, even risk libel!

The work felt relatively manageable, the atmosphere less tense.

If I spoke with some version of a Birmingham accent then, why did South Staffordshire folk seem so, well, backward and ignorant? It was their strain of Black Country dialect, of course, which in us City folk, believing ourselves smarter and slicker, stirred mirth and scorn. (These days, such ways of speaking, at once easeful and lively, frequently deliberately amusing, fascinate and warm me.)

Take some variant forms of the verb to be:

you are	yo'm
he is, she is	ee'm, she'm
we are	we'm
you are	yo'm
they are	they'm

And the interrogative?

are you?	am ya?

The negative:

is/are not	ay (to rhyme with *hay*, *pay*, *may*, etc

In use:

Are you going?	Am ya gooin?
I am not.	I ay
He is going.	Ee'm a-gooin

Dialect expressions:

Snap food, particularly packed and taken from home to be eaten elsewhere. 'Ah've 'ad me snap' = 'I've eaten my sandwiches/packed lunch'. In the late fourteenth century poem from the Cheshire area, the word *sanap* is used for a tablecloth or dressing. Other expressions have survived, almost intact or barely changed, since those times.

Cut	canal
Yed	head
Jed	dead
er doh	she doesn't
ee ay	he isn't
wor	was not
aar (long indef. artc.)	our/my
aar kid	my/our brother, cousin, young male family member or friend
er bawls at we	she shouts at us

My father once came back indoors gleeful with his most recent discovery. He had, he said, just overheard the local 'good sort' in the shop, telling another woman, 'If ah a-knowd yer was bad, ah'd a-come and a-dood for yer.' (If I'd known you were ill, I would have come and done things for you/run your home/looked after you/stood in for you.)

Moving away from the Midlands (and marrying a Londoner!) soon made me realise that words I took for granted were not standard English; for example, 'outdoor' for 'off licence', 'play the wag' or 'wagging' for 'truanting', 'pither' for 'dither', 'bost' for 'break,' 'broken,' and 'bosting' for 'very good' (cf 'smashing'). But generally, I was brought up with standard English, doubtless delivered with a variant of the Birmingham accent. There is, of course, no one Brummie accent, but a whole variety of pronunciations, inflections and expressions. One of my father's foremen could quite reliably tell you where you came from: West Bromwich, Aston, Nechells, Acocks Green, and so on. Moving and mixing have diluted my tones, to the extent that telling people where I was born and grew up frequently presses the switch that illuminates their delight: 'Oh, yo'm from Birmingham!' they triumph, crudely lingering on the first syllable *Birm*, in the most appalling travesty of an impression. Yes, and thank you for informing me. Please don't tax your wit any further by educating me that I'm bald. I noticed that on my own nearly fifty years ago, but I'm not going to lose any hair over it!

Many, indeed most, of those Staffordshire grammar school teachers were, in knowledge and effectiveness, of a high standard, *mutata mutandis* equal to the best I have worked alongside for over forty years. We all just took them for granted; I certainly did. When the bar is high, few if any stand significantly above it. At thirteen, I had no idea whatever that my new English teacher, R.F.Langley, would have such an effect on me, or that he would go on to earn distinction and recognition as a poet and journal writer. His sadly early death at only 73 from heart failure stunned me when I chanced upon it in the Farewell column on the inner pages of *The Week*.

How many secondary school teachers earn a full-page obituary notice in the *Guardian*?

Young, bearded, trim and smart in his grey suit, crisp white shirt and monocolour ties, perhaps mauve or yellow, RFL led us to ideas, experiences, riches. In just the two school years of our second and third forms, we became acquainted with the Egyptian *Book of the Dead*; Freud's psychoanalytical theories, particularly about the *ego, id* and *superid*, the subconscious mind and the interpretation of dreams; Sartre and Existentialism; Descartes' method of doubt and *cogito ergo sum*; Wordsworth and the Imagination; Gestalt psychology; macrocosm and microcosm in the Elizabethan world view; order and hierarchy in *Macbeth*; haiku poetry; the music of the spheres; allegory and symbolism … all these treats as well as the standard fare of comprehensions, grammar lessons, Shakespeare (*A Midsummer Night's Dream* and *Twelfth Night*), readers, poems. The last items were from the stock cupboard, available to all. Our form had extras, usually on duplicated sheets: Larkin's *Toads*, poems by Yeats and Pound. If continuity issues one challenge to an English teacher and predictability another, Roger Langley answered both, with fresh surprises and his own shared excitement. He carried around a foolscap (I think) hard covered book, which he kept as a journal, writing his thoughts and observations, illustrations and drawings, perhaps short extracts he wanted to record from his reading. As in our exercise books, he wrote with fountain pens, often broad-nibbed and italic, with unusual shades of red, lavender and brown inks. I believe he found pleasure in the physical business of writing, the production of attractive layout and design, the sensations of drawing the nib over quality paper, feeling its texture, savouring the aromas of special inks, observing the stylish formation of his characters, cleanly glistening wet till before assuming their final mattness.

But what I most treasured during those two years were the weekly invitations to write my own things. I cannot recall now how they were stimulated or triggered (to use our jargon); one old exercise book from June 1963 to March 1964, when I was 13-14 in Forms 2A and 3A, contains a number of my pieces, certainly uneven in quality, but really quite varied, and with one or two perhaps slightly more reasonable passages:

[from January 1964] '… Imagine a dark, dusty, Victorian style sitting room. Its decoration is brown and cream interlaced with drab cobwebs and outdated fly cards in the disguise of calendars. The room is small, its only relief a single chair, well past its prime, and a table of cane. The chair is occupied by a sweatered and trousered male, whose age it is difficult to tell; he has not shaved since his youth, obviously long past forgotten. He stares at a dark patch on the wall; dark because the damp has disgustingly oozed through the wall. The oil-lamp produces no effect, for the shade is hidden under a film, nay sheet, of filth …'

I have no recollection what stimulated this unsavoury meditation, but suspect that I was absorbed in recording it. Equally, I accepted that, whatever response I should encounter when our books were returned, there would almost certainly be a carefully considered reaction, often extending some way down the page, by no means entirely positive, but always constructive, thought-provoking and helpful. By a lamer half-line of a poem: a cross and 'stock idea', [of a short story] 'too confused as a whole to hang together', [of a silly statement] 'perish the idea' – they were all fair comments, and balanced by a kindly will to find *something* to approve of.

After he moved to Wolverhampton Grammar, three of us kept in touch with Roger Langley for a couple of years, even cycling uninvited over to his house in Aldridge, where we were always well received. My perhaps more than optimistic requests for him to look over a poem or two I had written elicited, through the post, a typed two sides of comment and advice. Generous with his time and indulgence, RFL would also lend – or even give – you books. I still have the copy of *The Penguin Book of Modern American Verse* he suggested I look at, particularly recommending poems like William Carlos Williams' *To Waken an Old Lady*:

Old age is
a flight of small
cheeping birds
skimming
bare trees
above a snow glaze.
Gaining and falling
they are buffeted
by a dark wind
But what?
On harsh weedstalks
the flock has rested,
the snow
is covered with broken
seedhusks
and the wind tempered
by a shrill
piping of plenty.

He told me 'poems grow on trees' in Hobbs Hole Lane, not far from where his parents lived in Leighswood Road. Skeats' Etymological Dictionary was 'an invaluable guide to thinking.' One important rule for writers (or was it just me?) was 'prune, prune, prune.' He spoke about 'particularity', which later made sense when I came across his poems and had learned about Hopkins' *haecceitas.* It meant everything to me when I pleased him, which was by no means always, though the mark of 48/50 for a discursive competition essay we all had to write and his response to our first ever English Literature exam (in Form 4, involving *Henry V*) both took me by surprise. Somehow, I came top of the year in the latter, with 70%.

I cannot explain what happened to me in the third form. I became competitive, being placed 1st in the Christmas exams. Secure at home, largely unintimidated at school, feeling at some advantage because of the start given to me by St Philip's, I came out fairly well in all subjects, top perhaps only in physics and German, but second in French and in the first few of most other subjects. Increasingly, they made sense to me, with one exception, geography, for which I could find no organising principles or rationale. We had hopped across a few topics, like sheep farming in Australia, coffee production in South America, offshore and onshore winds. One or two of the form just lapped it up and made sense of it, or at least could simply recall it all. Their exercise books were neat and colourful. For me it was too bitty and unrelated. I know now that if I had begun to suspect some connection between where and how people live, and so what life is like for them – and how they develop, of course, I should almost certainly have become at least engaged, more likely fascinated. Or, even more likely, if the *physics* of physical geography had been shown to us in some structured and sensible way, I might have taken things for myself. Worse was to follow!

I learned two major lessons in the spring and summer terms. I could take control of some things and make changes, but that they might come at a price. Whilst, I suspect, many of the form led more peaceful and balanced lives, thinking about the Beatles and fashionable clothes et cetera, mixing more with friends, I narrowed things down. I wanted to stay first in the form. Weeks before the summer exams, I made my revision timetable. These days, it is standard practice for form teachers to draw up plans with their pupils; we were left to ourselves. Many clearly did nothing at all till the last moment.

My strategy could not have been more basic, brutal even: prepare and learn everything. Make lists, go through exercise and text books, worksheets, processing *everything*. All the listed items were plotted on a daily chart over several weeks. Both at weekends and in the evenings I followed the scheme, dividing my work sessions into periods I relieved with listening to records or playing my treble recorder. The recording by Yehudi Menuhin of the Max Bruch first violin concerto (Opus 26), with the London Symphony Orchestra conducted by Sir Langdon Ronald, became my routine diversion and reward. (As far as I could, I played along, using Dad's violin part!) I allowed myself one movement between topics, the three movements being conveniently recorded on three 78 rpm records in 1931, when Menuhin was fifteen. (Dad had actually *seen* and *heard* him play the Bruch in Birmingham before the War. He had a small framed photograph of the violinist playing, with an autographed torn off programme margin.)

I had no idea how to tackle geography. I more or less gave up on it.

In those times, form teachers habitually posted lists of marks and placings on the classroom notice board. Our form teacher, David Maddock (Modern Languages) used blue-black ink on a torn off scrap of lined paper. So, he would be pinning up two lists for us, one in French and, finally, our form positions. I kept a page of percentages and positions in my rough workbook, my own on one side and those of the classmates I most feared nearby.

Our chemistry teacher, Mr Hamish Poulsom, seemed quite put out when he returned our papers to us. My 92% must have thrown him off balance. He certainly had not been expecting it, since he had already given me only C+ (Average) on my report, and it was too late to revise that: all comments were written in a black leather-bound, gold-lettered Report Book, designed to hold *all* our reports from the first form to O level. (How the staff coped with the stress of not making mistakes occasioning rewrites is beyond my imagination.) Shockingly, I actually came first in chemistry, and can still regurgitate, completely pointlessly of course, information about the hardness of water and the allotropes of sulphur! Poulsom, by the way, struck me as both clownish and unlikeable, with unnecessarily rigid discipline and his marked northern accent, never more garish than when he stressed the second syllable of *nahtrayht;* his idiosyncratic way of referring to us ('blue Margaret', 'red Margaret', for example, because of their spectacles frames); and his clumsy unpleasantness. He seated us around the front bench for demonstrations, frequently walking around the semicircle to ask questions. If you gave the wrong answer, he would rap you sharply on the top of your head with his raised middle knuckle. On more than one occasion, he brought his arm down with a force increasing with this annoyance, on five or six heads, only to realise that the *first* person had said the right thing! Safety, and hence the need for good behaviour, are questionless essential in a laboratory, but I could not respect him.

Before I left the school, I ruefully discovered that we might even be distantly related!

Annette Jones (in the Alpha form) was definitely something like his niece, and *she* was a cousin to Tony Cantrill (also Alpha), who was *my* third cousin, or something like that. (Someone can work it out for me: Tony's father was my mother's first cousin, Leonard Cantrill.)

I came second in English, second in French, first in German, second in both history and biology, and first in physics. I enjoyed all those subjects, and felt I was beginning to get a grasp of them. They made sense, especially physics, so clearly and expertly taught by Francis George Butler. Again, some of his practices would be frowned upon these days. After an exam, he used to ask everyone to wait at the very front of the room, before handing back each paper in order, the lowest mark first. I do remember who that was, but shall not publish it! That girl had to sit on the extreme end of the first bench. As the marks rose, so we were seated, snaking around in ascending order to the very back of the room. Was this unfeeling? Might it stigmatise? One possible benefit was that those who most needed extra help and support would be exactly under Mr Butler's very nose and attention, whilst those who were most competitively eager to do well – and excitedly interested in the subject - would be cheerfully vying for 'pole' position, and in future determined to hang on every word from the front!

Never unkind or unreasonable, Francis Butler nevertheless exerted the tightest control. We could not relax, but were always completely on task. He played the role, of course, sustaining it without faltering, of holding us in alert obedience, much as I have seen trained dogs expectantly watching their masters' face and every gesture. Regularly, he tried to catch us out. Every lesson started with detailed enquiry into what we had done just before – or even way back earlier in the course. It was a game many of us loved, not least for – was it really a twinkle? Dare we smile?

> [*Very gravely – everyone mute and motionless*] 'What [*long pause*] is a [*slight pause*] watt?'
>
> Or
>
> 'How does heat travel? Yes – by convection, conduction and radiation. Heat rises … you can tell me why? … exactly, the molecules of air are more widely spaced … so why do our thermos flasks have openings *at the top* instead of at the bottom?'
>
> [*Long silence*] 'Well? Hall? Come on then, say it!'
>
> 'Please, sir …'
>
> 'Yes?'
>
> 'Well, sir, all the tea would spill out!'
>
> 'Well, thank you! I'm glad someone's brain is working! You'd better all revise gravity!'

Even in art, where I was generally clueless, my water colour effort at a wayside country cottage mysteriously did not fare too appallingly.

At the end of the year, I came first in the form. On the last day of term, I should take home a *red* report. The Headmaster, E.B (Ted) Merriott, colour coded his report comments and signatures: blue-black for almost everyone, but green for a small few who were causing serious concerns and red for a similar handful of those who had done well.

Final assembly was shortly after lunch. With so much time and like others, I chose to make my own way home. The school coaches left. I walked with three classmates to a house in Bronwhills, leaving after a short time to catch the ordinary service bus, stunned by the afternoon heat. The simmering roads and pavements smelt of dust. I caught the bus, knowing I should have to walk from either Shelfield, across the fields, or the library at Rushall.

Shelfield. On the pavement. Alone. Light-headed. Never been like this before. Things not right. A sudden rush of something sweeping up inside my head. The 'Test Your Strength' indicator rocketed, ringing some bell deafeningly. Like dizziness, but not. Numbing. Feeling vague and paused. Paused, yet panicking. Standing still on the empty pavement. Standing.

Things calmed enough for me to cross the main road and begin to walk home, past rows of silent houses. Disconnected. Another world. Across the fields. The bridge. Our door. Home.

Anticlimax after weeks of pressured intensity, emptiness, disappointment – the words will not convey the other-dimensional strangeness of this state. My mother understood I was not well. I had no explanation.

The next morning, the doctor prescribed something. For a day or two, I could do nothing. I slept, woke, ate, sat in a chair. When I moved, just turning my head might bring on another of those sudden head flashes, a tightness in my breathing, a weird hot freezing of arrest. My parents must have been worried. When a few days later, we went to Somerset for our summer caravan week, I rode as an invalid in the front of Dad's pea-green Ford Popular.

As suddenly as they had arrived, these neutralising onsets just evaporated, like summer mists under the sun. A time came when I realised I had not realised that I was just all right again. ('I quite forgot I could forget' – Edward Thomas *The Other*.)

Something similar to this has occurred to me only once since. Perhaps I had put myself under sustained pressure with too much intensity for too long. Certainly, more balance and variety during the previous few months, with more vigorous physical exercise, would have done no harm. But had I sacrificed myself for a petty victory? The exam marks I had so eagerly sought were not even recorded on our reports, just very broad impression grades from A to E. In four whole years at Shire Oak, I ached, at times feverishly, to bring home a complete set of As, though that was withheld until the last possible chance, in July 1966. Before that at least one grudging A- would be recorded. Perhaps they deliberately followed the philosophy of the raised stick and dangling carrot; more likely it was justice; and just as possibly the final clear round was allowed as consolation. At least my final geography mark was not written down, though David Maddock had to refer to it in his summary comment: 'Except in geography, this is a splendid record of achievement.' A less generous man might have written 19%!

Discoveries

These, in all they write, confess still what books they have read last, and therein their own folly so much, that they bring it to the stake raw and undigested...

Now, because they speak all they can (however unfitly), they are thought to have the greater copy; where the learned use ever election and a mean ...

Ben Jonson

My friend Vernon tells me my emails are 'stream of consciousness', which I suppose means unplanned or unstructured, maybe lacking conscious control.

I do like following my nose. I admit that. My secondary school teaching showed it. Of course, we must cover the syllabus – but that did not seem to me to ban spontaneity, tangential departures, digressions, anecdotes … thoughts circulate through the mind, like fluids in one's system … what one read last night, or this morning … that item in the news … some amusing or striking thing that has presented itself … things connect – or appear to. Why not share them?

Take what I have been reading. In the Introduction to his *Tall Tales and Wee Stories*, Billy Connolly confesses (or maybe boasts):

'All I have when I step out on stage is a wee list of headings like this:

Parachutists
Alcohol
Marijuana
Army
Scrotum
Holiday
Cameras
Shampoo'

That is pretty well the way I came to 'plan' my after-dinner speeches or sixth form assembly addresses to about 200 students and twenty or so colleagues; it worked better than a full script or even topic cards – or at least I thought so. Best of all, though, were the live additions and departures, when the audience and I reacted to each other or some incidental occurrence, or I went off piste on a whim.

In *H is for Hawk*, my bedside book this week, the writer Helen Macdonald skilfully, indeed quite beautifully, tells of acquiring and taming her goshawk, Mabel. But she is very much concerned too with her own life, her experience with falconry, her relationship with her father, who abruptly died young, and her struggle to understand herself and the world.

One tries, then, to make some sense of something. Why am I writing this?

I like writing. I wanted to write something. My time has been in short supply till now – or I have chosen to do other things with it. It is pleasing me to remember. Looking back at people, places and experiences enables some processing to take place; some fresh understandings, insights even, into aspects of one's life. One's glories and blessings can be celebrated, the trials glanced at, some circumstances recorded, perhaps even injustices avenged – if only in scorn and satire! If anything I have done has ever been even slightly creative, it was entirely ephemeral. No record remains, no *high-pilèd books in charactery*, not even some a measly low pile! Every year, I have had no occasion to return their card to my college informing them of some academic or other achievement I have clocked up. Even the intended model railway layout has never been built, nor several constructive projects completed, though like Prufrock I hope *there may be time.*

Children are born, grow and separate, taking over life for themselves. Pupils pass through our classrooms. Photographs amass, are stored or discarded, their very fidelity somehow distorting things, disappointing as Larkin says.

I have an end in sight, a half dozen years on from where I have reached. I shall endeavour to be not entirely predictable, not exhaustive, not entirely chronological. From the inside, those years to me were a Tutankhamun's treasury: wonderful things; to anyone else most probably nothing, or worse banality!

*****

Whilst my world narrowed down more and more centripetally to Shire Oak Grammar School, it felt to me as if it was opening out! New courses and teachers, even a totally new subject. A fascinating arrival to the staff, rich in talents, an abundant store of information and anecdotes, even a proficient oboist who would give me lessons in lunch hours. The first time I played in a concert, just a year after starting the instrument.

A first, brief friendship with a girl, even a cinema date one Saturday evening. Adolescent intensity and tears.

That saint of English teaching, Raymond O'Malley, the most humane and understanding of men, once told me during my PGCE year that we should never be condescending to or disparaging about our past experiences or what we had been when younger: that was how we were then. It was inevitable and right to be ourselves.

Only seven of us chose to study Latin at O level. That addition to the timetable was to be taught by C.J.Cooper as well as English. This Mancunian, son of the Vice Chancellor of the university there, Sir William Mansfield Cooper, had followed his secondary education at Manchester Grammar School with a four-year course at the relatively new Keele University. I formed the impression that his father had, presumably for idealistic educational reasons, encouraged him to take a joint honours degree after the initial 'general' foundation first year being provided in the north of our county. Chris Cooper had, he told us, enjoyed and benefited in a number of ways from his exalted father's position, including attending a succession of parties in New York where Marilyn Monroe was present. We were told that, maybe surprisingly, Monroe was not just or even a dappy, pretty woman, but a person of considerable intelligence. Less sensationally glamorous, perhaps, but intellectually and scientifically eminent, Sir Bernard Lovell, first director of the Jodrell Bank Observatory, had connections with the Cooper family, as no doubt had many other celebrated men and women from different spheres. Several of them, I am confident because Chris Cooper could invite them, visited the school to address the sixth form as part of their weekly lectures programme ('General Studies'). For me, the most awe-inspiring celebrity our Latinist had known was the oboist, Evelyn Rothwell, Lady Barbirolli. For a fifteenth birthday present, someone had bought him some lessons with the great English player. We were invited to imagine his trepidation, as he neared the front door of the Barbirolli household, to witness his own regular teacher emerge in tears: she had drawn Mighty Wrath by wearing lipstick! (See the footnote on page 58 of her book *Oboe Technique*, which legislates: 'Women oboe players should realize that lipstick clogs the fibres of the cane and may thus spoil a reed. It should be completely removed before playing.' This is firmly enough put, but not accorded the italicised prohibition [on page 16] against succumbing 'to the temptation of taking alcohol before playing.' That *non fiat* appears in the main body of the text!)

It was inevitable that I should revere a man of such varied glamour, teaching the subject I had burned to discover, expert at playing the very instrument I was obsessed with, attended by such rare artistic and cultural spirits, but additionally open, chatty, amusing ... There were only seven of us in the set. We could relax and hear jokes: the little girl called her cuddly Gladly because of the hymn *Gladly, my Cross I'd Bear*. The laundry van, delivering towels to the kitchens, pulled up outside Room 4. We read the message superscribed over the cab: 'Anthony's Passion Wagon, Moses'. We all convulsed, without understanding why. We assumed the name of a group 'Unit 4 Plus 3' in agreement with our gender balance. Andrew Coleman even told a less-than-delicate joke which included the word 'shagged': universal mirth again. This was revolutionary.

So was the teaching method. To get us to O level standard in the mere two years remaining we were issued with P.H.Vellacott's idiosyncratic textbook *Ordinary Latin*, which I suspect was that remarkable classicist's lesson notes collected and supplemented. Original and challenging, it launches off *in medias res*, though without assuming epic proportions, with third declension nouns, a brilliant ploy, since that is about as demanding as it gets, and if you master it you have immediate access to the largest group of nouns in the language. Admittedly, there were some gaps that

Vellacott had not filled in his book, probably because he would have covered the points in the classroom anyway.

I loved it. It all made sense, fitting together, supplying information and connections. Finding the private time to go back over material, ensure accurate memorisation, look ahead even at future topics rapidly became no chore but a joy-bringing fascination. We all have our quirks. No other study has so well taught me, in the most practical way, both some methods of self-instruction and its incalculable worth.

Little pedant that I was becoming, I even caught out CJC once or twice after some months had passed, when I pointed out an error he occasionally made, perhaps in not allowing for some word's irregularity. He took it with wry good humour, probably half thinking about late-night image counts towards his Master's thesis, work on the novelist Conrad, which eventually spawned the critical book *Conrad and the Human Dilemma* (Chatto & Windus, 1970).

Each Monday morning, some minutes after assembly, the Headmaster would burst into our room: history! The History of the Great Powers, 1870 to the Present Day. Bismarck's Foreign Policy: 'To promote European friendship, the Dreikaiserbund was formed …' How did he get away with it – not the right-wing Prussian who became Chancellor of a unified Germany, dominating European politics for two decades, but Ted Merriott? I think he had a B.Sc. degree (from Liverpool?) in mathematics; more accurately he should have been M.B., Master of Bluffing. Booming and blustering, he informed us with threatening imperiousness that we were 'all going to get a Grade 1', and in just one year. We were impressed.

By the second week the route markers to this Holy Grail has been pointed out to us. We were given a serious textbook, to read more or less on our own. At the beginning of each week, duplicated sheets, typed by his secretary and run off on the office Gestetner machine, were handed to us. We should memorise each model answer by the end of the week, when we should have to write it all out in the last lesson. As for actual teaching or discussion … When our efforts were speed marked, often in front of us, we should jump at high-explosive comments, usually at some patent blunder, but just as likely a surprise plaudit: 'That's one of *my* phrases, isn't it?'

I now wonder whether he actually did write the stuff that was doled out to us, sometimes four foolscap sides of twelve-point typing. For most of each lesson we suffered away in a silence enforced by a pregnant chemistry teacher, knitting at the teacher's desk. How do you memorise dozens of pages of tedious prose? Why should you even think of it?

'You're all going to get a Grade 1.'

Running the world, or his small part of it near an ailing Staffordshire colliery, perforce meant that the HM *had* to be elsewhere most of the time when he was timetabled to teach us. As a compensatory gesture, he would at odd moments fire himself into our classroom and detonate himself fairly randomly where his gaze landed.

'Ah, Christopher Robbins! Copying in a test? You've got your notes on your lap? You're a CHUMP, Robbins, a CHUMP! Come and see me in my room at the end of the lesson.'

By a disconcertingly brilliant stratagem he circumvented his ignorance of most of our names by calling all the girls by one name, and all the boys by another. So, when 'Kathleen Hawkins' was suddenly tagged on to the end of some brutally abrupt question, none of our suffering sisters had the faintest idea who was being targeted, their perplexity being intensified by Merriott's deliberate insistence on keeping his eyes on the *boys'* side of the room.

Naïvely trustful, we accepted all this as masterly classroom practice. We were all going to get a Grade 1.

Much of my time that year was ruined by the disintegrating folder, bulging more with each week. Learn all this lot? How? Why? Even Hercules had had a free pass on that sort of thing, and as for Sisyphus, his boulder did not actually increase in mass every Monday morning.

We were all going to get a Grade 1.

Looking back, I see what probably happened. The school was short of a history teacher. The head said he could and would fill in. He chose the top set, trusting that some elements of our industry and native wit would help us along. The rest was bluster. He could get away with it because a few moments' gaining some superficial acquaintance with a topic would be enough. After all, he chose the questions!

A Spanish and French teacher called Ralph James played a similar trick on us once, but harmlessly. Standing in for our German teacher, he strode in, allowed us to stand in silence, instructed us 'Setzen Sie sich, bitte!' and gave us the set work, some exercises. After twenty minutes or so, he asked for some answers to be read out.

'That doesn't sound very German to me! Who can say the word properly? Yes? Eustace?'

'Frühstück, sir.'

'Thank you. That's more like it. Carry on with the next exercise.'

The next lesson, Miss Graves confessed that James knew no German at all. He had asked her how to say 'Sit down' earlier in the day!

Ted Merriott definitely conned our whole form the next year. For reasons that will emerge, we were left without an English teacher for a term, just before O level. Enter Sir Edward, minus rearing steed, armoured and armed for the rescue. Again, the sally in, sally out manoeuvre … 'Write an essay on Sir Toby Belch in *Twelfth Night*. Mrs White will bring your books to my office at the end of the lesson. That all right, Mrs White? Kathleen Hawkins! Are you listening? Yes, you. You're Kathleen Hawkins, aren't you? Linda Profett? No. Today you're Kathleen Hawkins! It makes a change, doesn't it? Collect the books up at the end for Mrs White.'

The next lesson, he galloped in, dumped the books on a front desk.

'Christopher Robbins: give the books out. You'll see I've marked them. More quotations needed, Christopher "Dost thou think because thou art virtuous there shall be more no cakes and ale?" All of you, write out quotations in your exercise books and learn them. Mr Briggs will sit with you.'

I could teach myself in English.

Though I gained the form prize for 4A, our August history results ('You're all going to get a Grade 1') turned out to be bitter-sweet, containing a deserved lesson for Merriott himself, but hardly acknowledging all the sacrifices most of us had made: grade 3 for a few of us, with others going down to bare passes at grade 6, and at least one *ne plus ultra* grade 9. I learned the news in his office that August Thursday.

'Never mind, Hearne. You can repeat it next year, and get a Grade 1.'

'That's what you think,' I thought to myself, closing the door. In two days we were going to Skegness.

Since I shall never be fifteen again, there is little or perhaps no point in thinking over the time I went to the cinema with a girl one Saturday night. I had to ponder very hard about writing that, because 'experience with a girl' or 'first date' could well be misleading. Young, shy, (inevitably) inexperienced, I didn't have a clue what I was at, or what to expect, or anything at all.

How exciting, nevertheless, to walk to a public phone box a mile from home in order to make the call privately. We sat through a comedy, I think with Shirley Maclean, until we began to walk home, to be picked up by her father. Maybe I put my arm around her shoulders or held her hand. We certainly did not kiss!

I do not look back upon times like that (yes, others were to follow!) with a Larkinesque bitterness ('Nothing, like something, happens anywhere' etc). I idealised, elevated, thought (what I suppose may be called) purely. I liked the talking, sharing of ideas, finding things in common. Girls and femininity were, if not sugar and spice, delicate, different and special, soft, gentle, fragrant … When the young lady told me, I think the following Tuesday, that she did not want to continue, for a day or so some emotional deluge coursed through me, bringing new strengths, if not depths, of feeling. It really was the end of well, not the world, probably all time … Then I thought of something else. Life continued. I was all right again!

Some months on and still at school, we became fairly good ordinary friends. From our university days and till now, through our marriages, child-bearing and now grandparenting years, we still exchange greetings and news, if only at Christmas.

If bad news is good news for the media, perhaps good news is no news at all. Life went on smoothly and comfortably, at home or at school. With the exception of the wretched Great Powers, schoolwork was not just fine, but increasingly satisfying. Once you knew the passive voice in one German tenses, which you demonstrated with a model sentence, starting with the present:

> Man treibt Wintersport hier … Wintersport ist hier getrieben …

you progressed to all the other tenses. That was it! There were splendid definitions to learn in physics: ' A coulomb is the amount of electricity required to deposit 0.001118 gm of silver in a silver voltameter.' Latin boasted grammar and vocabulary even more gloriously than French and German. Maths made sense, though taking some time; you could even understand many things from first principles.

No English teacher could have compensated for the loss of RFL, who would stay at the school for just one more year, his fourth in teaching, but take another fourth year class. His successor, Welsh Mrs Reed, the new Senior Mistress, worked us systematically at exam style questions. I wished she would leave us more to try things on our own instead of going over everything before we attempted it! I cannot remember her communicating any excitement over language or ideas. That I came first in the year in our first ever English Literature examination, marked by the way by Roger Langley, must have been because I had fortuitously read the introduction to Shakespeare's *Henry V*, encountering some useful ideas and remembering some quotations:

> 'In peace there's nothing so becomes a man
> As modest stillness and humility etc'

School went well enough. I took the form prize again, but in no way stressed myself as I had the year before. Perhaps having more diversions helped: for example, being prompter and curtain winder for the school play (*Caesar and Cleoptra*), to which we brought more genuine drama than Shaw ever created. In one dress rehearsal, RFL, playing the part of Apollodorus and being forced to abandon his spectacles for reasons of authenticity, moved speedily across the stage to leap the sea wall (a disguised piece of vaulting equipment from the P.E. department), and swim away to safety… he told me afterwards he had very carefully worked out how many paces he had to run before a one-handed clearance of the 'wall'. He was terribly short-sighted without glasses. The foot stool left from a previous scene by an errant stagehand normally would not have mattered … the sprawling, clattering crash shocked everyone, not least the hapless teacher. For some seconds he lay completely motionless. We all froze. The eventual florid curse relieved our feelings too.

Even though the stage manager made sure thereafter that the path was clear, Apollodorus made his subsequent exits much more gingerly, to be followed shortly later by Caesar. But it was a fated episode. On the first night, poor Jones, playing Britannus, had the curtain pulled on him before he could finish the scene, reducing the audience to raucous mirth, the stage manager's signal for some dramatic effect being mistaken for the end of scene curtain wind.

In the interval, we lost all lighting backstage. With moments to spare, our physics teacher unscrewed the green metal panel to expose the fault when he threw the mains back on: a firework of sparks and sharply pungent smoke showed the short circuit. Working by torchlight, Mr Butler put it right, just as the end-of-interval bell was rung.

Just before Christmas, I played the oboe in an actual performance when the school orchestra accompanied the audience singing of Christmas carols. Unlike the musing magus's comment on his Bethlehem visit of long ago, that large ensemble (violins, violas, cellos, double bass, flutes, oboe, clarinets, trumpets, trombones and percussion), was not (and never was) what anyone might judge satisfactory! Despite the contributions of some able and promising young musicians, the rest made a pretty appalling sound, individually and together, with such variation of individual pitch and poor playing intonation, that even parental love must have been taxed. To be fair, we were probably at our best with first nowells and heralding angels. Our interpretation of the Pilgrims' March from Mendelssohn's 'Italian' symphony might have accompanied resisting victims to a torture chamber, whilst our take on the Minuet and Trio from Haydn's 'Surprise' symphony liberally added some original bone juddering shocks.

Special dispensation allowed me to return a few days late for the start of 5A. Skegness blasted and chilled us from the East, though Dad was delighted by the conditions for kite flying. Against the level evenness of that part of the world, Boston Cathedral raised a splendid protest, whilst the county's windmills whirled spectacularly. One day I must finish Charlotte Brontë's *Shirley*, half of which I read in Lincolnshire before I had to return it to the library.

When I returned myself to Shire Oak, I was furious that Merriott had put me – and everyone else – back into the classroom, to go through the whole business of the accursed Great Powers again. After all, he clarified, we had all his notes! If we learned them this time (really?), we etc etc Grade 1. As a luxurious treat, we had been allowed four timetabled lessons to sit in a classroom and bone ourselves up.

For the rest of the year, he hardly visited us. I lugged my loathsome albatross around, that grubby, deconstructing envelope folder, in my school bag, rotting like some bloating seed pod, doomed never to quicken and yield.

At some point, I think quite early in the year, the Deputy Head, Mr Wemyss-Holden, asked me to join a newly forming orchestra, the Royal Sutton Philharmonic! I would be second oboe to Chris Cooper, whose wife Elspeth would play viola. Mr Holden himself would play his second instrument, the bassoon. It would be unjust of me not to acknowledge the Deputy's contribution to music. A clarinettist of some quality, able to give an accomplished recital of works from Mozart to Finzi, he devised and brought about all the instrumental music in the whole school, personally starting dozens of pupils off on his own main instruments, to which he added the flute, oboe, trumpet and trombone! He started and was responsible for (cynics might say was guilty of), the school orchestra, liaised with the County Music Director, brought in outside teachers and performers, and formed a wind quintet, where I first came across the medium and a range of works - all this in addition to being second in command of the whole school and teaching history. Ex RAF, he imposed fierce discipline, never more impressively seen than when, alone on the platform, he controlled the completely silent dismissal of the whole school from assembly. Black-suited and gowned, he stood tall on the edge of the stage, arms folded in a pose of Egyptian regality. He had to perfection the trick of quelling the slightest suspicion of incipient restlessness with a swelling intake of breath through the nostrils, almost a sniff.

Yet he was human. I recall one event, an evening of Christmas music and readings, when I could see JWH at close range as we sat in the orchestra behind him, facing the audience. As he stood at the lectern for his reading, the military sharp crease of his trousers was distinctly quivering with nerves no one could have detected from the rich and beautifully modulated voice. *'Tis true: this god did shake* as Cassius remarked about Shakespeare's Julius. Fittingly, Jack Holden actually *was* the Roman leader, or at least Shaw's version of him in the same production which sent Roger Langley sprawling. The school still having few older pupils at that time, he joined his English teacher colleague and our German teacher, Senior Mistress Miss Graves (Ftatateeta), on stage.

Grandly named, the Royal Sutton Philharmonic actually met in a dusty wooden scout hut! A local violinist, Howard Bonsor, conducted us, I think wielding the baton for the first time.

We all have to start somewhere! For me in a fairly serious orchestra, it was with Haydn's 'Clock' symphony, the overture to Rossini's *The Thieving Magpie*, the two *l'Arlésienne* suites by Bizet, Elgar's *Nursery Suite*, Schubert's *Rosamund* music, the overture to Strauss's *Die Fledermaus*, Mozart's Symphony 40 … I more or less coped with Chris Cooper next to me, but definitely struggled on the occasions he could not attend our Monday night sessions. Sight-reading was one issue, counting bars of rest another. Most taxing, though, and unexpected was the difficulty of playing quietly and sensitively enough, following the conductor's variations in tempo … The other players, all much older and all considerably experienced, found astounding resources of tolerance and generous encouragement. The halfway tea break brought welcome relief.

At home, I played the oboe, and sometimes recorder, manically, or listened to music for huge portions of the day, tuning to Radio 3 as soon as I came downstairs every day shortly after 7 a.m. It was hardly the most considerate behaviour in such a small, open-plan house, every sound from any room being painfully audible in any other. Even dad's love of music and paternal tolerance reached their elastic limits when I worked extensively at Hans Ulrich Staeps' *Virtuose Suite* for solo recorder. Tonally adventurous à la Hindemidt, this four-movement composition challenged me irresistibly when I saw it marked 'd' in Schott's catalogue, i.e. 'difficult'. As I recall, only the Sonatina by Lennox-Berkeley was also offered with this warning. For me, it has been a lifetime source of technical and expressive wealth, though only in my late sixties did I venture to perform the first three movements in a lunchtime recital. The final challenge remains of the last, marked 'Presto Possibile' requiring extensive use of double-tonguing, which I learned from Rowland-Jones' book *Recorder Technique*, more or less memorised along with the companion volume on the Oboe (Evelyn Rothwell). Ordering the latter, I recall, proved no simple matter in the Walsall branch of W.H.Smith, the poor Saturday assistant having to cross out at least four wildly wayward misspellings of 'oboe' before I quietly offered to fill in the request form by myself. Dad's background snorts and tuts cannot have helped the flustered pimply youth.

Though after a couple of sessions the lessons with Chris Cooper fell by the wayside, I worked through the tutor (Langey) he had loaned me, as well as through various pieces I got hold of. Doing so largely on my own inevitably led to limitations and restrictions. With no teacher to supply or adjust reeds, and absolutely no knowledge, tools or skills, I was dependent upon what could be bought from a general music shop. That meant a Saturday afternoon drive to Yardley's, near Snow Hill Station in Birmingham. They stocked Prestini reeds, sold in colourless plastic tubes with green stoppers. I just had to get by as well as I could.

When I went to a Saturday morning rehearsal of the Second Staffordshire Youth Orchestra, for the first time I met a professional oboist, Brenda Rees/Constantine. For some part of each rehearsal she would take you out of the whole group and give you some guidance. Susan Haycock, from Queen Mary's Girls', who I think went on to study at the Royal College and play professionally, was already Mrs Constantine's pupil, about to take Grade 5. Whether it was her instrument, reeds, natural ability or the tuition she had received, Susan made a better, more authentic sound that I did. I envied her. In one or two brief meetings, this tutor corrected some of my basic bad habits, certainly of posture and stance, but probably of embouchure and breathing. I went home and played till I ached, recharged.

Somehow it came about that I gained a piano accompanist, Carole from the year above, who sang Bach arias, played the viola in the County *First* Orchestra, and was preparing to play a piano concerto (*Miniature Concerto* by Alec Rowley) with the school orchestra – generally an all-round natural musician. After school, we went through whatever pieces I had, like Dad's volume of Handel's violin sonatas, using the upright piano at the back of the geography room. We talked about other shared interests, too, novels and poems.

All this sadly had to stop when Carol's family suddenly moved north. Her father, a local Superintendent of Parks, had been promoted to a similar position in the Potteries. Carol left the school, I think at Christmas. We exchanged a letter or two; she had started at Longton Sixth Form College, doing English, French and Music. She wrote out and sent to me Donne's *The Sunne Rising*, which spoke most powerfully to her:

> She is all States, and all Princes, I,
> Nothing else is.

Carol's friend, the Congregationalist minister in Walsall, was going to be in the massed choir of local churches performing Bach's B Minor Mass one Saturday in February. Carol would be travelling back south that weekend, staying with a friend. Would I like to go to the performance with them?

Walsall Town Hall might not seem the likeliest place for a life-changing experience. The scale of the masterpiece, the quality and power of the vocal soloists, the fine playing from the Orchestra da Camera, conducted by Hamish Preston (and with Brenda Rees playing oboe!) – all of these and much more began to teach me new depths and dimensions, from the sun-blinding charge of the first full choir *Kyrie*, the urgently overlaying orchestral lines, kaleidoscopically changing instrumental colours, vibrant purples from the oboi d'amore, shining silver from the flutes … The sheer inventiveness of each succeeding section: forms, ensembles, musical ideas … majesty, might, glory, compassion, sincerity … human totality. *Gloria in excelsis deo*, a Michelangelo wall; *et in terra pax* … exultant peace, profound and celebratory relief. Carole was leaning towards me to share her Novello vocal score. Her shoulder brushed mine, her waves of red hair my cheek. At the end of the Gloria, she put her lips to my ear.

'They're missing out the first three sections of the Credo. The Catholic men's choir couldn't cope with it.'

I breathed the weight of her warmth.

The next day, Saturday, we met in Walsall again, to go to the cinema, sitting twice through *Alfie* with the young Michael Caine. 'He doesn't learn,' Carole whispered at some point in the philanderer's shallow blunderings. I think she had read Bill Naughton's book. I put my arm around her shoulder and kissed her.

We met in town again on Sunday, to walk around for an hour or two in the afternoon. Around four o'clock, we said goodbye to each other at the top of a hill near the Congregationalist church from where her father would shortly collect her. We agreed to write, and exchanged addresses.

I was walking down the hill, back towards the bus station to go home, knowing that Carole was walking in the opposite direction at my back. We had become emotional, embraced and kissed one long, softly gentle kiss. Walking felt effortless. Deep inside me something was laughing liberally. The fine spring day would still be light for hours. Upstairs on the bus I looked over the trees of the Arboretum, freshly leaved. The lake shone its cool blueness back up to an almost cloudless sky. A fragrance was ascending from my paisley neckscarf. Carole.

I must be in love.

Over the next few weeks letters, maybe two or three a week, fluttered the fifty or so miles between Pelsall and the park-superintendent's house in Longton Park, where Carole lived: what we had been reading or listening to, trivial things that had happened, our teachers, how we were missing each other. Carole recommended *Where Angels Fear to Tread.* I read the library copy. I wrote out for her the programme details from a superb Radio 3 broadcast of Spanish Renaissance Church Music I had listened to from that ancient portable radio, smuggled into a steamy bathroom. What she fed me I greedily consumed: metaphysical poets, T.S.Eliot, the Shakespeare tragedy they were studying, Bach's fugues, A level harmony and composition, new French vocabulary, double and triple trills in Chopin … Meanwhile, the decade continued to deluge us with the Beatles, Mary Quant, Carnaby Street and all the rest of popular culture. Collarless jackets and pointy shoes meant nothing to me. I had been learning a different musical language, exploring inexhaustible mines of riches. I refused to try to 'do the twist'; my daemon spirit danced elsewhere more darkly, possessed. 'Fab' and 'groovy' were laughably valueless, 'great' a tired, unthinking gesture. At their most charitable, my classmates put me down as serious, but more usually with lip-lifting contempt as 'square'.

Some weekends later I travelled north for an overnight stay in Longton Park. Dad drove me to Wolverhampton Station, for a journey that these days can take only thirty minutes, but should not extend to a full hour. Of course, I checked the timetable for the time and platform. I was watching the station clock carefully. It was the right place and the right time. Just to make sure, I asked a uniformed station worker if the approaching train was the Stoke one. 'Yes, mate,' he promised.

There were families, parents and young children, in the carriage, lots of them. They all seemed excited.

We did not stop until we reached Prestatyn. I do not know how long that took. These days, a fast train gets to that North Wales resort in under two hours, a slower one taking sixty minutes longer. Oh Mr Porter!

It must have been well after lunchtime that I finally made it to Stoke, where I phoned a distressed Carole. Her father collected me. We sat behind him, holding hands in the Ford Escort Estate. I omitted to mention the scorn I had endured when I explained my mishap to the ticket inspector. In front of everyone else he had loudly remarked that some people needed their mothers to do everything for them. Mercifully, that release of disgust sufficed him: he left huffily without asking me to pay any extra.

In the afternoon, we went to the cinema again, where the only film showing was once more *Alfie*. Again we sat through it twice. It did not seem to matter. Back at the Park Lodge we played music together. After the gates closed at dusk, we had the whole park to ourselves. We walked around the lake. We could have taken a boat out.

Novel and glamorous enough, this unfortunately shortened brief stay was topped by the chance to play more duets on the Sunday morning, before catching this time the right train back. One piece I am certain we went through, probably twice, was the Concerto by Arthur Benjamin on themes of Cimarosa.

We continued to exchange letters.

*****

It's my turn now. My first time. Andrew and Michael did it two years ago. I'm hot. I'm nervous. I feel electricity in the air around me. Her pyjamas trousers are making the tops of my legs itch.

'Go on!' a voice whispers in my ear. 'Now!' I edge forward …

A wave of warmth surges weightily over me. The light is stunning. Beyond it, a dim impressionist tableau, hazy: the audience. First night of the school play. Two steps have brought me from the wings into full view:

Solanio *Good morrow, my good Lords.*

Bassanio *Good signiors both, when shall we laugh? say, when?*

The new Head of English, Mr Field, was putting on *The Merchant of Venice.* One afternoon after lessons, weeks before, he had auditioned me in the classroom where I had started that very first September morning over four years before. All directors cut their coats according to the cloth they have. He asked me to read the speech from early on in Act I, Scene I:

In Belmont is a Lady richly left, ...

Knowing nothing of either the play or the ambivalent young Venetian wastrel, I instinctively made a misty-eyed emotional crescendo in my appreciation of the tasty inheritrix: wealth, looks, virtues … naïve?

A couple of days later, Mr Field stopped me in the corridor between lessons to hand over a Penguin Edition copy of *The Merchant of Venice*. Over half a century later, the tattered booklet's school grid, stamped on the title page, claims it to be on issue to Hearne 5A, in the same red ink which records 'Bassanio' in the top margin.

Bounty hunter or beau idéal, the character assuredly has enough to say for himself, though his online count, which tells you 73 lines, compared with Shylock's 79, makes no allowance for his lungs' stamina. No wonder Portia compares him to the Roman hero just before he makes his choice from the caskets:

Go Hercules …

when his next three speeches fill 35, 35 and 11 lines each, which with his other contributions in that scene alone tot up to 113 lines, all but 6 of verse. So, a straight and wordy, maybe dodgy, romantic character, someone who can recall and reel off stuff … !

When our costumes arrived in a huge wicker basket from the hire department at Stratford, my outfit turned out to be in dark turquoise, the breeches puzzingly cut in two separate parts: puffed out shorts from the waist to crotch and some curious thighwear, held up by an elastic waist band, meant to be overlapped by the balloon pants.

As part of the fitting session we were inspected moving around on stage. On me, the two breeches parts did not meet, by a considerable way. Several square inches of upper inner thigh glared out whitely under the lights. They must have stretched in use or been made for a different physique … Miss Langley, helping with costume, took pity and called me aside. 'I'll do something about that,' she promised. Before the dress rehearsal, she handed me a carrier bag. 'Wear these underneath,' she said. They were her cotton pyjama bottom, acceptably blue-green. 'I won't tell anyone if you don't,' she smiled. 'I've cut the frilly bits off.'

The sweetest moments in the three or four performances were just before our entries for the last time in the last act. Portia and Nerissa, Gratiano and I waited in the corridor outside the school hall, excited and whispering. Pulling the blackout slightly away from the glazed door panel, we saw the bluely moonlit stage:

On such a night as this …

How many things by seasons season'd are! Indeed! Most of our living is automatic. It has to be. We repeat movements, routines, patterns; we assume habits, even consciously adopt them. You don't have to think about making your morning cup of tea or breakfast, nor any of the dishes and meals you've been serving up for years. You just do it. Oh, is that the time? I'd better put the oven on early. That chicken is a bit bigger than we normally have.

It is only when we do or experience something new or for the first time, something special for good or bad, that we become more sharply and perhaps deliberately aware of all that is happening, more alert and alive. That one occasion, out of unnumbered dozens, when your cycle tyre hit the surprise patch of black ice in early December just around the corner from home, over seven years ago. The split-second replays still: the stomach plunge before the eternally instant wait for the shattering crash and slithering slide, the simultaneous security floodlights of damage – shoulder, hip, elbow; the wet road inches from your eye, focused; the battlefield urgent inner scream to clear the road; jet roar pain, crescending; distressing damage to cycling tights, that favourite jersey, the Italian bike's pedal and gear lever … All these things and more register and are long retained; yet the actual event scarcely occupies seconds.

I must have waited outside the assembly hall dozens of times, at least for my first two years at the school. From the first day, I had been marshalled with the other Catholics, about thirty of us, to wait outside the religious part of school assemblies. The duty member of staff kept us quiet some way away from the door before lining us up. The hymning, praying and holying got through, the C of E multitude paused whilst we trooped into the front row seats left vacant for us. That was just ordinary.

This was different, better, special, magical! Each night, we felt that we had made it at this point. The rest would be relaxed, easy. The words delivered themselves, at the right paces. We felt the audience. They laughed readily at the rings and cuckolding business.

I suppose you could call it peaceful excitement.

One chance comment and reaction subsequently acquired added significance. Alfie Birch (Gratiano) had teased our Head Girl (Portia) just before we made that final entrance. To her *sotto voce*, over-the-shoulder protest as we lined up, 'Oh, I'm putting on weight!' he had innocently, though with a grin, suggested, 'You need a corset!' She spun round and, with a tightly furious face, thumped him heavily several times. It must have hurt. Alfie suppressed his cries with gulps. The next term we heard that Portia had left the school. She was going to have a baby.

When we came to write our O level papers, I felt fine, apart from nuisance considerations like Bismarck, Lenin, the Weimar Republic and a couple of worldwide conflicts. How amusing it was to look around at the start of each paper and see the surrounding dozens scribbling breathlessly. I surveyed the paper, chose my questions, jotted down the question changing times and worked my way through, with the kind of pleasure you can find in filling in crossword answers. We were entered for a maximum of eight subjects, unlike the luckier people at other local grammar schools, who were allowed ten. For me that meant English Language and Literature, Maths, Physics, French, German, History (oh no!) and Latin, the last being delayed until the November since we had started so late. In those early years, the school record for Grade 1 passes stood at six, clocked up by John Anslow the previous year.

We must have been more compliant or tightly suppressed than the young folk I have taught, since the next school day after the last paper, we were all back in class for, I think, another fortnight before the summer break. The people who did let go were our teachers, who did just what they liked now that the syllabus business was all dispensed with. For our German teacher, that meant teaching us some elementary Russian, from a tantalisingly small taster of which I retain only two sentences. I have never yet been called upon to tell a native of that country that my brother is not a physicist, or that there is a bright electric light, but maybe one day … In Physics, Francis Butler toyed with us yet again, getting us to derive the remaining equations of speed and time from the first one. Bernie Wight had already gone beyond the maths syllabus to introduce calculus, with some basic differentiation and integration. Why didn't we use that, Mr Butler demanded, pretending to be both surprised and a little impatient. You could never tell how serious he was. Did knowledge have to be narrowly kept in compartments? Couldn't we think? For me, this was just brilliant. What else were we missing?

Even though we had more freedom, I did on one occasion take an extra liberty. A day or two before we broke up, the French exchange pupils arrived from Châteaubriant. That meant that Carole, with whom I had been exchanging increasingly dreamy, rather lovesick letters for weeks now, would be driven down from Stoke to collect the exchange partner she had stayed with the previous year. I think she was called Anne. On the scheduled afternoon, I separated myself from the others and kept out of the classroom, hovering behind the pillars of the foyer where the hosts and guests would be reunited. Either before or after that, Carole arrived. With disgraceful innocence we slipped away to some remote corner for some fairly enthusiastic embracing and kissing.

A man's sudden voice made us jump. 'What would the Headmaster say if he saw you doing that?'

It was Mr Dowen, the school caretaker. Even at the height of summer he wore a faded blue boiler suit. Like other similar workers, he made a tirelessly massive contribution to the running and well-being of the place and everyone in it. I have no idea why we nicknamed him Clarence. His favourite question, frequently heard, was: 'Now, would you do that at home?'

Carole leaned back. My arms were still around her. 'Oh, he just turned a blind eye,' she replied. Clarence snorted and walked away. Moments later, with a startled wince she put her hand to her mouth. 'Oh my God!'

'What?'

'I'd forgotten. He's blind in one eye.'

It was true. The watery, immobile ocular prosthesis, lighter hued than its blue companion, told its own story, though I heard the full account a couple of years later from Bert Dowen himself. A German bullet had blinded and almost killed him. He had known nothing about it until he woke up in hospital some days later in England. He never complained.

A chatty new teacher once told us *his* understanding: the nickname came from Clarence, the cross-eyed lion in the television series *Daktari*. But we were sure that wasn't it. He was just Clarence because it suited him. And us.

I was at home on my own the July Saturday when England won the World Cup. I watched the game on our black and white set. When Mom and Dad returned from shopping in Aldridge they told me men had crowded around the TV shop window in the village, cheering and weeping openly.

At about 5 o'clock one July morning, for the first time in my life I saw a fox as I walked across the fields on my way to Shelfield, the urban creature still being fairly rare or at least reclusive, whereas in 2021 Surrey they are everyday sights, often passing you nonchalantly by on the pavements or in your garden, in our case as squatters under my garden workshop, where last year a pair raised a cub. I had started early to catch the coach on its pick up. The French exchange party was heading down the M1 to London. Whether Mr Maddock thought I really wanted language practice or just to spend time with Carole, he allowed me to tag on to the party for a number of trips: Chatsworth, Colwyn Bay, Bourton-on-the-Water, the Capital … I sat by Carole on the coach, smooching with her when the teachers were looking the other way. Before the party left, our boys played theirs at football in Rushall. Though the players were the same for two games, we lost the first 2-7 only to reverse the result 4-2 the next day. It was the last time we would play together after more than four years. Brian Eustace had kept goal with instinctive control and athletic skill throughout. Like others, he had already finished his schooling and had a training course lined up, I think in telephone engineering. When I took the ball off an attacking French boy, he stumbled over his own feet or perhaps the ball, ending up on the ground. The black-faced scowl with which he batted off my proffered helping hand would have done a professional proud.

Probability and an internet calendar suggest Thursday 18th August as the likeliest date for O level results publication. Carole would be travelling south to be with me.

I made my way alone to school for the 10 am release time. Members of my year were arriving, singly or with a friend or two, sometimes a parent, to wait in the foyer. In turn, we were sent down the narrow corridor to the Head's office at the end.

'Ah, Hearne!' Mr Merriott boomed. 'Well, you didn't do too well in History, though I suppose the rest were all right.'

He wasn't pleased.

'Grade 5!' he frowned. 'It should have been a Grade 1!'

He passed me two slips. The first was from the Southern Universities Joint Board. My class alone, as an experiment, had been entered for English Language for two boards simultaneously. The SUJB print out had just one result: English Language 79%. No Grade. I held it out towards the Head, for explanation.

'That's Grade 1.'

The second slip read:

English Language	3
English Literature	1
Mathematics	1
Physics	1
French	1
German	1
History	5

It wasn't quite what I had hoped for, in the JMB English exam at least; the History 5 said exactly what I felt for the beastly Great Powers from 1870 onwards and their pestiferous agent, but English? The *Language* part of things? That threw me.

Of course, it proved inconsequential, both immediately and much more so afterwards. The SUJB grade made things somewhat better. If you counted that, I had still equalled Anslow's record of six at the top grade, with Latin to follow in November[2]. Having in later years marked English Language papers I easily understand that failure to supply exactly what the narrow demands of comprehension questions expected, or perhaps not quite pleasing whoever assessed the more creative essay paper definitely would have made a difference. More likely, though, I committed some of those sins of carelessness which I detect only too often in myself: superficial reading, ineffective or absence of proof-reading, or just plain ignorance. The results of my own life's experiments bear out Father Hamish's hypothesis with irritating frequency: God indeed is alone perfect!

The sun was shining. On balance, I had done as well as anyone else – well actually better! And Carole was with me. She heard my news with noisy happiness, smiling and bouncy. We hurried up the drive holding hands, first to find a phone box. I wish I could remember whether I called home or my father's office. One or the other would have been agreed upon.

Carole had suggested a day in Lichfield. We caught the bus. On a bench near the Cathedral we ate soft bread rolls and Dairylea cheese, bought with apples from the Co-op. Before catching the bus back later in the afternoon we visited the Cathedral, walked around the city's sights. In the secondhand bookshop we found the floors – I think they were named after countries or continents – of our interests. I bought a copy of Vergil's *Aeneid IX* in the Macmillan 'Modern School Classics' red bound series as well as a small selection from Jacob Van Eyck's *Der Fluyten Lusthof*, edited by Dolmetsch. I had no idea then that all of the blind carilloneur's virtuoso works for unaccompanied recorder, some of them contractually written for his midday performances outside the cathedral in Utrecht, would fill three thick volumes of sheet

[2] Though the November result did allow me to go one better, any triumph was short-lived, since Patricia Cross in the year below made it the maximum eight the following summer. This yet again evinces that the Almighty is female, God alone being perfect! Pat went on to study Modern Languages at Oxford.

music. The Swedish maestro, Dan Laurin, has recorded every piece, all the sets of diminutions, on nine CDs! Of the five in my selection, the last one, *Malle Symen* 'Naughty Simon' became my favourite, played in solitude over the decades, then eventually to be included in my diploma programme. But that can wait.

In the afternoon we caught the bus back towards home, walking from Shelfield. In the second field from the road we lay out of sight in the warm summer grass, near where I had spotted the fox a month or so before. There were no passers-by. What next?

It is the same question now as it was then: how to make sense of one's wishes and feelings? What to think? What to feel? What to say? Where do I go from here? Where did I go from there?

How do I describe things now?

Everything was so good and happy – the results, Carole, the best day out ever, the perfect summer's afternoon; all was settled, complete, accomplished.

And uncertain. These stirrings might be a man's feelings. I was no longer just a boy, certainly not a child. But still at school, having to avoid being caught walking on the grass, a ready target of shouts and rebukes if I spoke, even murmured, after the Silence bell in the dining area; near penniless, with ten bob a week pocket money; in a sort of love, but inexperienced, emphatically lacking the audacity to suggest any significant intimacy. Besides, anything like *that* was unthinkable, not just because of the procreational risk. Sex, no doubt, was – or at least ought to be – very beautiful. But for *us*, in our lives then, impossible. I could not have dared. Did the others, Mick, Andy, Sherlock and Winnie, think like me? Were they, too, shy in their respect and reverence? Carole – a girl, a young woman – had come as close to me as she must. The mute ache in my chest, in my limbs – was it yearning? was it doubt? – must persist. Like Edward Thomas, whose poetry I would encounter in future years, I must 'be content with discontent'. Like him, I could not 'bite the day to the core.'

Carole was staying with a friend in Brownhills. We spent a few hours together the next day, walking to the village, where we sat a few yards into the green of the common, beneath trees. We were both quieter, wistful. She returned to Longton in the evening.

Our letters continued, even when I went again with the family to a caravan week in Somerset. When I wandered off on my own in the evening, over the dunes to the empty levels of beach, I let the breezes coolly travel over me, silently overviewing the expanses to the far off, flattening waves, greyly rippling. After a time, my sister and father called me from behind. Was I all right? Sylvia was worried.

One day I bought a small charm to send to Carole with my letter: Skillywidden, a metal imp to attach to a bracelet or chain necklace.

The holiday ended.

Loosening Reins

Not yet old enough for a man, nor young enough for a boy—as a squash is before 'tis a peascod, or a codling when 'tis almost an apple. 'Tis with him in standing water, between boy and man.

William Shakespeare, *Twelfth Night*, Act 1, Scene 5

I could have felt cheated. It was back to the beginning in September: a public rebuke from Ted Merriott for being a sidestep from the line-up during fire drill, nailed to a particular time and place even to eat my lunch sandwiches, in a sort of love that could go nowhere, penniless apart from ten bob a week from Dad, most particularly regarded as not very good by the new English teacher. My first offering to him, some sort of response to *Concert Party* by Siegfried Sassoon drew the sub-mediocre mark of 12½ out of 25 and a few belittling annotations in spidery red ballpoint.

John Bell had read English and been taught by F.R.Leavis at Downing in the 1960s. As far as I can work out he must have been ten years older than I, and so only twenty-six or seven when he rose to Head of English. He made an impact: six feet tall, rugby-shouldered, large in gesture, dramatically poised and attention arresting. He walked on stage with every classroom entrance. The wave and cheery facial and vocal greeting, the immediate reaction to something he spotted: heaven-raised eyes at the girl (Goodness me - hopeless!) who scatter-dropped a pile of books, a head and jaw-lowering suppression of mirth at the upturned rump (Oh, I say!) of a portly boy rummaging in his schoolbag … you just had to watch him. His gift must have been comedy, if not melodrama, though perhaps not too remotely hung an optional sinister mode, suspended.

Raised in Derby, he had returned to somewhere near home for his first teaching appointment before coming south to us. There was no discernible East Midlands accent, rather a relaxed, gentle, caressing lilt, accompanied by some delicately light hand movements, feather stroking the invisible air, when he described the fine qualities of some poetry we were considering. I took this for Cambridge refinement; the Derby voice could still be caricatured with energetic *thees* and *thas*. Early on, he shared the joke of some locals' puzzlement at the forthcoming school play he had once been producing: 'Ey, dost tha knaw what this *Volpone* is all abaht?' Of course, it was pronounced as two syllables, rhyming with 'phone'.

Our first text *Othello* established the pattern: dramatised classroom reading in sections followed by detailed, appreciative elucidation, fluent, articulate, vital, at once charged and skin-shaved sensitive. He relished reading the part of Iago, assisted by his deepset eyes, darkly glittering. After undergraduate acting he had spent some months at least with a theatre company, but turned to teaching after spending most of the time fetching and carrying for others, rising to a one-line bit-part announcement now and then. So much – or so little – could have only dampened his fires, but the theatre always drew him. From early on we went on evening trips: to a cinema for the Olivier/Frank Finlay/Maggie Smith *Othello* film (he liked only Iago), to Stratford for various Shakespeares, to Keele University's student *The Alchemist*, the second text we studied. He found the last affair so offensively awful that, after a snorting removal during some early scenes, he spent the next hour or more sitting on the steps outside, reading his newspaper with noisy ostentation. And he seemed to have connections with the business, attending courses at Stratford, securing good quality costumes from them for our productions, bringing actors and their road shows to us. Theatre-Go-Round brought us their *Waiting for Godot*, presented on a circular wooden stage erected in the afternoon. From wonderfully close range we watched *The Play in which Nothing Happens – Twice*. On another evening, we experienced a splendid piece of synchronicity. *The Hollow Crown,* three or four actors reading extracts from the sixteenth century, included a passage from James I's *A Counterblaste to Tobacco* (1604). The actor must have reached somewhere in this part, making us alternately squirm and smile with his own reactions to the text, delivered in a perfect Scottish accent:

> And for the vanities committed in this filthie custome, is it not both great vanitie and uncleanenesse, that at the table, a place of respect, of cleanlinesse, of modestie, men should not be ashamed, to sit tossing of *Tobacco pipes*, and puffing of the smoke of *Tobacco* one to another, making the filthy smoke and stinke thereof, to exhale athwart the dishes, and infect the aire, when very often, men that abhorre it are at their repast? Surely Smoke becomes a kitchin far better then a Dining chamber, and yet it makes a kitchin also oftentimes in the inward parts of men, soiling and infecting them ...

It was at this point, or somewhere just like it, that one of the two prominent 'No Smoking' notices, at least three feet by two feet on either side of the stage, just floated down from the wall. Uproarious laughter. 'I can't go on!' the actor wryly sighed in his own, non-Scottish voice. And sat down.

If by now you are wondering what happened to Tony Field, producer of *The Merchant* (and composer of the production's music, as well as a fabulous organist, pianist and composer), he had during the spring been granted compassionate leave. His wife was suddenly terminally ill down south, from where they had not yet moved to be near us. That explains how Ted Merriott nominally kept some sort of watch over our English classes. Mr Field's lower set clearly needed the specialist attentions of our regular teacher, Mrs Reed, who was shunted to their siding. It was a sad departure, though would have been worse had we known the full story and sequel. It was only when I met Chris Cooper again, at an examiners' meeting three decades on, that I learned

Tony Field had suffered a massive heart attack, dying shortly after his wife. Hence the acquisition of John Bell.

Mercurial Tony Field! Bald-pated, quixotic, sharp-moving, hard-smoking, he crackled with life, firing off creasingly witty comments, never forgotten. When he wanted the singer to get on with the song *Tell me where is fancy bred*, he called out, 'Let's have it then. *Où est la pâtisserie?* Waiting for stagehands to move some things around, he might just sit at the keyboard of the grand piano and play something like the soloist's first entry to K488, the A Major Concerto, jumping up immediately after the last note (bar 82) to clap his hands and speed the team up. A Shakespeare production in your first term as Head of Department in a new school, with a full teaching load, and then the drive back to London for a weekend of family life before the Sunday evening return to wherever he was staying – all that would have been tiring enough. The M1 was only just being completed north of Rugby, and certainly did not take you right into London. Besides, the kinds of cars that schoolmasters could afford were generally not the motorway cruisers that can effortlessly purr along at the national speed limit. We had no idea when Mrs Field became ill. Our first awareness of something wrong must have been after Christmas, when one morning we were kept behind after assembly. All the staff left with the Head, whilst Mr Field and a music teacher remained. He directed a hymn practice with tight authority whilst his colleague played the piano. Meanwhile, the emergency meeting was deciding how to release him immediately, and cover his classes. For all the raging anguish that must have been flooding him, he did not appear any different from at play rehearsals: brisk, no nonsense, very sure of what he wanted, even jauntily scathing of our efforts.

I see him still, a small and slight figure, smart in his navy-blue suit and polished black Oxfords, one overlong lock of swept-across black hair fallen down under its own weight, to dangle. His nickname, Mad Harry, prompted by the skew-whiff spectacles and hanging strands, was entirely affectionate; he was fiercely respected and admired. It would be comforting to know that the hauntingly peaceful mood music he composed for a wind quartet to play in Portia's moonlit garden has survived somewhere. When in later years we came to the casket scene in my classes, I always sang them Shakespeare's words to his tune:

> Tell me where is fancy bred,
> Or in the heart or in the head …

At home, things were gradually changing. The new house increasingly became shabby. The mignonette emulsion blistered in places, some white bathroom tiles just fell off the walls, never to be replaced, the back door swelled with laundry and cooking steam until it would hardly shut again if you heaved it open, the exterior woodwork was in need of paint. One morning, a gust of wind blew a garage door back so violently that the frame came away from the brickwork. After that, every time you used the garage the door would drop down and have to be hoisted back into place.

Mom cooked, washed, cleaned, shopped and did almost everything else, seldom if ever questioning her onerous and repetitious life. Dad took himself to work, returned for lunch and tea, read the paper and watched the television. On Saturday, they did some of the shopping for the week at the butcher's, the greengrocer's and after a time a newly opened supermarket in Bloxwich. It was understood that I did all the 'heavy' lifting of bags and boxes.

A weekly annoyance was the unscheduled and uninvited arrival of Mr Knight, usually in time for Saturday lunch, after which he would sit in the lounge area the whole afternoon talking steel and picking Dad's brains for his next week's dealings. He wrote down measurements, prices, names of potential customers … It was the 1960s, boom time for steel trading. In five or six years Fred Knight had moved on from the modest Austin A30 of Newport Road, to an A35, then Austin Westminsters, by which time his accountant was urging him to upgrade and take benefit of tax relief on company cars. The 3 litre Rover of 1961 gave way to a light green 3.5 litre coupé, then a couple of top Ford Granadas models. All of these were very powerful automatics with an organ wrenching kick-down lurch, either at odds with or perhaps compensating for the driver's thin-nosed weedy puniness. His hand always trembled when he reached to take something from you. The partnership of his dreadful myopia and the stamping alternation of brake and accelerator made riding passenger little more comfortable than being jolted awake to find yourself clamped to the north face of the Eiger in a blizzard. He invited me once in 1961 to go on a Day 1 test drive in the 3 litre Rover. He had never used the kick down on an automatic before. From perhaps fifty or sixty yards behind a traffic lights queue, he tried it. Then immediately stamped again. He had to. We choked to an arrest six feet behind a van. 'Brakes work, Mart!' he said.

Quite early on in their succession, the Saturday visits ceased for a while. I think we all were relieved. Our time was our own. Mom did not have to make extra provision at lunch. The respite would not last. It had two, related, causes. For some months Mr Knight met a married mother regularly. She must have been the first woman in his life apart from his mother, who lived with him. As with his driving, so in his love life he fired precipitously forward. That he could so cheerfully *talk* to others about, never mind get up to, the beauty spot escapades he had with the woman, whom he nicknamed Fanny Craddock, jolted my idealism quite sickeningly, but he was losing his mental balance. Just before he was admitted to a psychiatric ward, he showed me, perhaps for a second, a Polaroid print of the woman, naked from the waist down except for her tights. He seemed to think that was clever. Or funny. Instead of alluring, she looked to me silly, immature, cheap. At the height of the depressive episode, he had wandered off in the darkness to find a road where he could get himself run over and end it all. I understood that he had pinned everything on the woman's leaving her husband and bringing her little son to settle with him. That never happened. She probably wanted to keep him as a sugar daddy. He had money, a smart car, could buy her things.

Whatever he had been like before, from this point onwards in his life, Mr Knight was obsessed with mental illness, primarily his own. He bought whatever the pharmacists' standard reference book was, spent hours in it, read successions of books on mental disorders. His favourite terms were *neurosis*, *psychosomatic*, *nervous energy* and *neurotic*. Anyone who had had a mental illness was one of *the magic circle*. He would eventually persuade himself he had become wise and insightful in these areas; he would get himself educated, starting with O levels, train as a doctor and then specialise in *nervous diseases*. The true pathos was not the delusion, but the sincere thought that he would be able to help other suffering people.

Out of friendship, and perhaps gratitude, Fred invited us some Saturday nights to his house, which he called 'Elmfield Palace', a small detached 1930s crescent property he had bought for himself and his mother, now deceased. He wore a bow tie and poured Riesling or Barsac into long-stemmed glasses. Dressing and making up, going there to be looked after, even treated, lit my mother's smile. Dad mildly flopped in a chair.

Every now and then there would be a special invitation, either to a smart restaurant or to a meal at the Highfield Club, in Park Road. The dinner-jacketed security men, huge and surly, acknowledged our host, who signed us in. The downstairs dining room of this Birmingham businessmen's private residential club provided fine food and service. Gambling went on upstairs, both at the tables and in the bedrooms, where the evening dressed ladies' clients risked their sexual health, and possibly their reputation, if they had any care for either. It was a curious place for my Good Catholic father to spend the evening.

At Christmas, Fred brought us all presents, quality things, probably wrapped by a female office worker, most likely from the pool of seasonal smoothers routinely applied to customers. The black early edition Parker 17 (with unhooded nib) prompted me to slope my writing forwards from January 1963 onwards, as an old exercise book shows. I used it exclusively from then, through O and A levels and university times to the end of my first year of teaching, in 1974. It was stolen from my pigeonhole in the staff room over the summer holiday. I suspected a teacher who was later dismissed *inter alia* some years later for stealing chickens from the school kitchen. When older, I received luxury adult gifts: five-star brandy, a wooden box of King Edward cigars.

Not only did Dad continue to help Fred, but Mom had growing concerns for him. The rest of us wearied most heavily, unable to ignore their hour-long phone conversations, trying to follow a television programme with the sound greatly or totally reduced. We were all impatient. Dad sighed, but said nothing, bar a few muttered comments to us about 'nut house talk', 'old neurasthenia' and so on. But Mom lapped it up, fully subscribing to the notions and language. No doubt she had her tensions and troubles, not unsurprisingly. So had Dad. They always had a supply of Valium (now

Diazepam), yellow 5 mg tablets. I cannot remember when that started, but in those days the doctors prescribed them almost on reflex. When she felt that things were too much, usually in the early evening, Mom would take a pill. After a few minutes she would lean back on the sofa, benzo-stunned, talking at length and unnecessarily. She had no idea that her brain had gone slurred, out of focus. Why did that irritate me?

The non-prescription tranquilliser came in four-pint cans: when one Saturday afternoon Dad drove to collect his evening paper from the village, he brought back a four pint can of beer to be shared among us, Sylvia and David, I think, having weak shandies. That became a routine, progressing to a seven pint can, all to be drunk before bedtime. In my late teens I probably accounted for a couple of glasses. It loosened things. Dad took his tie off. After a time, he would start yawning.

Not even our withdrawing 113 miles, from Pelsall to Towyn, Merionethshire, shielded us. Fred visited us on the caravan site, staying a couple of nights at The Corbett Arms, where he invited us to dine. Increasingly, Mom saw him as a special, even distinguished guest, who must be provided for and cosseted. The ancient Greeks' sacred xenia (ξενία) could hardly have been more punctiliously observed: the special place to sit, even in a caravan ('let Mr Knight sit there, our Martin – he's had a long drive'), the full late meal, prepared an hour after we had finished lunch and ached to be on the beach. ('Here you are, dear. That will make you feel better.' 'Thank you, chick.') Even if our seething had not been mute, no one would have heard it above his breathy, slurping ingestations of the heaped plate and full pudding bowl, followed by one or two cups of sink-gurgled down tea. Worst was the imposed vigil, while he lay full length ('you just take your shoes off and relax, dear') and slept on his back for an hour or more, extending our purgatory ('be quiet, all of you – Mr Knight needs to recharge his nervous energy'). The sands and waves would have to wait until perhaps half past four.

Photographs record Dad and Mr Knight in beach chairs, wearing ties and jackets despite the fine weather. A rarer moment has them each in black swimming trunks, backs to the sea, smiling big-bellied in full sun.

And Dad's thoughts? The most we learned of them emerged from the usual comments, snorted aside to us: 'that nut case,' 'old neurasthenia,' 'God send!' and so on. As we said goodnight outside the small Welsh hotel one evening, Mom's goodbye kiss to Fred was no cheek peck, but full-mouthed, lingering. What then? Was that the same holiday before which it had devolved upon me to walk to the nearest phone box to ring her younger sister, Kate, blond, attractive and separated from her first husband, to turn down for her the last-minute self-invitation to join us all for some days in Wales. What might Zeus or Athene have done? Even some surprise descenders apparently did not qualify for ξενία!

Things carried on.

My 1966 birthday fell on the actual Saturday. Carole came south for a few hours. I later used her £10 book token as she suggested, to buy a Latin dictionary, the Cassell's still on my shelf, used at least several times most weeks over 53 years. A short while after that, her letters dried up for a long gap, possibly a fortnight, before the 'Dear John': it could not work. She had thought hard about it, and struggled etc. When I had bought that Aeneid volume on results day, she had turned to Nisus' words:

> dine nunc ardorem mentibus addunt, Euryale,
> an sua cuique deus fit dira cupido
>
> [Do the gods put this yearning in our hearts, Euryalus, or does each man's dreadful desire become his god?]

On the bus, she had explained to me that these two hexameters expressed her own raging psychomachia. Was God indeed calling her to become ordained and enter His ministry, like her much loved friend, the Reverend Jan Pawson, or was she misinterpreting her own inner prompting for His supra-astral whistles? The duality of *ardorem* and *cupido,* the latter all the more ravaging because of its destructive potential (*dira*) probably stayed beyond her precocious grasp – for all our intensity, we both were very young – but suggested the dilemma: eventual marriage or the ministry? Professedly, I was being given the elbow for a Good Cause, the Best! It was at least a kind gesture. Whatever pangs I felt, they faded disarmingly rapidly!

The library and BBC radio, especially Radio 3, fed my other appetites. For a new state school in a working-class colliery village like Walsall Wood, surely a cultural backwater, Shire Oak's shelves were richly and comprehensively stocked, with many reference books, texts, critical works and resources. The miniature scores section alone surpassed the town library's, supplying almost all of the works I was getting to know from the radio. From them, I learned the oboe and recorder parts of Bach's Brandenburg Concertos 1, 2 and 4, still in memory. Gems like John Earle's *Microcosmography*, Donne's Sermons, selections from Thomas Nashe, never mind standard editions of all the major authors, even multiple copies of all the Arden Shakespeare edition *and* Dover Wilson's red Oxford paperbacks of the plays – these and fiction from the eighteenth century to recent years abounded on the shelves. I have never regretted being always required to have a French reader on the go. David Maddock recommended titles, with brief indications of their content and interest, regularly checking on our progress and engagement. Finishing our first A level text, Sartre's *Les Jeux Sont Faits*, really satisfied and pleased me. In two years we read widely and well. Apart from that film scenario, we studied *Roux le Bandit* (André Chamson), Molière's *L'Avare*, *Quinze Contes* of Maupassant, some of Voltaire's *Contes* and *La Peste*, but then individually read five to ten 'standard' works as well as attending French films and plays acted in French, usually by Birmingham University students. In voluntary extra classes, some of us read and discussed extracts from major writers like Baudelaire, Apollinaire, Racine and Corneille.

This is worth mentioning because it characterises the prevalent attitude: these authors, their ideas and intellectual backgrounds, were all in themselves exciting and enriching; moreover, we absolutely should experience and acquire as much of everything as we could. Education was definitely not only the narrow pursuit of qualifications and experience useful for gaining employment and making money. Similarly in my other subjects, we were given informed and authoritative histories of English literature, and a highly detailed Roman history course. Apart from our set Cicero and Vergil, we came to know something of all the major prose and verse writers, as well as some less familiar ones. I read the poems over and over till I knew many by heart; much remains, forever part of me. When (rarely now!), after a snow fall the temperature rises and green patches begin to appear in winter's white covering, I say to myself:

> Diffugere nives. Redeunt iam gramina campis
> Arboribusque comae.

I feel and smell with Horace the relaxation and release!

> Donec gratus eram tibi …

> Nunc est Bibendum …

> … nam mellitus erat, suumque norat
> ipsam tam bene quam puella matrem

Only in later years have I discovered the duality of Lesbia's *passer*, not necessarily just her avian darling, but also possibly the writer's lifeless little fellow! Curse the Fates indeed!

No one at home seemed to mind my total editing of *Radio Times*, underlining and asterisking the music and other broadcasts I would listen to, including a cycle of Schubert's symphonies and weekly organ recitals. The radio could even be annexed to my bedroom for lengthy evening programmes or Bach's Passions on Good Fridays. Radio 4 Shakespeare dramatisations could be followed in the tiny font of his Collected Works. A production of *The Winter's Tale* so moved me that the play has remained a lifelong special. The real wonder is not in the statue's resurrection, but the poignant realisation of deepest human needs and values:

> Let no man mock me; for I will kiss her.

The soundest sanity emerges from Leontes' unashamed, apparently crazy act:

> O she's warm.

This, after violent madness, cruelty, discord, suffering, death and waste, especially of time and life, is all, for Leontes and us.

Do my enthusiasm, appetite for learning, and idealism appear youthful, perhaps naïve? If so, I must apologise: they are so still!

One day, Ted Merriott committed another corridor assault. He wanted me to form and chair a new group, the Sixth Form Social Services Committee. This, he explained, would involve our providing voluntary help, enacting the 'Service' part of our motto. Whether he included having something to mention in my university application I do not recall. In the same one-way conversation, he notified me I had been identified as the School's representative in another concern, the Brownhills Fellowship for the Physically Disabled, motto 'Help the Handicapped to Help Themselves.' At this age, I smell the device. At one of his Thursday Rotary Club lunches at the Shire Oak Inn, someone had prompted him to involve his older pupils. Ever pragmatic, he seized the opportunity for publicity, promoting his school whilst allowing some of us to earn some useful Brownie points.

Though chaired by a local GP, Mrs Bagharutti, the Brownhills Fellowship belonged to Councillor Blundell, who devised, formed, directed and controlled it. 'L'Etat, c'est moi,' proclaimed Louis XIV of France; Bernard Blundell's Versailles was a low-ceilinged, dimly lit, claustrophobic room in a community centre. I sat on a plastic chair at the back. And listened to Bernard Blundell. We all sat on plastic chairs. And listened to Bernard Blundell. After our two hours' sentence we were released. I had said nothing.

I loathe committees. I am incompetent and useless on them. Some wonderful beings calmly and creatively make good things happen and please many by their means. But committees sadly attract and encourage not only egoists, misfits, windbags and dolts, but (perhaps worse) expertly treacherous schemers, exploiters, suavely poised, voluble and sparklingly sharp-witted vipers. How and why is it, then, that I have been cheerfully sucked on to them so many times over my whole adult life, even triumphantly backslapped into the Chair now and then? Best of luck to the some who have this greatness thrust upon them!

The next day, Ted Merriott congratulated me. 'Ah, Hearne! Publicity Officer for the Fellowship! That's exciting, isn't it? Hmm!' he boomed. I would have chosen a different word, perhaps 'awful' or 'appalling'. I had no clue what to do or where to start. Mercifully for the Cause, Blundell had yoked me with a police Inspector, who knew how to get leaflets, pamphlets and posters printed, with occasional mentions in local papers.

'Do something,' a Dunkirk survivor once told me in jest, 'something good, if you can. But do something!'

I have no idea how much actual good we did for any Brownhills citizen. In my year and a half on the committee, I can promise, I did not *once* set eyes on, let alone speak to a disabled person – with the daily exception of my father, who had become officially registered 'disabled' partly to help his firm meet an employment desideratum. A group of us got together and made some sort of show at doing what either Councillor Blundell or Ted Merriott passed on to us. At Christmas, we accompanied Rotary Club members to distribute hampers to unsuspecting retired folk. Old ladies peered nervously round their doors into the darkness at us, puzzled and hesitant. In the warmer months, we prepared for a special event. This Blundell Bonanza was grandly described as a carnival. Putting up posters, which I believe some clever girl and boy designed in our art room, selling programmes and collecting items to sell on stalls all more or less took place. The success or return rate in such affairs has always seemed to me disappointing – disproportionate to the expectation and effort expended – but some things did happen. One Friday night in early summer, a group of us spent hours decorating as well as we could the brand-new flatbed lorry, loaned by a local builder, which was to convey the Carnival Queen in the procession. Boxes and buckets galore of plastic flowers, bunting, flags and other bright trappings took ages to arrange and secure – to dishearteningly poor effect. We could have used as much again, many times over!

The next day, we worked in teams of car parkers, programme sellers, rattle can collectors, marshalls and – another Blundell Brainwave – running Tea with a Slave Girl! For five shillings, you were ushered into a large tent, guided to a garden table and served a cup of tea and a home-made cake by one of our Lower Sixth girls in bikinis, with improvised gauzy drapes and flimsy lilac half-face masks. Safeguarding may not have existed then, but how some sensible senior member of staff did not raise concerns or impose a veto might well be wondered; however, the event proved to be almost disappointingly tame and low-key, the good people of Brownhills being much more interested in a short sit down with tea and cake than anything spicier.

Johnny's event car parkers fared less well. The Land Rover drivers towing their horse boxes flatly refused to pay to park. 'It's costing me enough just to come here and do you lot a favour. So you can jolly well bugger off!' one equestrian lady eloquently reasoned. Similarly, my roaming team of collectors had little to rattle by five o'clock. Many programmes ('You'll sell dozens on the day' – B.J.Blundell) remained unsold.

At the end of the afternoon, a mixed group of about ten of us went back to Anthea's nearby house, by invitation of her parents, who had voluntarily chaperoned their daughter and the other slave girls all afternoon. Her mother and I had spent quite some time chatting. This time we were served Mrs Baggott's cakes and a drink, tea or lemonade.

Before the sixth form, I think like others I had lived within a very narrow circle. The inevitable mixing from other forms and sets when we moved up from the fifth form, combined with collaborating in activities like the Brownhills Carnival, widened things. When David Mott, a scientist who had come from the fifth form below, held up his sprig of mistletoe to challenge me ('Come on, Hearnie – you and Maddy') to kiss Madeleine Hughes (also not my form), on her last day in December 1966 ('go on – she's leaving') (she had decided the sixth from was not for her), I gave her a long, close kiss. ('Ok – that's enough!') How warm and soft she was! ('Blimey – steady on, you two!') We were both surprised, startled. I had not kissed another girl before or after Carole, who had withdrawn ten weeks before. 'Happy Christmas,' she said, squeezing both my hands and looking straight into my eyes. There were other ways to learn than from books.

The carnival team became a social group. We formed a number of couples. Slave girl Anthea became my girlfriend. That was after about ten of us formed Phoenix, a group I hoped would discuss arty things like music and writing. Cornily enough, the name came from my reading of Lawrence. Predictably, we met about once a week, at various houses in rotation, usually sneaking into the quiet corner of a pub for a glass of beer or cider. (We were all a few months underage still.) In the Baggotts' back room we ate sandwiches, chatted aimlessly and laughed. Initially it surprised me that Anthea drew closer to me. She had previously not hidden her disapproval of my open displays with Carole some months before on the French outings. She had in any case probably thought me too full of myself.

At some time in my lower sixth year I took an execrable decision: I would, like my father, smoke a pipe! Dad was delighted. He bought me a Falcon, like his, and an ounce tin of Three Nuns. Of course, I had to learn all the performance of this new habit. It took perseverance, determination. After my first serious practice, I suddenly discovered things were not altogether right. I felt peculiar, not daring to turn my head, which appeared to have a gyroscope whirling round inside it somewhere. Sweat broke out on my brow. I became wobbly. Confession, especially to Dad, was unthinkable. Over weeks I kept going, building up tolerance in manageable bouts. Two years before I had begun to shave. Now this. Both just had to be.

I kept up pipe smoking for a decade, all through my university days, into my teaching and until we were married. My happiest smoke was probably of St Bruno Flake one snowy Christmas Eve before I left home. No pressure presented itself for me to stop. I just did. It happened to be a few months after we got married in 1977. No withdrawal occurred. I have never missed it, although I have many times dreamed that I was still smoking, and with the full enjoyment which I genuinely came to attain, progressing through various tobaccos to the hard-core strength of Condor flake or even long cut. Stupid and disgusting as the reader may concur with me in judging this to have been, I shall finish the subject for ever by stating that, in my second year of teaching, for example, of thirteen men on the staff, nine or us smoked pipes, certainly in common rooms and even walking between lessons. The air in the Masters' Common Room was always blue, sometimes in two senses!

I added a seventh O level Grade 1 in November 1966. Our new teacher, J.N.Daunt, fresh from the University of Hull, taught us simultaneously for that examination and for the A level that two of us were progressing with. Revising our portion of *Aeneid IX* took about an hour for every twenty lines – exactly my sort of ploddingly thorough work! Very much a poor, unaccommodated subject, Latin was not always even found a room. Medical screens hiving off part of a draughty, thronging corridor hardly promoted either our comfort or status!

What, apart from the subject content and techniques, did I learn during this stage?

Being intolerant and impatient as only a young person can be with ideas, attitudes and practices I found unsympathetic in no way prevented me from seeing most other people's points of view! When you came across a different way of doing things, it could often, almost always, be worked with or around. Thus, new teachers' requirements, initially annoying or apparently lacking sense, could be complied with. To almost everyone else, the Headmaster was just intolerable; but I could after all work and get along with him. (I either forgot about or forgave him the history of our History!) The RE teacher, who also taught us some French, turned out not to be as poor and silly as we first thought to be, but a sensitive human being. When he left at the end of the year, our French set clubbed together to give him a present, and had shared his joy at becoming a father, even if we giggled to ourselves that, on taking the phone call from the hospital, he had put the receiver down on learning he had a perfect baby daughter, totally omitting to ask how his wife was doing! The classmates you had not really taken seriously until recently suddenly became interesting and credible. Tchaikovsky might be continents apart from Mozart, or Monteverdi from Chopin or Stravinsky, but you could 'see' things from their points of view too. It was possible to agree with F.R.Leavis or Samuel Johnson about Milton, and still find much to admire and even be fascinated by in *Paradise Lost*.

Oh dear! Life was neither simple nor easy. My first, disgracefully superficial, glance at Jane Austen's *Emma* made me dismissive. Silly boy! In no time I began to see it for the astounding masterpiece it is. You could be cocksure one moment and writhe with shame the next … Why was there no word for that? Not *cocksure* but *cockignorant*? *Cockup*?

Do something … something good if you can…

I.A.Richards' *Practical Criticism* afforded some reassurance. The misreadings his volunteers – all English graduates – made of the 'protocols' he provided (unseen pieces of verse for response and comment) confirmed how mistaken many of us can be, but more comfortingly I generally seemed to read the protocols without falling into the illustrated traps.

In his first year, John Bell directed and produced Shaw's *St Joan* as the school play. I think he chose it because he had seen the young Judi Dench's revolutionary performance under John Neville at the Nottingham Playhouse, though the actuality of living with Shaw's wordy prosings and statically undramatic stretches of largely unexciting language quickly palled. We cut whole swathes without any noticeable injury, introduced irreverent clowning to bring some leavening, caricatured at the merest opportunity … My part was Richard Beauchamp, Earl of Warwick, the English military leader determined to dispose of Joan on account of her threat to feudalism.

It is a tribute to Shaw's verbal artistry that I am unable to quote the shortest phrase of all the lines I force crammed and disgorged! In her review for the school magazine *Ilex*, Shura Boyko from the year below said that Martin Hearne had presented as a 'worldly and cynical nobleman, very different from his offstage self.'

Our next school play, the following year, likewise originated from a Nottingham visit, though this time our French set had seen Christopher Hancock as Harpagon in an English version of Molière's *l'Avare*, again under John Neville. What had so powerfully struck me was the knife edge uncertainty how to take the climactic scene when Harpagon *solo* rushes on stage beside himself:

> Au voleur! au voleur! à l'assassin! au meutrier! Justice, juste Ciel! je suis perdu, je suis assassiné, on m'a coupé la gorge, on m'a dérobé mon argent.

Serious? Funny! Ridiculous? Tragic? You were arrested, troubled, disturbed even. The play would be worth putting on our stage just for that moment. We spilled all this out in the next English lesson.

It was decided: I would translate it, Sheila would type it … John Bell would do the rest.

Of course, it was doomed, some of it anyway. My wordings, though probably fairly accurate, could not be delivered on stage. Sheila might have coped with the sheer load, but it would have been asking much. The Monday after we had handed in our efforts, Bell off-handedly told us it was all right. We need not bother. He had felt keen over the weekend and done the whole thing himself.

That might not have mattered, but a pretence had to be maintained: the word had spread that a pupil was translating a French play, to be directed by a teacher … Someone arranged for the local paper to send a photographer. A shot appeared of the two of us sitting at a table in the library. I look abstracted, troubled, a mess; Bell is looking sideways at me, calmly smiling. He had told me to go through with it, as it would do the school good … I could not have felt more uncomfortable at the deception and dishonesty, but the worst was to come. Though not among the cast, I watched many rehearsals, out of interest. It had genuinely been my initiative. As they progressed, Andrew Coleman as the Miser became more and more impressive, masterly even. The whole production was slick, fresh, original, powerful. John Bell said school plays should not be much inferior to professional theatre; in so many ways he realised this aspiration.

The worst moment for me was at the end of the last performance, on the Saturday. Bell suddenly alerted me that I should have to go on stage during the speeches for a round of applause. I was wearing the shabbiest pair of Dad's holiday slip on soft shoes. I felt my failure most keenly. John Bell was a traitor. So was I. All the people on the stage must have known it.

Something good if you can … it was the best I could make of a bad job … not good enough.

Yet I did get away with some things. The next project that came the way of the Social Services Committee, whether offered to or imposed upon us, seemed to have all-round positive effects and benefits. Ted Merriott executed another corridor raid: good for the School, our UCCA forms etc. An elderly lady in Kingstanding, living alone, needed contact and cheering up. Young people should do the trick. Her council house also could do with decorating throughout. It was not so much a 'How about it?' conversation, as 'Over to you now!' Social Services would pay for materials.

What did Sir Thomas Beecham say? He just hired the best musicians and told them to play? Somehow we formed a team. Sue Chambers cheerfully did much of the rounding up. Phil Rhead could drive, and would borrow his decorator father's van, providing transport and equipment. On site, he directed our efforts, making us rub down any area with drips and paint it again! Two girls looked after the old lady herself, washing and styling her hair for her, making her lunch and cups of tea. Thus, for both days over several weekends, as well as over some of our half term, we redecorated the whole house. This not being a Blundell scheme, we were spared publicity. The household cat, scared we were told of men, spent the whole time hiding in an understairs cupboard. Though I put in as much time and toil as anyone else, the others supplied most of the necessary qualities, certainly the bright ideas. Yet, strangely, they all seemed to look towards *me* as *their* leader! Whoops! Whatever the truth of things, we had camaraderie and collaboration, the old lady a smart and fresh-smelling house.

Though the Royal Sutton Philharmonic never gave a concert in my time, the Old Marians regularly did, in town halls and large parish churches. At the dress rehearsal of Beethoven's *Egmont* overture in Walsall's parish church, St Matthew's, the superstitious were not the only players to feel a thrill or chill. A split second after the final, fortissimo F major full orchestra chords, the whole building shook at a thundering full organ blast in the same key. All our heads turned to the console, behind us on our right. No one at the manuals. They were fully closed, probably locked. I had understood that a large organ could make windows rattle, and send vibrations through the wooden pews you sit on. That was sympathetic resonance. But could it work the other way round? We all listened keenly for a repetition in the actual concert. Nothing.

More and more playing came my way, including the solo part in the *Domine Deus* of Vivaldi's *Gloria*, a Mozart piano concerto and Schubert symphony, a week's run in Humperdinck's *Handel and Gretel* at Sutton Girls' High School. Apart from the rather lovely music, too little known if challenging – first flute complained the composer thought, like Wagner, that any sequence of notes on your instrument, at any speed and any volume, was a reasonable expectation – we had the sort of incidental fun almost guaranteed at any amateur production. When Hansel's father, no bristling baritone, but a piping, slender sixth form girl, arrived at the cottage with food, 'he' showed 'his' excitement by spinning round, holding the mushroom basket with their supper. That, we realised in the dress rehearsal, was a couple of pounds of King Edward's best that would be centrifugally fired right into the orchestra. An unfortunate viola player got one or two of them right on his bald patch. After that, we ducked and covered our reeds for a couple of bars at the key moment. I suspect the girl left it in because it could be relied upon to get them a good laugh – except from their crusty Headmistress, the Queen Bee, who sat impassive and glaring in the front row.

When she heard about the playing I was getting in adult orchestras, Brenda Rees moved me up to the First Orchestra. On the first Saturday of every month, I caught the contract bus, from Cannock to Rising Brook School in Stafford. Here, the County Music Director, Miss Maude Smith, a formidable woman in late middle age, held centre stage for some very fine performances, possibly her greatest. It was not just the music. Grey-haired, slightly portly, to a passer-by in the street just another grandmother, this lady had presence, authority, assurance, poise and steely command, of both music and musicians, students and professionals alike. I do not remember her as having a remarkable stick technique or platform manner. She was not all eyes, like Mahler. The sounds we produced, both as individual soloists and as a full symphonic orchestra, were of the highest quality, explaining why overseas audiences reacted so well when the orchestra toured, something I never did. I joined too late, was too peripheral, needed a better instrument. Besides, the existing players were too good to dislodge. I enjoyed the thrills: of hearing first flute, a boy called David, play the Bird solo from *Peter and the Wolf* faultlessly first time, of the massively powerful brass section, raised behind us and physically sending shock waves of air in Wagner's *Die Meistersinger* overture, the fullness of the string sound, getting my fingers to manage the key slides for Prokofiev's Duck … One Saturday, I sat next to John Lawley. Miss Smith welcomed him back for a special appearance. He had just finished at the Royal College of Music and astoundingly landed the job of cor anglais at Sadler's Wells. (From that he moved on to be principal oboe for English National Opera for over a decade as well as second oboe in the London Symphony Orchestra.) His playing in the first tutti of the last movement of Beethoven's C major piano concerto stood out like diamonds against pewter from the rest of the orchestra, good as they were: crisp, articulated, projected, super agile. How could anyone inject so much tonal body and substance into the shortest staccato notes? Other players also went on to full professional careers.

There were shows, operettas and musicals that needed bands. One illustration should suffice.

Someone, maybe a violinist from another orchestra, had passed my name on. Could I play in a run of *San Marino* (1932) by Alfred J.Silver? One Sunday morning after that Dad gave me a lift to St Margaret's School in Great Barr. You just walked down the drive to the nondescript post-war building, pushed the swing door open, continued down the corridor into the school hall, and like other people found an empty few chairs in the seating to put your coat down and take out your stand and instrument. You knew no one else. Few players spoke, but tuned fiddles, blew reeds, tried a few notes. You did the same, without trying to be noticed too much.

The tuning fork business, trying to see whether the A was right. You could never tell. In the end, you would just blow it when asked, long repeated notes, trying to disregard the glares of some others. Why do violinists always have toothache when they tune?

‘You’re Martin,’ a bald, brown-jumpered man informs you. ‘Do you know Norman?’

You’re taken over to a huddle near the conductor’s stand, two violinists and another man bent over the score. Your escort introduces you to Norman Satterthwaite, conductor.

A thin, ordinary-looking man. ‘Ah hello! Thanks for coming. Got your part? No? Mary! Got the oboe part for this young man? Could you sit just there, please, next to the flute?’

One run through of the whole show, with a break midway. It’s a corny American comic thing:

> San Marino, island fair,
> Home of the brave and free …

A silly story, some solos and chorus items, suburban Birmingham’s Broadway for middle-aged mums and dads.

I have never seen such smiling and good humour. Their collaboration is almost incendiary. It’s all so killingly funny for them. Shame about the jelly wobbling vibrato of that made-up fifty-year-old housewife, the plump one. She sounds amplified when she isn’t. But they really love it. I suppose they do it very well.

Only it’s wretchedly poor stuff, lacking wit, originality or point. Even so, I have to work very hard, sight-reading the hand-written part, picking up the tempi and changes. Every so often, I lose count of rests, and have to feel my way back in. Norman lights a cheroot just before the last couple of numbers, moving it to and from his mouth with his left hand, narrowing his eyes as the fumes rise. The show ends, with full chorus and soloists on stage. Universal joy. Smiles and laughter. Back home, I go over my part several times in the next few days.

The dress rehearsal and run of several nights pass without disasters. I am invited to the after-show party, but that will be only a middle-aged continuation of the several days’ long jollities that have been sustained, only this time with glasses of wine and crisps. I suspect most of them belong to the Church, which would explain the pathological bonhomie. As the audience ease their way out, I hand back my part, pack up and go to find where dad is parked in the Cortina. It has actually been instructive playing experience, but it’s not Mozart.

Most Saturday evenings are spent with Anthea, in her parents’ lounge. We chat, eat her mother’s sandwiches and cakes, practise our snogging. Now and then we go to the cinema, or for picnic walks. In school, where we have both become prefects, we behave with the seemliest decorum, not even sitting near each other in shared lessons, meeting during the day to talk maturely. During holidays and revision times, we sit on opposite sides of the dining table, working silently at our books for hours on end. The company and friendship feel right.

Blond, of solid medium build, broad-faced, bright-eyed and excitedly breathy – inclined indeed to asthma – she is the only child to doting parents. Walter ('Wallie') in pre-war days worked as a butcher, thereafter in factories. Quiet, undemonstrative, loyal, decent, he belongs to a definite but small and diminishing class: the solid, principled, modest, simple good father, husband, friend and worker. He says little, is bright but not highly educated, satisfied and happy with his lot, content to work endlessly to sustain it all, uncomplaining, grateful for his life, peaceful tending his garden, expert with his roses, vegetables and shrubs. 'Our Anth' means everything to him. He has never smoked since he made a solemn vow to quit if she survived some appalling illness as a toddler, possibly pneumonia. He doesn't drink, deliberately making himself bring back a couple of pints when forced to be convivial at a family wedding.

His wife, Dorry, formulates and articulates thoughts and words for both of them. Chirpy and quick-eyed behind her thick lenses, she provides both necessaries and comforts for the three of them, makes the home, baking, knitting, planning and cosying. While Wallie reads little other than the newspaper and cowboy stories, his wife knows the classics and modern authors, from D.H.Lawrence to Somerset Maugham, Conrad to Priestley. She does crosswords. They live for and through each other, for their daughter more than anything else. When Anthea will be called to interview at the South London college where she wishes to train as a teacher, Dorry will accompany her. I don't try to work out why this feels strange to me.

In the summer holiday between our two sixth form years, John Bell took me to Cambridge in his red VW Beetle. We walked first around his college, Downing, then along the Backs, into King's Chapel, into several colleges, where he showed me a cleaned up medieval ceiling, once dowdy, then startlingly vivid in its reds and blues, at some point to Sidney Sussex. He thought the chapel, museum mournful empty, one of the best modern ones. Some months earlier, Merriott had – I surely do not need to explain how – cursorily raised my higher education plans:

> 'Ah, Hearne, you're thinking of Cambridge.'
> 'Yes, sir.'
> 'Sidney Sussex, then. That all right?'

It may not have been said. The larger, richer, grander colleges were above my class. Maybe all of them would be. How astounding it must be to walk daily around King's or Trinity. But just possibly Sidney might consider a lowlier applicant. The idea may have been mentioned in the HM's *en passant* briefing. Or did he have a connection with the Master, David Thomson? That distinguished historian had carried out the official opening of Shire Oak in 1963 or 1964, an exclusive occasion we were not invited to. Over the months, I did what extra reading and thinking I could – never enough – but did become very familiar with our A level texts. It would surprise, maybe overwhelm, many students these days to hear that we studied ten texts for English, counting Arnold Wesker's *Trilogy* as one, and faced critical questions on unseen material. No plain texts were allowed then; you learned the book, including quotations. I was to be entered for S level in English and Latin, though I had attended the extra French classes too. As a Merriott experiment, a few of us were to be entered for a fourth A level, in General Studies. The HM told me that no preparation at all was needed, but there should be the chance of an additional good grade. 'Here's a book on Darwin,' he mentioned. 'Could come in useful. There's a science essay.'

Just before Easter in 1968, I took the bus to Lichfield in the late afternoon. Anthea was singing in a combined Staffordshire schools' choir in Bach's *St Matthew Passion*, performed in the cathedral. Though my seat was fairly far back, I could see the orchestra and soloists. Maude Smith was conducting the work, given in English. I think it started at 6 pm. It was a fine spring evening, the late sun coming in from the west behind us, casting colours on slanting rays downwards to the stone floor.

In all my life, the next couple of hours were to prove some of the very richest, most illuminating, moving and deeply felt, very much a total experience. Anyone who knows the masterpiece will need no further words. For other curious parties there must exist volumes of appreciation of Bach's genius, though they may not necessarily mention the purple richness of texture added by the oboi d'amore, played on this occasion by John Lawley and Brenda Rees.

In all of the sixth form, I was not required to attend one P.E. or games session, Latin being timetabled against any such opportunities. Unfortunately, clashes meant I missed out on quite famous visiting speakers, including Mrs Mary Whitehouse and the already mentioned Sir Bernard Lovell. Worst of all, I was also unable to attend a recital by the visiting oboist Janet Craxton and her husband, Alan Richardson. Whilst hundreds of mostly uninterested teenagers sat through their programme, I wrote a Latin exam in the library! Was I fated? Though able to be at another recital, this time by a wind quintet, the one thing I looked forward to most could not happen: the oboe player cannot have been too proficient, since he failed to produce a sound from his cor anglais reed, just giving up altogether after a few breathy attempts. I keep at least one and usually two back up reeds in my pocket, even though I have never had to resort to one in a performance. Is that another invitation to Fate?

In those times, most applicants to Oxford and Cambridge submitted their forms after their A levels, staying on for a seventh term. The public schools, and maybe some established grammar places, timetabled specialist lessons, even provided full programmes of individual tuition, often delivered by quite distinguished academics. Shire Oak and similar establishments had no such resources. We reckoned there would be no harm in trying a fourth term application. In time, Sidney Sussex wrote that, whilst they would consider a pre-A level application, they advised me to defer for a year, when I might be in a position to apply for an award. So, I would be having the best part of a year off! My deferral was sent to UCCA.

A whim the school indulged was my growing a moustache during the A level session. Am I the only male to have responded to stress in such a way? As far as I remember, the actual papers required sustained concentration and fast writing, but otherwise were just work, not uncongenial and even satisfying. The two novel General Studies papers proved fun, with something of the challenge of puzzles and quizzes. Match the composers to the operas, the artists to the paintings. The maths questions were no harder than O level, the spatial reasoning section straightforward. As for the science essay, the book on Darwin did it all, sourcing material for an answer on effective scientific methods and practices. E.B.Merriott 1 – Examiners 0.

During one week of the industrial fortnight, while we were waiting for our results, I went with Anthea's family by coach to Butlin's at Pwllheli. She already had a place at Southfields in Wimbledon. She had been working in a supermarket over the summer, to save extra cash. We had been good, close friends; I certainly liked and was fond of her. It was lovely to have a female companion. But I was sensing it would not, could not last. She was moving away; I was staying. One of the Redcoats entertaining at evening shows was the young Frank Carson, slender and agile. Even then he had the catchphrase 'It's the way I tell them!' I remember and have – to the surprise of many classes – used one of his cheeky offerings. It illustrates what doggerel is neatly enough:

> I wish I were a fairy,
> And if it came to pass,
> I'd climb up all the hills and trees,
> And slide down on my [pause, while their eyes widen] hands and knees!

The Saturday morning of our departure, Anthea and I went on our own after breakfast, for a final dip. Apart from us, the beach was deserted. It was a still, misty Welsh summer morning. We were quiet, subdued. We changed in the open, under towels. I took some photographs with my Kodak box camera. The week was ending. Part of me had been hoping for a future together, hoping to hope. Realistically, I fully understood she would be going her own way, and honestly I accepted that I did not feel strongly enough to believe things could or should continue between us … I had to swallow my sadness to myself, silently. Were things going anywhere?

Was I taking off anywhere? The results a week or two later would clip my wings:

English	A (S level 2)
French	A
Latin	D (S level U)
General Studies	A
Use of English	1

I did not argue or protest. At least Ted Merriott was able to pat himself on the back:

'Well, Hearne, it's a good job I put you in for General Studies, wasn't it? Mmmm? Wasn't it? Hm!'

Interim

I said nothing. I slipped away.
Edward Thomas *The Other*

Mid ocean. The sea marble, pale periwinkle like the indiscernibly joined sky, endless, unmoving. The air imperceptible. Engines stilled, we drift, unnoticing. Our hearts have not paused, beating.

Walking out of school for the last time that November morning, passing through the gateway, descending the hill unaccompanied, carrying nothing …

It is impossible to say just what I mean too, Mr Prufrock! How does one describe a feeling, a taste, an aroma? A major experience?

One morning in November 1968, at some moment between 11 o'clock and noon, I left school. No one else did that day. I do not recollect that anyone commented. I probably took my leave of the Headmaster. Something had ended. I felt neither glad nor empty. There was neither climax nor let down. Things just were. A good, mild feeling, like aimless peace.

For the first time since the school's opening, three of us had stayed on for part of a seventh term, to attempt entry to Oxford or Cambridge. Lesley was applying to Lady Margaret Hall for Modern Languages, Max to Pembroke, his uncle's Cambridge college, for Natural Sciences (Physics). The three subject departments made some arrangements for individual tuition and preparation. No doubt they did their best, with heavy regular timetables, and scarce, if any, experience of either university or preparing applicants. In that respect I had an advantage, on account of John Bell. He provided me generously with texts and critical books of his own as well as giving me sessions over the summer at his Lichfield flat and then in his untimetabled periods once back at term. Other English teachers saw me once or twice on special areas of their own interests, Brian Simmill on older literature. With him I read, very laboriously, the Anglo-Saxon poem *The Seafarer*, and then, faster but still painstakingly, *Gawayne and the Grene Knyght*. Brian had already introduced me to the Old Marians' orchestra, where he played horn. A late starter, he braved the inevitable hazards of that fiendish instrument with a modest persistence that defied normal embarrassment tolerances. He made me think of a suddenly blinded man blundering his way through a waiting room of orthopaedic casualties, jarring them shockingly with his jolts, wincing and apologising perpetually. A huge bear of a being, he was said to have been a line-out specialist in his Oxford college team. For a young male teacher surnamed Embley I wrote about D.H.Lawrence's novels, especially *The Rainbow* and *Women in Love*. Mike Bowen (who had at school kept wicket to David

moments of sociable chat with the customer and of course increased security for the store, the cash being stored and handled in a remote, locked room somewhere. Only dishonesty there or an intruding robber might have made things go wrong … or an absent-minded salesman, who became so occupied with another customer during a rush, he forgot all about the patient Pakistani gentleman and his £9 16 s 1d change from the £10 note he had paid for some day-glo blue nylon socks, price 3s 11d! The mild soul must have waited several minutes before he politely reminded me!

The number of mistakes I made surprised even me. Every day, you had to total the sales in your book, so that your bonus could be calculated. For every £1's worth over a certain amount you sold each month, you would be paid 1d, which at 0.42% of the price could not be considered generous. I soon worked out the mark up on items. The buyer had coded his cost price in pencil on labels next to the selling price, but so transparently he need not have bothered! Anyone who could not see that e/f meant 5s 6d or ci/aa was 39s 11d probably remained happier anyway. The average mark up on all items seemed to be roughly 50%. Congratulating myself on seeing that hardly compensated for all the other errors I committed. Every time I added up my figures wrongly, Mrs Sudlow would crow and chortle, 'There's another O level gone!'

Each day started slowly and rather horridly, for my suit especially, with dusting. All the displayed items, the boxes opened to show the cellophane protected shirts, the counters and all hard surfaces, had to be wiped over with yellow cloths, a filthy business. Customers rarely arrived until till well after 10 am, which meant standing achingly for almost an hour. Only the elderly and pregnant ladies were expected to use the single wooden chair. It was strange how moving briskly around when things picked up brought much greater comfort. My attempts to have a book on the counter to fill empty moments met with an icy disapproval approaching shock levels. Such effrontery! Such idleness! How it might have made the remotest bit of difference was never explained. You had to *look* as if you were working in case the manager walked by, even if there was nothing to do.

Old-fashioned, gloomy and largely female-staffed, Richman's might have been thought a quality store. The goods were generally of fair quality and mid-range in price. Miss Beebee, in Fabrics upstairs, having worked there since leaving school at fourteen more than forty years before, a cheerful energetic woman, red-cheeked and rounded, infinitely skilled in her business, embodied what virtues the place had. Customers seeking advice on what to choose for the articles they wanted to make, and exactly how to do certain things received generous expert advice; Miss Beebee's reputation drew them in regularly. She had found her calling early in life, and loved every moment of it.

I ate my lunch in the back of shop rest room. In shifts, the middle-aged women sat along the sides of a huge square table, discussing their interests, generally making me welcome and indulging me. I understood that, with me there, they restricted their conversation, though on occasions as I moved around the store I overheard a couple now and then giggling together, rapidly straightening their faces on my approach. Their nickname for manager Thomas would hardly have flattered him: Soft Cock! He may well have been a perfectly decent man, but was known to drink, hardly ever spoke to anyone, smiled with rather a leer, kept hidden away upstairs, and indeed in all the weeks I worked there never once visited our department, except to walk through it every day to go for his lunch. I could not imagine what his work consisted of, though our buyer, Mr Simmonds went to see him every now and then. They seemed to get on cheerfully together.

Mr Simmonds! Portly and pompous in his double-breasted mid-grey suit, approaching fifty, he was of the McCarthy type from my first school: self-important, oracular, rather overbearing and authoritative. He held himself in check for much of the time, speaking little, and then often after a controlled pause.

'Mr Simmonds!'

[*two seconds*] 'Yes?'

'There is no price marked on these.'

[*two seconds before he looks down at what I'm holding*] 'No price?'

'Yes.'

[*two seconds. A sniff.*] 'Mrs Sudlow!'

'Yes, Mr Simmonds.'

'Will you tell the young man the price of these socks?'

After some days, he melted enough to ask me about myself, what I did, where I would be going. A few hours later, out of nowhere he informed me, 'Of course, I myself play the cello. [*pause*] And the organ. Mostly dance music.' The instant picture of him letting himself go with some Blackpool Tower outburst, or even more outrageously, actually tripping his bulk around a room more or less in time to a beat, presumably with some smart-stepping female, made me bite my cheeks.

Hard going, Simmonds liked nothing more than his elephantine flirting with perfumed Enid, dark eyed and shapely, from neighbouring Cards and Wrapping Paper or, perhaps better, to catch you out. 'Ah-ah! Leave those boxes alone! They're only for the sales! Just do what you're told to!' Expert on every subject, he was once in a rarely expansive moment holding forth about gardening. He had a whole patch completely covered in weeds.

'We cleared ours with sodium chlorate,' I offered.

'Sodium *Chloride*!' he corrected me.

'Isn't that what you put on your fish and chips?' I queried.

'No. It kills weeds. Sodium *chlorate* is used for culinary purposes.'

It was just as well I would never be eating at his place.

He did rescue me once. By that time, I knew the stock and had become quite competent at assessing a customer's shirt and other sizes at a glance. ('Pants for you, sir? I'd say Medium.') I could wrap boxed items in striped paper torn from the roll and tied around with ribbon from the reel. But one morning the largest man I had ever seen was standing before me. He wanted Meridian underpants. I had never served the item in more than Double Extra Large (44-46 inches). My own waist was about 31 inches. He must have been worth several Pickwickians rolled into one. 'The usual ones, please,' the Brobdingnangian being wheezed. 'My size.'

Mr Simmonds came from behind. 'You can leave this gentleman with me,' he quietly said. With the stepladder's aid he brought down a lidded brown cardboard box from a top shelf at the back of the shop. From it he drew forth a thick cream thing. He unfolded it and stretched it across the glass counter, spreading his arms wide. You could have made a small sail from it. 'These, I think, sir?'

There were moments when I was left on my own. Early on such a Saturday afternoon, a threatening-looking character advanced on me. He clumped his outsize working man's fist on the glass counter, causing it to tremble. 'Give us a shairt,' he said.

'What size is that, sir?' I asked, guessing at least 18 inches, maybe 18½.

'Give us a shairt!' he insisted, leaning forwards. Our reasonable quality items cost just under £2. For £3 you could buy a classy Louis Philippe. I moved to the cheapest display and picked the loudest striped shirt we had in the biggest size, for £1 5s. He paid in cash without speaking.

In the weeks before Christmas, especially on Saturdays, we were deluged. Shoppers swarmed around, pulling at your sleeve as you navigated the displays to serve your customer. It was amusing how so often a lady would want *exactly* the shirt and tie you had put on a dummy in the window! I must have sold hundreds of white handkerchiefs, in packets of three. At the end of one afternoon, Mrs Sudlow shrieked, 'That dummy! Did you sell those things?' Two hours before it had been dressed with an expensive shirt, silk tie and luxury, cricket-style V-necked long sleeve cream jumper. None of us had. The thief had taken everything, totalling at least a working man's weekly wages, from two or three feet away from us.

One icy morning in the New Year, when I was the only person to have arrived at our department, a heavily pregnant woman entered by the double-glass doors at the end of our section. When she let the door swing back on its own, it caught on its fellow, instantly detonating into thousands of pieces of thick safety glass. The swollen lady stood there, catching her breath, covered in fragments from her hair downwards.

Mercifully, Enid took command. She rushed to the imminent mother, told her to keep still, brushed off what she could and then gently escorted the lady by the arm out of the store to a back room. We learned later that they had to strip her to her underwear and supply brand new clothes from the upstairs department. At least she was probably fairly warm, whilst for most of the day we shivered until workmen came to board up the massive gap.

Since mid-September, Anthea had been in Wimbledon. We wrote each other letters. I should see her at Christmas. I went out playing in orchestras one or two evenings a week.

Things resumed with Anthea after her return, though I detected some uncertainty on her part. Early in the New Year I learned that she had developed glandular fever. Soon after that I also was not well. With a very sore throat, aches and pains, I was directed by my GP to go to Walsall Hospital for a blood test. I took the bus there on my own.

Like many, I suppose, I had some apprehension in those days about needles, though the actual experience of seeing the insertion, followed shortly afterwards by the dark red fluid filling the reservoir of the syringe fascinated me. A day or so later I learned the result: confirmed mononucleosis, glandular fever, what the Germans call Studentenkrankheit, for imaginable reasons. By then I was struggling.

I have never, before or after, ever been so ill in my whole life. The fever was extreme, lasting many days. I was bedridden, weak, aching. My throat became so raw I could scarcely endure another swallow. My mother kept renewing sodden sheets and pyjamas. Work was impossible between the beginning of January and mid-March. I could not leave my room. Eventually, I was able to feel my way downstairs, a slow step at a time, to sit for an hour or so in an armchair. A few days later, I could sit, still in dressing gown, at a table placed before me. A large jigsaw, a London scene in 1500 pieces, was bought for me. I worked at it for days, much slower than I normally would be. I had not done a puzzle for at least ten years. Placing each piece represented a small part of recovery. The red London bus, a black cab, street traffic, monumental buildings, whole areas of tree foliage, a largely blue sky, cyclists, pedestrians.

The day came when the doctor said I should go for a second blood test. The outside air felt unfamiliar, chill. I walked with a vague lightness to the bus stop. But the result proved negative. I could return to work the following Monday. Mr Thomas allowed me to resume, whether I was necessary to him or not. At some time in the previous weeks Anthea had written to call our relationship off. I understood she had a replacement called Frank. Perhaps he was physically more adventurous than I had been. After all, they were both living away from home. I did not grieve particularly.

After a few days back at work, Anthea's parents came into the store. Wallie asked if I would like to work in the factory with him. It would be harder work, but I should earn more. He would look after me. I told Mr Thomas I would leave at the end of the week.

I took with me, and have kept ever since, a fairly reliable ability to size men from among the standard sizes, accurately predicting collar, chest, and waist sizes, even what glove will fit, though I suspect that the trade no longer uses the measurement in inches around the knuckles of a clenched fist. As for folding garments and speed wrapping boxes with paper and ribbon, I could probably earn a silver badge even now! This knowledge also informs me that the average size of a male has increased over the decades. In 1969, the average British man, Mr Medium, took a 15-inch shirt, had a 32-34 inch waist, was 5 feet 8 inches tall and took size 8 gloves and shoes. By the time I had finished my teaching career, such an eighteen-year-old sixth former would be well down the line when we arranged them in height order for the leavers' year group photograph.

*****

I wonder what a Roman forge was like. The poet Vergil almost certainly visited one, at least once; otherwise, how could he possibly have created his picture of the Cyclopes' workshop under Mount Etna in Book VIII of *Aeneid*? He heard the deafening sounds of heavy metal workings, saw and felt the wonder and shock of molten steel and copper flowing, witnessed the rhythmical working of men heavy hammering in numbered sequence. His smiths were giants, fashioning thunderbolts for Jupiter, a prophetic shield depicting the history, present glories and future destiny of Rome: remembered reality was fashioned into poetry and legend, perhaps *aere perennius*, to borrow from the writer's contemporary. We made car wheels.

Waiting for the bus home, late afternoon on my first day of factory work, the heavy drop hammer forging from Armstrong Stevens bumped me upwards off the pavement every now and then, an almost amusing additional shock to me, bombarded since early morning. My ears would roar scarred for another hour or so still, as they were to do every working day; my lungs and muscles ached; my T shirt and underpants were sodden with sweat which left darker patches on my navy blue boiler suit, the front and sleeves stiffening and dark with suds oil, sparkling with swarf flecks, silverfish sharp. Cold trickles dribbled down my back. I smelt like a hot car engine.

I felt good, so tired I was empty, peaceful. It had been a total experience. Nothing more had to be done; I had nothing more to give.

After a few weeks, I started to cycle to and from work. That not only saved two bus rides each way, but proved a small daily adventure. The secondhand Dawes Debonair, nominally a ten speed sports bike, set me back £5 from a schoolmate's big brother. The front mechanism for changing between chainrings, a cable-less chrome plated affair with a topmost knurled knob you supposedly reached down and turned, had been removed and was handed over separately. In five years, I never attempted to replace it. The chain stayed on the smaller ring.

My first serious bike! I had longed for one for years, but Mom and Dad decreed bikes too dangerous. Then one Sunday afternoon when I was sixteen and the family was walking on some isolated patch of common ground, David *found* an abandoned bike under some bushes! Flat-tyred, ancient and rusting, it clearly had not been ridden for an era. And it fitted into the Mark 1 Cortina's boot – more or less.

Black (faded to matt dark grey), sit-up-and-beg, rod braked, the discarded machine had Sturmey Archer gears, shifted by a vintage quadrant lever frame[3], crossbar mounted. In the two or so years I made do with this relic, I fiddled endlessly with the cable adjuster, hoping to activate all three gears, but never managed to persuade all three to co-operate, dispensing with the middle ratio.

Cleaned, oiled, supplied with inner tubes and tyres and tinkered with, it worked, in a ponderous, trundling way. So did I work! Just progressing moderately on fairly level ground was an uncompromising work out. Out of folly or pride, I persisted, pushing myself around local circuits, building up to maybe six or eight miles.

Each wheel alone weighed more than any of my current five bikes (two of them carbon framed), the rear one a perplexing oddity, with a rim width of 1¾". Fred Spencer, who ran the interconnected village cycle and toy shops, told me the tyre size was commonly found on small, powered machines, cycles with tiny two-stroke engines. It must have made pedalling all the harder. Toiling up hump-back canal bridges, for some reason I imagined carrying a cast-iron army bed frame up flights of stairs.

Switching to drop handlebars on the lighter, nippier Dawes took some adjustment. Braking needed delicate caution to avoid rear-wheel skids or launching yourself over the front end. The first time I rode to school, on a chill autumn morning, I chose lanes and back roads: quieter, more relaxed, more attractive … and in the shadier frosty hollows more treacherous! When a dog burst from the left-hand hedge and shot across perhaps fifteen feet ahead of me, a quick snatch of the rear brake had me sliding across the tarmac, my left hip flaring into pain. I learned to rely more on the front brake, applied progressively.

As spring turned to summer, I relished my six-mile rides increasingly, the early morning ones especially, threading quiet lanes, seasonally aromatic, to the straighter, untroubled main roads, to build momentum. This, in boiler suit and heavyweight protective footwear, thick-soled and with steel toe caps to withstand a ton weight falling twelve inches vertically, could not have looked too elegant. Only in bucketing rain did I bother to add the huge yellow plastic cape, as much a danger and encumbrance as aid. One morning, I caught sight of a loose dog, padding proudly

---

[3] Recently I have discovered that some Sturmey Archer gearings had high, low and *neutral* settings, though I remain utterly unable to guess why such an option should ever be made available!

along on the pavement opposite, a huge floppy, furry rabbit limp in its mouth, no doubt some bereft child's back yard darling. Applying the brakes for a red traffic light another time, I heard a ping, to be followed a hundred yards further on by at least two more: completely snapped front spokes! Thinking the wheel would collapse if I rode further, I continued on foot for half a mile or so, before cautiously remounting and finishing the ride at a gingerly slow speed that avoided heavy braking. In my lunch break, I rode round the corner to Dad's workplace in Willenhall, leaving the bike for him to have the wheel fixed, which he did by the following afternoon, when I walked to collect it. The nearby bike shop man was yet another of the local characters he had somehow got to know well. Perhaps Dad had done him a favour or two, like the occasional free offcut or two of steel for his shed or workshop. That wheel stayed sound and unbuckled for the rest of the bike's life with me. As Gerd Shraner tells us in *The Art of Wheelbuilding,* a properly built or corrected wheel should stay forever true unless exposed to violence; Black Country fingers were often as skilled as oily. Of course, I went as fast as circumstances allowed. Belting once down the slope from the railway bridge to the works entrance, I chose to go for a gap in the oncoming traffic, somewhat underestimating its speed so that I had to supply a final frenzied burst. I did clear the approaching Ford, but then had to bank right at racing speed to avoid smashing into the brick security building on the left. My left shoulder feather-brushed it, without mark or injury. 'Bet yo dint need yer Ex-Lax this mornin!' a machine operator from the next line commented when I walked past an hour later.

Motorwheel was only one of several huge manufacturing sections on the Rubery Owen site at Darlaston, reputedly the most profitable. Steel in coils, such as some of the material my father dealt in, was unloaded from lorries outside the main works building, before entering which it was 'pickled' by Mick the Pickler. With his heavy dark orange apron, this curly-headed extravert spent most of his working hours outdoors in all weathers. He would hoist coils delivered by forklift truck, on chained block and tackle apparatus, swing them up from the ground to level with him on his platform, several feet above ground level, hoist them higher, and then swing them over a huge vat, a rectangular tank filled with concentrated sulphuric acid which steamed at all times. Lowered into the hellish liquid, the coils emerged steaming and dripping, but also rust free, rinsed of oil and gleaming. When dried off, they would be ready for use.

Inside the building, entered by two rubber push-flaps of small cathedral door size, they were forklifted upon demand to one of two production lines, where loaded on to dispensing reels they were unbanded, fed between rollers and drawn in controlled lengths for the first machine operation, to be cut into blanks. Subsequent machines down the two lines shaped them in stages, one producing rims and the other the centres or 'plates' that would be rivetted or welded to the rims on the assembly lines. A separate modern and automated line assembled wheels for Minis, huge numbers delivered, I think several times daily, to Longbridge.

The blanks for the rims passed from machine to machine, being slid along steel rails between operators, who lifted them from one side, placed them in their machines, performed their own operation, and then moved them to the other side, to the next set of rails. To start with, the rectangular blank passed between revolving tools which curved them until they were circular, after which they passed to be placed in a welding machine, which clamped them in place for the operator to press his two buttons, well back from the machine and one with each hand, for the flash weld, which sent fountains of yellow sparks spraying in arcs upwards and outwards. Polishers with pneumatic handguns cleaned the weld smooth before it passed up the line to be shaped and sized in stages, each machine bringing the article nearer to completion. To put the curves and flanges on the steel bands, machines with two revolving machine wheels when operated drew and rotated together exerting forces of sixty tons per square inch; the sizing and final shaping into circularity were carried out in stages by 'stretchers' and 'shrinkers', the latter metal structures perhaps twelve feet wide, with a central tool in segments that made a circle of exactly the required diameter when brought together under pressure, again with the standard two remote buttons behind the safety line. Completed rims went to inspectors, who clamped them to a stand-mounted chuck, to be spun against needle gauges and tested for tolerance. Each job had an accepted 'run out', an allowance of a few thousandths of an inch either side of central zero. Recoverable deviations were instantly corrected, by the crude yet effective method of well-directed clouts from an orange plastic club hammer; a few were thrown into the bin for scrap. Passed rims received the inspector's stamp, which identified not only the man but also the date and shift. They were then stacked by hand in walls built as high as the stacker could reach, a new stack for each change of size. Some rims were simply laid flat on top of each other like bricks, whilst others, usually the narrower ones, were 'laced', that is, placed at angles formed by laying some rims flat, then angling the remainder on them and each other, with mounting lines angled alternately. This form of stacking required skill and experience to remain stable and safely unstackable for use, as I was quickly to find. The counterweighting of locking rims bound all together securely; a poorly laced stack was as inferior as a grannie knot to a reef one.

Plates, being smaller and lighter, were more easily produced. The coils fed into guillotines which cut squares, subsequently chopped into circles and up a line of smaller presses, each one of which modified the shape or added a feature, like the cut-out windows. This was after all the very place where the ROSTYLE wheel (RO for Rubery Owen) originated, when some designer had the idea of cutting oval or other shaped holes in the discs of wheels' centres. If, for example, a particular plate had twelve 'windows', one of the operators would secure it in his or her machine and punch a hole in it by operating the machine with a pedal, then rotating the disc to a stop and punching every next hole until the number was made up. Stacked on base-mounted steel poles, they were in turn wheeled by 'move men' on two-wheeled trolleys like porters' barrows to the beginning of an assembly line.

I was to be another sort of move man: with one or two others, I would take rims from the built-up stacking walls, load them on to trolleys, and wheel them to the assembly lines, three or four of which would be running constantly. More modern systems had already dispensed with move men, officially 'inter-line feed men', in reality only unskilled labourers, sweating for hours on end. It was £20 a week, though, nearly three times what you got for selling socks and pants, and for fewer hours.

Wallie had fixed it so that I should permanently work the day shift with him, although for years he had suffered the three-shift system, as two or three other teams still did. (I think they earned a small extra supplement.) He had climbed, over the years, to become an inspector, and was additionally respected not only as a wise old hand, but as a shop steward. He and the rest of the day team had spent two decades or more, certainly all the time since the end of World War 2, working together. In the six months I worked with them, I do not think the team ever changed: Des assembled plates to rims, Harold pierced the rivet holes, Jessie and Tom inserted and hammered the rivets pneumatically, Billie operated the 'snapper, finishing the hammered rivets to round heads, Wallie inspected and stamped them. Piercing, riveting and snapping all required one foot to be permanently on a pedal lever. Wallie jested that Billie, who had, apart from his National Service years, stood on one foot eight hours every working day since leaving school, used to move his foot up and down in his sleep. On rare occasions, Tom or Harold might briefly stand in for Des, perhaps when he needed a toilet break, just to keep the line moving. Unlike me, they were paid on piecework rates. We worked from 7.30 am till noon, and then from 1 to 4.30 pm, with short, timetabled tea breaks.

The first morning, Wallie took me to foreman Vernon, a lugubrious stooping man in a grey plaid suit. He initialled my first weekly timecard for the day's clocking on, after which it was my responsibility to queue and time-stamp it at the start and end of every morning and afternoon.

Till the shifts changed at 2 pm I worked alongside Sylvester Fleming that first week. A friendly and communicative Jamaican, he showed me what to do, not just how to work, but also how to avoid pinching my fingers or bring metal crashing down on myself. Warm and entertaining, he would tip you off about workers to be wary of: 'Take no notice of him, Martin; he's all talk!' I loved his stories of working with the sugar cane in Florida, of feeling the snakes moving over his arm, reliving the memory of his wide-eyed alarm. Sober and responsible, he followed the horses, ensuring minimal risk to his family's finances by never entering the betting shop with more than four shillings in his pocket. 'I picked a great horse last night, Martin. Real stamina. Must have had. Bloody thing's still running!' He was very happy with his wife and little boy. Generous hearted, he sensed if I was tiring and occasionally pushed an extra trolley to give me a break. On one occasion he skilfully saved me from at least a very unpleasant battering: we were extricating the last few rims from deep within walls of rims lace-stacked. Leaning and unstable, they were beginning to waver. I was at least ten, maybe twelve, feet in the middle of all those tons of metal. Sylvester rushed over, screaming at me to get out. Knowing exactly where to put pressure with maximum effect, he arched his whole straining body against the moving wall whilst I scrambled out on all fours. Immediately he leapt back, everything caved in. The sustained crashing noise made all the operators look round. There were shouts and whistles. Then laughter and cheering. Sylvester was sitting on the floor, legs outstretched, puffing his cheeks. 'Bloody hell, Martin!' he finally said. Then he tipped his head back and howled till the tears rolled down. We were all laughing. Saying goodbye to him after months was to be a wrench. He gripped my hand and quietly wished me all the best.

Short, tubby, balding and late middle-aged, Len Dutton lived a single life, No 6 cigarettes and Atkinson's Bitter being his only companions. He smoked constantly, was frequently leaning forward with the back of his hand on his chest, reporting a pain 'atween me shoulder blades, cock.' He regularly drank more beer in one night than I would over several weeks, though never seemed to suspect a possible link between 'fifteen pints, cock' and his physical miseries. Pushing laden trolleys sorely taxed him. From my first week I put in more work than he did, although to start with I was not paid the full rate, on account of my youth, and would need two more birthdays to be granted that. Though I just accepted things, Wallie and the others saw the anomaly. They reasoned that, though we were paid on a day rate, which was age-related, our work was so inextricably bound up with theirs that it was effectively a piecework job. It was only because the assessors, the time and motion folk with clipboards and stopwatches, had found the move men's movements so confusing and variable that they had given up the job of fixing a rate for us and settled for a fixed one. But 'that warn't fair,' as I was seriously told. From Day 1 I was a member of Wallie's Amalgamated Engineers and Fitters Union, the other one in the shop being the Transport and General Workers. Older heads were put together. Walllie and the other shop stewards went to see the managers. At first their request was denied. Wallie knew the game. He grinned as he told me, 'We'll request fifteen minutes for a shop meeting. They car say neow.'

The meeting, held with everything weirdly silent, actually took only a minute or two. The situation was explained, and a show of hands taken. Everyone supported the move men's claim, which actually had only ever applied to me alone. But there was a principle. And those directly in the know understood that a nineteen-year-old, especially one fitter and quicker moving than Len, dripped as much as anyone. The shop stewards returned to the manager, Parker. At the end of the afternoon, Wallie toddled over to me, grinning. 'The boss is going to pay you chaps all the same, with back pay. Just look busy when he comes round.' In my remaining months I think that happened only once. An extra couple of pounds a week was worth having.

I had two other direct work mates, Moaz and Wayne. The former's first and very much main language was Urdu. We struggled to communicate, which I regretted, since otherwise we worked very harmoniously. I could have wished that Jamaican Wayne said less, or at least less uncomfortably. Shorter, younger, less alert and responsive than his fellow islander, he claimed to have had some incapacitating injury, the nature of which never became clear. His slow-wittedness even made me wonder whether he had been brain injured. Sylvester would say very little about him, but changed the subject if he was mentioned. 'He's a bloody liar,' he would mutter, and look away, worried. Wayne liked to hold your attention and recount his exploits and triumphs, over opponents he had fought with horrible consequences or women he had exhausted in bed. 'I kep going for two hours until she al dried up,' he leered. 'She was cryin out for me to stop cos it was gettin sore.' He made a point of leading you away from others and standing very close when sharing these intimacies. Mercifully, he did not stay long, or perhaps switched – or was moved - permanently to the night shift.

'A fair day's pay for a fair day's work' was the assumed and declared basis of Wallie and the other older workers I was fortunate to be associated with, an altogether different race from the younger, brasher, more militant and altogether less pleasant younger teams I also kept supplied with rims. Frenzied and demanding, they maintained the fastest possible rate, pushing the massive welding machines to their limits and exploding with foul-mouthed rage whenever the line had to pause for repair or maintenance. At the same time, they were constantly alert for the flimsiest pretext to down tools in defence of their perceived rights. One twenty-something year old could not have been more different from his father, Ernie the fitter, one of Wallie's friends.

The duty fitters, elderly workers who had operated all the machines and knew them intimately, lived a mysterious and impressive life, moving quietly around keeping an eye on things when all appeared to be going smoothly, perhaps not doing very much for whole stretches until something failed. Since much of the plant dated back at least three decades, there could be a sudden bang or uncanny silence, a firework display of sparks or – most concerning – a pipe burst under hydraulic pressure. The assembly presses, which our direct job was to supply with rims, exerted 100 tons per square inch when the safety cage was drawn down by the left hand and the righthand lever moved forward. Under many thousands of constant rapid pressure changes more or less every day for decades, any pipe or joint might, even without warning, simply shatter or fail, shooting a gush half the length of the entire shop, flattening and drenching anything or anyone in its way. There were tales of men – and women – being lifted off their feet and slammed against hard and sharp surfaces, or even having some of their clothing blasted clean off. 'You should 'ave sin er back! She wos black as black from neck to backside. Said she had to sleep on her belly for a fortnight, poor wench!'

‘Bloody ‘ell, Martin!’ Sylvester would greet me some mornings when he had already been working for an hour and a half. ‘We need to keep a eye on that feller.’ He would nod towards an assembly press, which was shooting a radiant spray every few seconds. ‘’E’s goin to blow before very long.’

There were then dangers and fears. One Saturday morning, when we had gone in for some overtime, the usual half-day, higher-rate lighter mood vanished at the shock wave of a ‘bad un.’ During a stoppage of the rim line, an operator had restarted his spinner completely unaware that a toolsetter’s mate was still working behind it. As the two revolving wheels came together, exerting their many tons of pressure, they caught up the concealed man’s hand, all but amputating it. From some distance behind the scene I saw the near-collapsed man, sitting slumped on a steel chair someone had given him, his injured hand still encased in a heavy red rubberised glove like the ones I wore. A manager stood nearest to him, legs astride and frowning, doing his best to comfort and reassure the casualty, as a silent group of others, both co-workers and office staff, stood facing the stricken young man in a semicircle. Within perhaps five minutes, the works ambulance team arrived to take the man away. The following Monday Wallie told me he had in fact lost the hand. ‘It wor such a shame. He’s a nice young chap. Wife and babby too.’ I never saw the man again.

Other workers reputedly lived with their injuries’ effects. One fitter, Lanky, walked with a loping limp. Even with his slight stoop he dwarfed me by a good foot. The story was that, one drenchingly sweltering summer night shift he had been towards the top of a ladder attending to a derailed pulley belt when a pretty young machinist called Jenny had called to him from the ground. ‘Hoy, Lanky! Look!’ Just for his benefit, she was holding her button-up lightweight overall gown wide open, briefly revealing her complete nudity underneath.

That floored Lanky in more ways than one; hence the limp. If, as I think, that had happened a decade earlier, during the heatwave of 1959, Jenny must then have been in her early twenties, even prettier at that time than she still was as a working mother of two small children.

I never learned exactly what Old Tom did. He regularly walked back and forth across one side of the factory, waddling softly from side to side on his heels. One lunchtime, Wallie spotted him. ‘See him?’ his breadcrumbs sprayed. ‘That’s Tom. Years ago he squashed ‘is right thumb in ‘is press. It was in the middle of the night. Such a scream he set up. It was a real mess. So, because he was right-handed, they cut his *left* thumb off and sewed it on ‘is right ‘and. Only that dint tek, and ‘e’d lost both ‘is thumbs. So they cut his big toes off and sewed them on ‘is ‘ands. To mek it ‘eal they opened a flap in ‘is stummuck and placed ‘is ‘ands inside for ‘em to ‘eal. Only that dint werk neither. So ‘e ended up losin both ‘is thumbs AND ‘is toes.’ He nodded and grinned sideways at me. If this was a leg pull, it was uncharacteristic, Wallie being no ironist.

His teasing took very physical forms: moving your cup out of range when you were not looking, tickling you from behind a stack with a long stick …

There were undeniably dangers. You could slip on the grease-caked floor, bring rims crashing down on your head, pinch your fingers between weights of metal, bruise and scrape yourself as you raced around keeping up with production. These risks, though, were nothing like what the machinists faced, or even more what they used to have to brave, before safety guards were installed on presses and aids supplied. Wallie remembered having to *lift* the tools, weighing around 2 cwt, on and off his press every time the job changed. By my time, toolsetters with block and tackle hoists did that for you, sliding the tools onto the machines from wheeled roller platforms. Even they needed to take proper care, though. Setter's mate Kevin ruefully showed me his suede shoe one morning, with between one and two inches chopped off the end. 'I war wearin me work boots, was I? Just dropped a Mini wheel on me foot. Good job I bunched me toes up!' You could always fork out £1 in the market for another pair of imitation Hush Puppies.

The sizes and weights of rims and wheels varied considerably, Minis actually being the smallest and lightest. You could easily pick up six or more Mini rims at a time, maybe eight. Mid-size Cortinas and Saabs also proved manageable, though larger. Swinging one in each hand to overhead height on your trolley demanded little effort. Chromed Rover rims, on the other hand, even worse Land Rovers, took much more out of you. The most dreaded job, which mercifully came up fairly rarely, was simply called 'Agricultural', 36-inch rims in the heaviest gauge metal we used. Both hands were essential for just one of these, though gap-toothed Big Des occasionally demonstrated the knack of swinging one from just behind him on to the press in a one-handed power lift, which required timing, balance and impressive accuracy. (Hoots and cheers!)

Wallie's team more or less adopted me. I have mentioned Snapper Billie, 'strong in the arm and weak in the head', as Wallie repeatedly reminded me. He lived with his sister and her family. Rivetter Tom, mild and quiet, simply did his job perfectly and calmly, gently smiling at all of us, rarely speaking, reserving his real living for his family and garden. Occasionally he and Wallie would talk plants and vegetables. 'Want some young tomato plants, Tom?' 'I can use 'em for yer, if yer like, Wallie. You got room for a few beans?'

Harold the Piercer and Rivetter Jessie were engaged. They had been for fourteen years! Already in their fifties, they each looked after elderly parents, having promised to defer their own lives until the time came … I occasionally saw them shopping together on Saturday afternoons in Walsall market. To anyone's eyes they were a married couple. Press operator Des, at perhaps 40 the youngest and fittest, was married with two children, one of each. A fellow inspector also worked alongside Wallie at the far end of the line. Also undemonstrative and undemanding, he just got on with things.

I cannot recall his name; he rarely came my way. I do not think any of the team ever showed temper or stress, though Wallie sometimes 'straightened someone out' by having a firm and measured word.

The weeks passed. I started a bank account and paid amounts in, saving most of my wages. For £33 12s 6d I bought my first 35 mm camera, a Yashica Minister III. Most weeks I bought *Amateur Photographer*, which Wallie seemed to think a reckless indulgence. I became fitter and stronger, loving the bike rides. I slept better than at any other time of my life.

When the Industrial Fortnight came, I went with the family to a caravan in Towyn. We left Pelsall, all five of us, in a red Hillman Minx. Dad's Mark II Cortina was being repaired. The previous Saturday, when he was having a cup of tea at the Baggotts' on Watling Street, having collected us both from a morning of overtime, a ring on the doorbell announced a frowning lorry driver. 'Is that your green Ford?' he wanted to know. 'If so, I've just nudged it a touch.' He could have added, 'with my 126-foot Pickford trailer.' So we travelled away in a loan car, on the understanding that Dad would have to drive back halfway through the holiday to make the exchange.

One disaster seems to lead to another … on his way home after breaking up that Friday night, Dad somehow trapped his shrivelled left hand in the locked driver's door, and had to plead with a passer-by to take the key from his pocket and release him. Every gear change on the drive the next day was accompanied by a whimper of pain. The roads were busy, with many delays and hold ups. But we arrived.

So did the Americans, the next day. On Sunday 20th July, Neil Armstrong stepped on to the surface of the moon, followed by Buzz Aldrin. 650 million people worldwide watched the event. We did not. The caravan had no electricity. There was no television set. If there were screens in any public places then, the small Welsh town certainly did not have one. To this day I have never seen the whole sequence, only stills and short clips. Fifty years later I contrived to miss the anniversary reshowing. One day, one day … The fortnight, though, was probably the last fairly happy one we had as a complete family. The weather co-operated. I had my new camera to play with, *Bleak House* to read, a few pounds in my pocket. I think Sylvia and David still recall the two days we spent on our own whilst Dad and Mom drove back to exchange the loan car for the Cortina. Some Kodachrome slides survive.

Back home, I worked in the factory for another few weeks, leaving myself an interval of freedom before starting at university. At the last tea break, a small group of workers gathered round to say goodbye.

'Yo'm off to college, then,' one remarked. 'Ruskin?'

'No, Sidney Sussex at Cambridge.'

‘Yo’ll be all right there then,’ a new move man commented. ‘Out on a punt.’ He mimed pole action.

‘Yes, there’s plenty of that there,’ little Derek chipped in. Everyone knew him to be solidly deaf. No one explained to him why we all laughed. He was laughing too.

And so the last few weeks at home. From V.L.Skuce’s in Walsall I bought a secondhand typewriter: £10 for a veteran standard Royal, just like the one my mother had learned on before the war. I worked through most of *Teach Yourself to Type.* Of course, the weight and size of the antiquated machine would always be inconvenient, but I have never regretted the decision. How other people get along using only a couple of fingers and having to look constantly at the keys has always mystified me. On several shopping trips I provided all the items I thought I should need.

Of the cutlery and tableware I bought, only one white side plate (3 shillings), a still very stylish small milk jug and some Woolworth’s soup spoons have survived over half a century. Goodness knows why I thought I needed four of everything plus umpteen other items. A couple of mugs and maybe a teapot would have been more than adequate! But they filled part of a sideboard.

The trunk I bought was toughened with stainless steel covering. It just about held all the items I took, the breakables carefully padded with towels and items of clothing. But the weight! I could only just lift it. It needed two people anyway, since there was no central handle. I took far too many books, but the shelves they filled looked suitably studious and otherwise homely. I felt buoyant: kitting myself out, about to begin something I had longed for, physically fit on account of the last six months cycling and labouring. Knowing nothing of what was ahead, I nevertheless felt no apprehension. I was sleeping well.

A few days before my twentieth birthday, Fred Knight proposed a trip to the West Country for the two of us: a short hotel stay and a visit to Plymouth, where some of his army training had taken place. That meant two nights at the Five-Star Imperial Hotel in Torquay, on fine September days with warm evenings, the illuminations around the bay gently swinging to the breeze, gourmet meals … the second night Fred ordered a bottle of 1947 Chambertin. The wine waiter clearly approved. So did we! Of the wines I have tasted over my whole life, I remember it as the best ever, never repeated or even nearly equalled, lighting inner lights and fires, filling lungs and nostrils with wondrous delights, suffusing wellbeing throughout. I could not withhold the smiles that everyone was returning. I did not want to.

The certainty that this happened will survive as long as I have memory; the evening ran the usual length, rather too rapidly.

Something was coming to an end.

On that second day we had driven to Plymouth, uniformly naval grey, and walked to the Citadel, where Fred loudly asked the guard on the gate if we could look around: he wanted to see where he had been stationed in the war. The private choke-swallowed his sandwich, spluttered he would ask the sergeant and went into a back room, wiping his eyes with the back of his hand. The sergeant would be with us in a minute, sir.

Very little seemed to be going on in the seventeenth century fort. The sergeant proudly showed us around the chapel, pointing out the paintings done by a soldier, then left us to look around on our own. Fred particularly wanted me to see a wall, to which they had all been marched in full kit and with rifles, and told to jump down to the grassed area below. It must have been ten or twelve feet. That had been too much for his nerve. ‘I can’t do it, sir!’ he said. To his amazement, the sergeant major simply replied, ‘Oh, all right. Run round and join the others then.’

We were on an A road, driving home, somewhere in Gloucestershire. As we were passing a stationary car that had halted on our left, I could see that it was creeping forwards to us. We must have been travelling at 60 mph. For a slight nudge, just behind the front passenger door, the thump and jolt were shocking. Exchanging particulars, the other driver immediately apologised. It was his fault. He had taken his foot off the brake pedal, not realising his automatic car would creep forwards. The damage looked surprisingly superficial.

A couple of days later, I left home. Leaving my sensible sister to look after our brother, my parents drove me to Cambridge. The porter called me ‘sir,’ told me I had been allocated to share room Q9 with Mr Thomson. I signed for the key.

The door from the corridor was already wide open. The building echoed. From the first floor, the main room looked out on two sides to another court, the street, the chapel, the garden trees …

Mom and Dad could not stay in the car park long. I walked back down the stairs to say goodbye to them. By the time the car was beginning to move I was already re-entering the building.

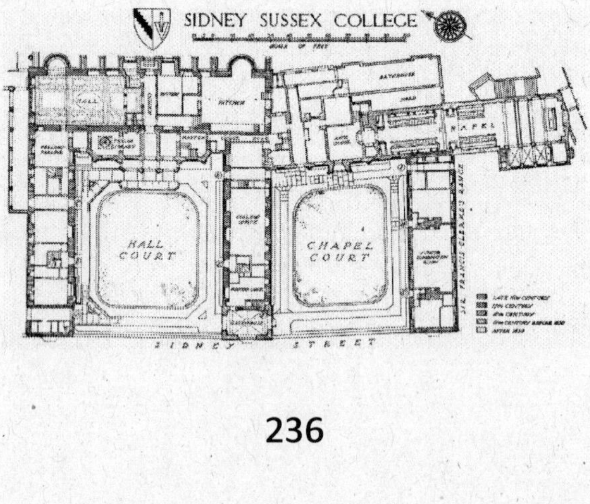